Law and Ethnic Plurality

IMMIGRATION AND ASYLUM LAW AND POLICY IN EUROPE

Volume 13

Editors

Elspeth Guild
Kingsley Napley Solicitors, London,
Centre for Migration Law, Radboud University Nijmegen

Jan Niessen
Migration Policy Group, Brussels

The series is a venue for books on European immigration and asylum law and policies where academics, policy makers, law practitioners and others look to find detailed analysis of this dynamic field. Works in the series will start from a European perspective. The increased co-operation within the European Union and the Council of Europe on matters related to immigration and asylum requires the publication of theoretical and empirical research. The series will contribute to well-informed policy debates by analysing and interpreting the evolving European legislation and its effects on national law and policies. The series brings together the various stakeholders in these policy debates: the legal profession, researchers, employers, trade unions, human rights and other civil society organisations.

The titles published in this series are listed at the end of this volume.

Law and Ethnic Plurality

Socio-Legal Perspectives

Edited by

Prakash Shah

MARTINUS
NIJHOFF
PUBLISHERS

LEIDEN • BOSTON
2007

Printed on acid-free paper.
A C.I.P. record for this book is available from the Library of Congress.

ISBN: 978 90 04 16245 7

Koninklijke Brill NV incorporates the imprints Brill, Hotei Publishers, IDC Publishers, Martinus Nijhoff Publishers and VSP.

http://www.brill.nl

Printed and bound in The Netherlands.

Table of Contents

Introduction: Socio-Legal Perspectives on Ethnic Diversity

Prakash Shah

This book emerges as a result of a series of lectures held at the Institute of Advanced Legal Studies in London from January to March 2006. The initial invitation to organise the series was focused on the issue of religion. Given the prominence of religion in public debates in Europe and beyond, this seemed an obvious heading to which speakers could have been asked to lecture. The prominence of terror activities drawing inspiration from extremist religious doctrines, debates over the *hijab* (Muslim women's headscarf) issue in many EU countries, and the recent furore over the publication of cartoons portraying the Prophet Muhammad in undignified ways are all leading to ripples, if not waves, being felt in the legal realm. However, it soon appeared that religion could not encompass the full range of contemporary debates about the situation of diasporic minorities in Britain and in Europe and I switched to an uneasy compromise with the title "Cultural Diversity and Law". As can be seen, this has now been converted once again to "Law and Ethnic Plurality: Socio-legal Perspectives". All this requires a bit of explanation.

Over the past months I have increasingly felt strong doubts about whether religion is an adequate analytical category on the grounds that its meaning is strongly contested, it arguably has strong Eurocentric overtones, and it is of dubious cross-cultural relevance beyond the constituency which British Prime Minister Tony Blair has referred to as the "children of Abraham", that is, the followers of the world's three main monotheistic traditions – Judaism, Christianity and Islam.[1] It is also true, as the above paragraph already indicates, that religion nowadays serves as a proxy or

1 Tony Blair's speech to the Labour Party Conference, 2 October 2001: see *Guardian*, 2 October 2001 http://politics.guardian.co.uk/labour2001/

Prakash Shah (ed.), Law and Ethnic Plurality: Socio-Legal Perspectives. *pp. 1-8.*
 ISBN 978 90 04 16245 7.

euphemism to cover discussions about Muslims while, in my experience, Muslims in Britain themselves tend to agree that religion adequately covers the issues about which they are most concerned in so far as they are connected with law. There are of course culture-specific reasons for this position to do with the core religious reference points or *grundnorms* for the *sharia* (Islamic law).

Nevertheless, I would maintain that over-reliance on the concept of religion to frame our discussions on the legal status of diasporic minorities carries the serious risk of discussions on such minorities, including Muslims, and the law getting trapped in what Chetan Bhatt (1997) refers to as the problem of "epistemic overreach". While one can certainly claim, with some validity, that religion, notwithstanding disagreement over its meaning and its proper place, plays an important role, it cannot be a sole focus for legal analysis since we are liable to overlook much of the socio-legal reality that lurks beneath its cover. Since law is an inherently plural phenomenon we need to take on board the fact that it has other elements which we also need to address for a more holistic perspective to be developed.

Notably, law quite obviously has a strong political flavour. While from a 'pure' positivistic and modernist approach that is all that it has, the political or state dimension of law is also not enough, even where combined with religion. Indeed, many of the legal crises in today's world appear to arise where a strong emphasis on religion is combined with a strongly political use of law. This leads in the extreme to a sort of religio-fascism. Conversely, looking at law from a combination of religious and modern political perspectives might cast the spotlight on terrorists and tyrants, but little else.

A related and justified claim, articulated most often by Muslims nowadays, is the tendency of modernist, political law to marginalise religion altogether. It is in Europe where the doctrine that religion and state, and therefore law too, must be kept separate developed, with the former confined to the 'private' sphere. While no European state manages to really see through the logical consequences of this ideal – a result of abstract modern legal theory having to cope with the messy details of real life, with some states according a constitutional role to Christian religious bodies – modern law making, and public debates more generally, certainly carry a strong flavour of secularism. In its modernist, secular form, therefore, political law tends to become highly culture-specific and parochial if considered in light of alternative, non-Western cultural paradigms which do not admit of the separationist claim in the way that is advocated in the West.

A stronger version of what we might call methodological legal pluralism needs to take on board the sociological dimension of law too. In so

story/0,,562007,00.html or *Telegraph*, 2 October 2001 http://www.telegraph.co.uk/news/main.jhtml?xml=/news/2001/10/03/nlab103.xml&page=7.

doing one needs to take culture seriously as Cotterrell (2004) has argued recently. However, culture in its links with law can entail many things as Cotterrell also makes clear and, while it is unrealistic to expect scholarly agreement on what culture means and how to contain it for analytical purposes, neither does it help us to focus on the core concerns of this volume as much as ethnicity does. Bhikhu Parekh (2000: 3-4), who uses the term "cultural diversity", qualifies it to mean "communal diversity". Ethnicity, unlike culture, has a greater containability given that many scholars who have examined its terrain remark on its dual role in helping to identify elements of a group culture as defined by oneself – what Meena Bhamra calls "identity markers" in this volume – which, at the same time, distinguish one's own group from outsiders. It is this constant making and re-making of boundaries and its implications for law, existing in virtually all complex societies, that is one of the key issues of interest here.

In using the word ethnic, we should not be taken to refer only to those non-European bits of the social field that appear somehow 'exotic'. Ethnicity, in its analytical sense, must refer to *all* the different communal elements which make up larger social fields like Britain, the United Kingdom or Europe. This includes people who might describe themselves as English, Scottish or Welsh. Although the focus of this volume is upon those ethnic components that might be otherwise described as diasporic minorities, we always need to keep in view the fact that these minorities are continuously in interaction with other proximate ethnic elements. We might also hear the objection that the English, Scottish and Welsh are really *national* and not *ethnic* groups. It is true that this has tended to be the dominant nomenclature, endorsed by prominent theorists like Kymlicka (1995). The way in which the label 'national' is used, however, is a political device to indicate the prior claims of those groups so described over those labelled 'ethnic', an aspect of nationalism which this writer would reject, at least for analytical purposes.

The abovementioned problem also touches on another issue which all the writers in one way or another address in this volume. And that is the accusation that in arguing for the social-legal realities of diasporic minority groups to be taken seriously, one is somehow making a claim for *special treatment*. As the ensuing chapters amply demonstrate, such assertions tend on the whole to remain blind to the fact that, particularly in the case of the dissemination and transmission of political law by theorists, politicians, lawyers, judges, the media and so on, there is an in-built bias in favour of the indigenous territorial ('national') majority group. The fact that this bias is often implicit makes it all the harder to challenge and renders the task of the analyst more difficult. Yet the writers here demonstrate that what special treatment there is exists in favour of the dominant groups, while minority groups are generally at the receiving end of what the inquiry into the investigation of the murder of the black teenager, Stephen Lawrence, chaired by Lord Macpherson (1999, para. 6.34), defined as "institutional racism":

> The collective failure of an organisation to provide an appropriate and professional service to people because of their colour, culture, or ethnic origin. It can be detected in processes, attitudes and behaviour which amount to discrimination through unwitting prejudice, ignorance, thoughtlessness and racist stereotyping which disadvantage minority ethnic people.

While the Macpherson inquiry report was concerned mainly with police malpractice in conducting the murder investigation, the potential application and implications of the definition employed by the inquiry are huge and it is submitted that, in many ways, the chapters in this volume can be seen as a continuum in efforts to address this critical issue facing minorities in Britain and Europe today. In so doing, there is not just one approach that can be, or needs to be, taken. Thus the team of writers represented here further reflects the sort of methodological legal pluralism mentioned above – they come from various disciplinary backgrounds – from political philosophy, sociology, criminology, anthropology, geography and law, and all of them are necessarily crossing disciplinary boundaries.

In the first two chapters our writers deal with the conceptual problems of justice for diasporic minorities and their integration. Meena Bhamra addresses the problem of the lack of normative bases for responses to cultural diversity. She argues that prominent legal writing about ethnic minorities is not grounded sufficiently in a normative framework. In other words, she argues, it fails to ask the question why it is just that minorities' claims be recognised in law. She critiques Kymlicka's theory on the basis that, while he shows that culture is valuable to people, he fails to follow through this argument by also applying it to immigrant groups and their descendants. Drawing on writing by Ballard and Menski she shows that anthropology and socio-legal theory demonstrate that culture is valuable also to people of immigrant heritage, and that this provides a more appropriate normative foundation for legal attempts to argue for their protection.

Valsamis Mitsilegas focuses on EU institutions and examines their production of policy documents and legal instruments in so far as they deal with the highly contested question of 'integration'. He quickly makes it clear that the EU institutions are working with shifting definitions of integration. On the one hand, thinking at EU level shows that the targets of integration tend to vary depending on the context and the policy being pursued – sometimes it is only immigrants, and at other times it includes people of immigrant descent who may well have acquired the nationality of a particular EU Member State. Mitsilegas also demonstrates that, while some earlier policy statements emphasised integration as a two-way street of the hosts and immigrants/minorities meeting each other, in more recent documents there appears to be an 'us and them' approach with 'they having to integrate to us' – basically an assimilationist approach. This shift in part indicates the increased securitisation of the debate on the immigrant/ minority presence in Europe, but probably also reflects the deep unease with ethnic plurality in Europe as a whole. Lastly, Mitsilegas shows that EU institutions have achieved little in terms of hard law on integration, although he finds some minimal indications in EU legislation on immigration.

Anita Kalunta-Crumpton discusses the situation of black people in Britain and how this minority group has been projected, in discourse and praxis since the 1960s, as drug dealing criminals. She juxtaposes this treatment to the ways in which the 'drug problem' has been approached in official policy. She shows how, especially from the 1980s, the drugs problem was tackled through a policy of criminalisation, while the drugs supply chain was put down to an 'alien threat' to the UK's citizens. She argues that crime fighting was focused on the low-level end of the supply chain whereby black people came to be disproportionately targeted and criminalised. Thus Kalunta-Crumpton considerably widens our focus of the process of criminalising black people through concerted official legal policies, building on the already widely-known facts about the disproportionately greater number of black prisoners, so far mainly explained by criminologists focusing on discriminatory chains in the criminal justice system. Conversely, she shows that treatment was geared towards heroin use which disproportionately affects white addicts, while black people who are more likely to be affected by crack fare poorest in the treatment regime. Kalunta-Crumpton thereby convincingly demonstrates the double-edged nature of discrimination in the 'war on drugs' – the disproportionate subjection of black people to criminal penalties and gearing of treatment regimes to suit white people.

Roger Ballard provides a personal account of his role as an expert anthropologist who finds himself in an almost unique position as a provider of knowledge about South Asians in various litigation arenas, ranging across the immigration, family and criminal courts. He takes us back to a time when jurors in England were drawn from local communities *because* of their knowledge of local circumstances and of the litigants and how this role has since declined, and he also shows how expert juries, once required to supply information on an area of technical knowledge, have also largely been dispensed with. The legal process in the courts has thereby come to be intensely controlled by lawyers and judges, even as the necessity for information to be fed across ethnic lines in legal processes has heightened significantly. Providing an example of a case in the criminal courts in which he was called as an expert, Ballard discusses the sorts of problems that can arise when anthropologists enter the frame as transmitters of vital information regarding the social contexts which led to litigation, particularly the difficulties of successfully inputting such information through the adversarial legal processes.

The following three chapters have a local focus while addressing issues of much wider relevance in Britain and the wider Europe. Ralph Grillo places his analysis within the larger European context which has not so long ago witnessed the *Satanic Verses* affair, and much more recently seen events such as the Danish cartoons and the killing of Theo van Gogh in Holland as a consequence of a documentary film he produced. He then focuses on the controversy in Birmingham surrounding the play, *Behzti*, providing the global and local contexts in which the controversy took place. He thereby argues that such controversies are complex phenomena, not amenable to an analysis based on the simple opposition of artistic freedom and offence to religious feelings, while also showing how the *Behzti* affair became a case study of just such a dialectic, which in turn helped to define the terms of the ensuing Racial and Religious Hatred Act 2006. While we await to see how that legislation will be enforced and interpreted in due course, and despite the political message to Muslims that this law now takes their interests more seriously than earlier laws which had excluded incitement to 'religious' hatred, the thrust of Grillo's argument reveals that it may not help to calm the unsettled waters that might lead to controversies about offence to religious feelings in the future.

Richard Gale analyses the processes involved in obtaining planning permission for mosque development in Birmingham. Using records from the local planning authorities he demonstrates the sorts of considerations that went into the process of obtaining approval for the building and location of Birmingham's Central Mosque and the subsequent desire for approval of the *azan* (call to prayer). He contextualises this case study by providing information on the success rates of planning applications by different religious groups in Birmingham, as well as by using interview records detailing how the planning process is viewed by people on all sides of the approval process. Gale's important research provides evidence that the whole process of applying and obtaining planning permission for religious buildings can be ethnically skewed in any of several fronts – in the location of the building, its style, the level of noise and traffic thereby likely to be caused, which particular group in the local community applies for permission, the feelings of local residents, the level of knowledge about the needs of the community available to local planners, and in the personal relations enjoyed by those applying and those approving the applications.

From Birmingham we move to a local study based in Hounslow to the west of London. Here Mohamed Keshavjee presents the results of a study of dispute resolution processes followed by the local community of South Asian Sunni Muslims. Keshavjee sets his study within the wider context of discussions and debates in the field of alternative dispute resolution (ADR). His study is the first of its kind to provide a local focus on a community of Muslims in Britain. He thus takes further research done on *sharia* councils by Shah-Kazemi (2001), by providing an account of the whole range of dispute processing avenues pursued by Muslims, including the Muslim Law (Sharia) Council based in Ealing. Keshavjee shows that Muslims approach a whole range of persons and bodies ranging across *imams*, influential members of the local community, advice and counselling centres, the police, solicitors and the courts, as well as the Sharia Council. Thus no one body is exclusively regarded as being the proper sphere within which to resolve disputes, thus demonstrating the inherent legal pluralism involved here, while the need for culture-specific forms of dispute resolution remains quite apparent. Keshavjee also draws out the lessons for the broader ADR debate and praxis, which also needs to equip itself for the culture-specific challenges of Muslim communities.

My own chapter deals with how marriage solemnisation among ethnic minorities is treated within British legal systems and, in particular, focuses on judicial decision making. I trace through a number of recent judgments in which the validity of marriage has been an issue and examine the extent to which British judges have been willing to recognise culture-specific ritual forms as leading to valid marriages. While we find that members of minority communities generally build the official demands of registration into their solemnisation processes I consider a series of recent cases where registration has not occurred for one reason or another. This latter set of cases presents the most challenging scenario for judges since they have to deal with marriages which obviously exist at socio-legal level but which they find difficult to recognise because of the failure to follow official requirements. In some cases we see judges using concepts such as the presumption of marriage to facilitate recognition, but in others the marriages are considered to have no legal effect. Lastly, I discuss a recent case in Scotland where the Court of Session denied recognition to a 'marriage' registered but not solemnised at socio-legal level. This judgment is cast in terms so wide that it risks doing damage to a whole swathe of marriages because it could easily be ruled by officials that the requisite intention or consent was not present at the time of registration. On the whole we find the judges having to struggle to recognise ethnic minority marriages, the underlying reason being the failure by the state to be sufficiently responsive to the demands of the socio-legal sphere.

Finally, Tahir Abbas presents us with the results of recent research on the possible reasons why the judiciary of England and Wales does not represent its ethnic plurality. It appears that the problem of under-representation is being overcome at lower levels of the judiciary more speedily than at the senior levels of the High Court and above. In order to get to the reasons for this lack of diversity Abbas explores what factors inhere in the selection of judges which make it difficult for ethnic minority judges to be appointed. Notwithstanding the popularity of legal education among ethnic minorities he finds that a specific factor hindering later progress in the profession is the choice of university as well as not having access to a network of practising lawyers. Then there are the linked problems of finding employment as a solicitor or barrister, the tasks of applying to become a judge, and being selected through a process that remains largely clouded in informal soundings and peer recommendations. Abbas also highlights a number of areas where further research would uncover the underlying mechanics of non-selection.

Chapter 1 On Cultural Diversity: The Importance of Normative Foundations for Legal Responses

Meena Bhamra

In this chapter I consider the way in which lawyers in Britain respond to and try to resolve questions related to cultural diversity. In particular I focus upon how their approach differs from that adopted by political philosophers. Philosophers who concern themselves with cultural diversity deal mainly with the normative issues it raises. In contrast, lawyers tend to make rights the starting point of their enquiries. They think about cultural diversity in terms of anti-discrimination, civil rights, minority languages, religious rights, human rights, and so on.[1] This is not to say that lawyers never concern themselves with normative issues; legal philosophers certainly look at normative questions, but their field of enquiry is the question of what 'law' is, and while the answers to this question would certainly inform the ways in which law should deal with the issues of cultural diversity, few take this further step. In this chapter I aim to demonstrate that the dominant approach in law, the rights-based approach, skips a vital, normative, step which has a significant impact on the role of the pursuit of justice in legal responses to cultural diversity. The claim that I am endeavouring to justify is that the challenge of cultural diversity in Britain has a salience in legal realms that goes deeper than just raising questions of rights.

1 See, for example, Robilliard (1984), Poulter (1986, 1990, 1998), Gregory (1987), Hepple & Szyszczak (1992), Bradney (1993), King (1995), Mason (1995), Townsend-Smith (1998), Hepple & Choudhury (2001) and Weller et al. (2001). I list these merely as examples of dominant legal responses to cultural diversity in Britain, it does not represent a list of responses whose conclusions I disagree with. I am concerned in this chapter with the method used and route taken to reach these conclusions, not with the substantive contents of the conclusions themselves.

Prakash Shah (ed.), Law and Ethnic Plurality: Socio-Legal Perspectives. *pp. 9-30.*
 ISBN 978 90 04 16245 7.

By focusing on rights alone, legal responses to cultural diversity implicitly see the normative question of whether diversity should be encouraged as superfluous. This exclusion of normative and conceptual issues is based upon the factual situation of diversity, which acts to render the question of the desirability of diversity otiose; if cultural diversity is a factual reality that we must deal with, why should valuable time be wasted considering whether it is a situation that can be normatively justified? There is much to be said in favour of such an approach, especially since it represents a pragmatic and direct response to extremely sensitive and difficult issues. However, my argument here is that without clarifying the underlying normative issues, responses to diversity are shaped without any clear statement of the presuppositions that give them meaning and purpose and that this has a significant, and damaging, impact on their ability to put forth a just solution.

In order to illustrate how a particular normative base can influence the pursuit of justice in political and legal responses, I begin with a normative argument in support of cultural diversity. In order to construct this illustrative normative position I draw upon Will Kymlicka's Theory of Multicultural Citizenship. There are two main norms which I consider to be vital to Kymlicka's theory. First, that cultures are valuable because they provide us with meaningful options in our lives; and secondly, that we have a strong and deep bond to our *own* cultures which means that we cannot easily be expected to give them up. I then use these normative foundations as reference points to assess the justice of different responses to the challenge of cultural diversity. First, I consider Kymlicka's own response which claims that voluntary immigrants should, to some extent at least, be expected to give up their own cultures, and I demonstrate that this response is unjust. Secondly, I consider two examples of dominant legal responses and, by using these normative foundations, illustrate not only that these responses are in themselves unjust, but that their failure to take the necessary normative steps displaces the very pursuit of justice from its location as a central motivation, making it a peripheral concern in their endeavours.

In order to illustrate the importance of normative foundations for legal responses, it is useful at this juncture to introduce two examples of dominant legal responses to cultural diversity. David Pearl has written extensively in this field over a number of years, later focusing on Islamic family law.[2] Whilst this later material differs markedly in its approach to his earlier work, an excerpt from one of his earlier pieces provides us with a classical example of a dominant legal approach to cultural diversity in Britain (Pearl 1972: 20):

2 See, for example, Pearl (1972, 1981, 1986, 1995) and Pearl and Menski (1998).

> When Pakistanis and Indians emigrate to this country, they do not discard their family customs. Many immigrants still retain their domicile of origin which law would be applied by the English courts as the choice of law in many disputes. Furthermore, most immigrants who adopt a domicile of choice in this country still follow family customs dissimilar from those of the indigenous population. These customs, deeply engrained into the way of life of the immigrant population, cannot be cast aside by the English courts in an attempt to integrate the immigrants into the English community around them. This country has a multicultural history and the recognition of alien customs, so long as they do not fall below minimum standards of public policy, would appear to be a valuable contribution to the enhancement of racial harmony.

Sebastian Poulter is the second legal academic whose work I wish to consider here. He has also written extensively in this field and, whilst his general approach to the presence of diasporic immigrants in Britain has not changed, his writing has evolved in a way that reflects broader developments in legal responses to diversity.[3] For example, he moves from writing about how English Law should deal with 'ethnic minority customs' (Poulter 1986) to viewing the challenges of diversity as something that must be resolved by the application of human rights (Poulter 1998). The following extract, taken from one of his earlier books, captures well the tone of his writing in this field (1986: v-vi):

> Should the ethnic minorities who have come to live here conform to English ways or should they be free to continue to practise their own customs in this country? More specifically, should English law adapt its principles and rules to accommodate foreign customs or should new arrivals bear the burden of any adjustment? Is the political objective to be the 'assimilation' of the minorities into the wider communities or is a pattern of cultural pluralism and diversity something to be officially welcomed and encouraged as valuable in its own right? ... Legal recognition must be afforded to many ethnic minority customs on grounds of practicality, commonsense, individual liberty, religious tolerance and the promotion of racial harmony. However, a few restrictions and limitations must equally be imposed, in the interests of public policy, to protect certain core values in English society...

Both could easily be described as sensitive legal responses to the question of cultural diversity in Britain. However, I want to re-evaluate this conclusion in light of the normative argument I construct.

3 For Sebastian Poulter's main works see Poulter (1986, 1990, 1998).

Before moving on to consider Kymlicka's Theory of Multicultural Citizenship, there are two preliminary assumptions that situate this thesis which require statement. First, I have limited the field of consideration here to the challenges of cultural diversity in contemporary Britain. In particular, I am concerned with cultural diversity in Britain as a consequence of the presence of Afro-Asian diasporas, and it is this concern which prompts my criticisms of Kymlicka's response to the challenge of plural societies. Secondly, it follows that I proceed on the basis that both the concept of 'culture' and the phrase 'cultural diversity' are adequate and appropriate expressions of the challenges that exist by virtue of the presence of Afro-Asian diasporas in Britain.[4]

1.1 A Normative Argument in Support of Cultural Diversity

1.1.1 Culture as a 'Context of Choice'

In the first part of this chapter I consider *a* normative argument in support of cultural diversity. I draw upon Kymlicka's liberal defence of minority rights and there are two elements which come together to make up the core of his defence. First, he explains the importance of culture, and secondly he explains why we need our *own* cultures, as opposed to being satisfied with leading a life that involves the culture of the host society (see Kymlicka 1995: 82-93).

For Kymlicka (1995: 83) cultural structures, in a general sense, are valuable: "Put simply, freedom involves making choices amongst various options, and our societal culture not only provides these options, but also makes them meaningful to us". Understanding cultural narratives is vital to our capacity to make judgments about how we should lead our lives. Thus, culture not only provides us with options in life, it also makes those options meaningful. Culture "provides the spectacles through which we identify

4 I am of the opinion that this second assumption sits on shaky ground, at least as far as legal analysis of the consequences of British Afro-Asian diasporic diversity is concerned. However, its accuracy does not impact upon the heart of my claim in this chapter, namely that in failing to consider their normative bases, dominant legal approaches to the challenges of diversity in Britain skip a vital step that has a detrimental impact on their pursuit of social justice. The epistemological question of how best to conceptualise the challenges of diversity in contemporary Britain will most certainly shape the normative base that is vital to constructing a just legal responses to these challenges. Nevertheless, the key to sustaining my claims in this chapter is to use *a* normative position and illustrate its impact upon both political and legal responses to plural societies. It is not critical to my claim to settle upon an epistemological position and use this to construct *the* normative position. Kymlicka's normative base is instructive for my purposes, and he proceeds on the basis that the challenge of plural societies lies in the presence of *cultural* pluralism.

experiences as valuable" (Dworkin 1985: 228 cited at Kymlicka 1995: 83). Cultures, therefore, are not an end in themselves, but they provide us with meaningful 'contexts of choice'.[5] Thus, the very value and worth of our lives is derived from access to culture.

Culture acts as a guide to how people act and react, it orients choices, it defines what people consider to be desirable, and what is unacceptable; as such it provides colour to our lives. What Kymlicka convincingly argues is that culture has value because of its character as a meaningful context of choice. However, this norm does not support the claim that we need our *own* cultures, and it is these cultures that we need access to. Why not let minority cultures disintegrate, as long as we have access to a culture, any culture, what does it matter which culture provides colour to our lives?

1.1.2 The Value of Cultural Membership

The second element of Kymlicka's normative claim seeks to explain why we each need access to our own, many diverse, cultures, and therefore why it is not legitimate to allow minority cultures to disintegrate. He does this by stating that we have strong bonds with our own cultures, and by explaining that the depth of this bond means that access to our own cultures is more than something that we enjoy and like; it is actually a human need.

In order to illustrate this Kymlicka (1995: 85) challenges Waldron's (1992) claim that "examples of successful 'cosmopolitan' people who move between cultures disproves the claim that people are connected to their own culture in any deep way":

> On [Waldron's] view, an Irish-American who eats Chinese food and reads her child *Grimms' Fairy Tales* is thereby 'living in a kaleidoscope of cultures'... But this is not moving between societal cultures. Rather it is enjoying the opportunities provided by the diverse societal culture which characterizes the anglophone society of the United States.

He concedes that it is legitimate to ask whether people should, on balance, assimilate into the host society. However, he (1995: 86) points out that whilst it is possible to leave one's culture, such a choice must be viewed as "analogous to the choice to take a vow of perpetual poverty and enter a religious order". By using this analogy Kymlicka is illustrating that whilst it is a physical possibility to leave one's culture, to require someone to live without their own culture is like asking them to live an impoverished existence. Just because it is a physical possibility to leave one's own culture, it does not follow that it is desirable or legitimate to require individuals to

5 I have taken this phrase from Kymlicka (1995).

abandon their own culture. The deep bond we have to our own cultures is "normally too strong to be given up" (1995: 90).

He goes further in justifying this conclusion by evidencing wide acceptance of this view amongst liberals. In particular he considers Rawls (1993), and Margalit and Raz (1990) and explains that the importance of this bond is consistent with liberalism (1995: 88-93). If a liberal society is one where individuals are free to choose their own conception of the good life and engage in a process of open-ended revision of these choices,[6] then it follows that a liberal society is not one where cultures or ways of life are imposed upon individuals. Thus, a liberal society is consistent with a society which respects the depth of the bond that individuals have with their *own* cultures.

Whilst Kymlicka provides a compelling account of why our *own* cultures should be respected by any theory of justice, it is useful to refer to some anthropological and legal anthropological works which further reinforce the validity of this norm in the British context. The Irish-American who eats Chinese food and reads German folk stories to her child is, I submit, typical of the diasporic minorities in Britain which are the focus of this chapter. To briefly explain Waldron's argument, he (1992: 762) sees the Herderian argument for the importance of cultural contexts collapsing because this cosmopolitan Irish-American illustrates that there is no distinctive human need for culture. It is this distinctive human need for culture that formed the basis of Herder's claim that we need our own cultural contexts. However, I argue that Waldron's view of this Irish-American as living within a kaleidoscope of cultures misunderstands the very nature of culture. Kymlicka (1989: 167) hits the nail on the head when he explains that culture is not a snapshot of a way of life at a particular moment in time. Culture is more accurately understood as a continual process of renegotiation, re-evaluation and reconstruction; it is never finished, nor is it finishable. This is best illustrated by considering anthropological and legal anthropological accounts of South Asians in Britain.

Roger Ballard (1994: 1-34) provides an anthropological study of South Asian diasporas in Britain that is instructive in understanding the processes of culture. He notes (1994: 5) that South Asians in Britain continue to draw inspiration from their cultural, religious and linguistic heritage and are actively engaged in a process of reinterpreting and rebuilding "their lives *on their own terms*". This process of reconstruction on their own terms stands in opposition to the official expectation that Afro-Asian diasporas would assimilate into mainstream society. Ballard observed that migrant families were, in fact, recreating around themselves familiar cultural struc-

6 It is beyond doubt that this is Kymlicka's interpretation of a liberal society, see, for example, Kymlicka (1995: 80).

tures; though familiar in nature, these structures varied from the original structures in the migrants' country of origin. Instead, this reconstruction was intended to take into account the changed circumstances of Britain. Indeed, Ballard (1994: 4) describes this process as an "adaptive strategy" born of a need to cope with a new environment.

This creation of what Ballard has termed '*Desh Pardesh*'[7] can be understood in more concrete terms when one considers the celebration of life-cycle rituals amongst South Asian diasporas, such as those of marriage and death. Menski (1988, 1993) has written of the two marriages that take place amongst these communities – there will be, for example, a Muslim, Sikh or Hindu marriage as well as a civil marriage which complies with the requirements of English law. Moreover, the religious marriage is sometimes adapted (reconstructed) to accommodate the elements required by English law. For example, Menski (1991) has written of the incorporation of the English registration ceremony into the Hindu wedding with the development of "new rituals out of the traditional patterns" to suit the occasion; a sort of Hindu-isation of the English registration ceremony, in order to incorporate it as part of the Hindu wedding ceremony. Menski goes further and also writes of this reconstruction beyond the bounds of just life-cycle rituals, and explains this phenomenon as the creation of hybrid laws by which day-to-day life is to be lived; he has termed these hybrid laws *angrezi shariat*, *angrezi dharma* and so on.[8] In many ways Menski's work on cultural diversity in a legal context parallels Ballard's conclusions in social contexts – one writes of legal hybrids, the other of cultural hybridity.

Ballard's work also provides a helpful concept that he terms 'skilled cultural navigation'. Later generations of South Asian migrants, those who are born in Britain, or who migrated at a very young age, are active in wider social orders than merely those of their own culture, and these other social orders can, in fact, contradict the conventions of their own culture. Ballard (1994: 30) asks whether this code-switching between different social orders will create psychologically confused individuals. He (1994: 31) concludes that the ability to switch conceptual codes does not result in cultural con-

7 *Desh Pardesh* is Urdu meaning 'home from home' or 'home abroad', and Ballard uses it to describe "the embodiment of the self-created worlds of Britain's South Asian settlers" (1994: 29). Given the linguistic proximity of Urdu and Punjabi, Ballard's use of *Desh Pardesh* resonates with the Punjabis that are actually the subject of his own chapter in this edited collection of papers; in Punjabi the same phrase would be *des pardes*. The term has also been adapted and translated into Bengali to denote a similar process amongst British Bangladeshis: see Gardner (1993), cited in Shah (2005b: 126), who writes of *desh bidesh*.

8 See, for example, Menski (1988, 1991, 1993) and Pearl and Menski (1998).

fusion anymore than being bilingual confuses speech. Those individuals who develop an accomplished capacity to switch codes are 'skilled cultural navigators'. It is this notion of 'skilled cultural navigators', together with an understanding of culture as a process of 'reconstruction on their own terms' that better explains our Irish-American.

Waldron describes this Irish-American who eats Chinese food and reads German folk stories to her child as an individual who is not rooted in any particular culture, an individual who is cosmopolitan. However, armed with the concepts of skilled cultural navigators and culture as a continual process of reconstruction and renegotiation, this Irish-American can be explained in a very different way; she is an exemplary skilled cultural navigator who is actively engaged in rebuilding and reinterpreting her culture on her own terms. (Perhaps this individual can be described as leading a hybrid American cultural life.) By virtue of incorporating aspects of other cultures into her life, it does not follow that she has abandoned her own; in fact, the incorporation of Chinese food and German folk stories can be said to illustrate a dynamic and fluid reconstruction and renegotiation of Irish-American culture that is typical of diasporic minorities.[9] Intrinsic to the nature of culture is that it is neither reified nor absolute in the way that Waldron's explanation of this Irish-American suggests, so that it is not possible to abandon one's own culture by simply skilfully navigating the diverse cultures that exist within various social orders. It does not follow that people lose the ties that bind them to their own culture merely by virtue of this capacity to navigate.

Ballard's study brings out another crucial element to culture which also assists in explaining the bond that individuals have to their own culture. The reinterpretation and reconstruction of culture by members of diasporic minorities takes place "on their own terms" (1994: 5, 34). Vital to the processes of cultural reconstruction is the individual agency that it involves, and I would tentatively suggest that this individual investment not only assists in explaining the depth of the bond that individuals have to their *own* culture, but also sheds some light on why it is even possible to begin to talk in terms of cultures that belong to individuals.[10]

9 See Kymlicka (1995: 104-105) for an elaboration of the dynamism of societal culture.

10 My suggestion here represents one small corner of a complex field which requires, *inter alia*, consideration of descent and heritage in identifying how and when we can write of cultures that belong to individuals and/or groups. My cursory explanation may suggest that individuals are able to construct their own cultures without any boundaries. However, this ignores the dynamics between individual and group agency in the reconstruction of cultures. It is not possible for there to be limitless reconstructions and reinterpretations

I reference both Ballard and Menski's work here to reinforce, in the British context, the validity of the norm that individuals have strong bonds to their own cultures, such that any theory of justice must consider how best to ensure these cultures do not disintegrate; and also to provide a more lucid explanation of the culturally hybrid phenomena typical amongst diasporas.[11] However, my focus in this chapter remains the construction of a normative position which supports cultural diversity and Kymlicka provides me with a compelling account. First, culture is valuable because it is a context of choice which not only provides us with options in life, but also makes those options meaningful. Secondly, access to any culture does not provide the meaning that makes cultures valuable; we have strong and deep bonds with our own cultures, which means that a life without our own cultures would be impoverished.

It does not implicitly follow from this normative position that I am also arguing that all aspects of culture have a valuable and worthwhile impact upon our lives. Indeed, I believe that Kymlicka's take on culture does not represent such a view: in acknowledging the deep bond that we have with our own cultures, and the meaning that cultures give to our lives, it does not follow that all aspects of cultures take on a valuable and worthwhile role in our lives. British policy on 'forced marriages' provides an illustrative example here. Britain has a policy of intervening abroad when its citizens are forced to marry against their will.[12] Consular services will stage

---

of cultures, and there appear to be external boundaries which are connected, *inter alia*, to one's descent, heritage and group membership.

11 This reflection upon social realities and existing relations echoes an approach taken by critical theorists in the field of political philosophy. Young (2000: 10) describes the approach of critical theory as a "socially and historically situated normative analysis". Regrettably, the relationship between jurisprudence and sociology/anthropology is far less explored. However, the approach taken here recognises the validity and importance of socio-legal approaches in dealing with questions of plurality. Menski (2006a: 15-16) explores this very question and provides a gateway into such debates. Citing Hinz (2003: 117) and Twining (2000: 10) he convincingly demonstrates that any theory which endeavours to deal with the issues of plurality and globalisations must not only have a strong socio-legal approach, but also "challenge the prevailing 'black box' approaches, as well as 'black letter' law and the predominance of authoritative law-making by rulers and nation-states" (2006a: 16). I agree with this and would argue that sociological and anthropological texts provide insights into the creation of 'laws' and social orders that cannot be ignored in formulating a theory of justice which focuses on the questions raised by plurality.

12 For further details of the Forced Marriage Unit and its work see http://www.fco.gov.uk/servlet/Front?pagename=OpenMarket/Xcelerate/ShowPage&c=Page&cid=1094234857863

an intervention and take these individuals out of the situation they find themselves in and return them to Britain. However, a *Guardian* newspaper report on this policy (Walsh 2005) followed a couple of girls in this situation and noted that after the intervention the girls had attempted to reconcile with the parents who had forced them to marry against their will. Whilst these girls were clear that they did not want to marry against their own will, it did not follow that they wanted to abandon their cultures. This is the consequence of being attached to one's own culture; to live outside and without this cultural context is an impoverished existence. It is entirely possible, therefore, to be attached to one's culture, and also for that culture to have a detrimental and damaging impact upon one's life. The deep bond that we have to our own cultures is a complex relationship that cannot simply be understood as implying that all aspects of culture will lead to worthwhile and valuable experiences, or that where there are (personally acknowledged) detrimental practices this will drive us to leave our cultural contexts.

In this particular example, the damaging nature of forcing these girls to marry against their will stems from a denial of their individual agency within this cultural context. Let us suppose these girls freely consented to having their marriages arranged in this way. As autonomous individuals with free will, their choice ought to be respected, regardless of the fact that a significant number of individuals would choose to find their partners in a different way. Alternative examples would illustrate the many other ways in which culture can give rise to damaging life experiences. The disadvantage that women continue to live under in European societies immediately springs to mind as another way in which cultures can oppress individuals. The examples are numerous, but my point is that it is wrong to assume that the cultures that we are deeply bonded to must only provide us with valuable, life-enhancing experiences, or that we are deeply bonded to our cultures only because they provide nothing but empowering, life-enhancing experiences. Furthermore, we ought not to assume that where our cultures are a source of detrimental, agency-denying or oppressive experiences we will want to completely move outside of that cultural context. If I accept these assumptions I will be leaping too far from our norm that individuals have strong and deep bonds with their cultures without good reasons to ground my leap. I argue here that we have strong and deep bonds with our own cultures, which means that a life without our own cultures would be impoverished, not that cultures only provide life-enhancing and emancipatory experiences; the two are separate norms and I am using the former here.

1.1.3 Kymlicka's Response to the Challenges of Cultural Diversity

I can now consider how Kymlicka moves from these two core norms to construct a response to the challenge of plural societies which expects voluntary immigrants to give up their own cultures. How does he reach this conclusion after he has so convincingly argued for the importance of our cultures? Having outlined his response, I use our normative foundation to argue that not only is this response incongruent with social realities in contemporary Britain, but it also fails to do justice in that social reality. Additionally, I claim that it is a flawed argument on a philosophical level. Finally, I venture that Kymlicka's response is motivated by a fear of nations where ethnic groups can legitimately make separatist claims.

Kymlicka claims that voluntary immigrants should be expected to live without their own cultures by making two distinct moves. First, he explains that he is not concerned with the survival of all cultures; he is concerned only with those cultures that fall within his definition of 'societal cultures'. Only these have grounds to survive into the future, and voluntary immigrants do not have and cannot develop their own 'societal cultures' (1995: 76-80). Secondly, he makes a distinction between 'national minorities' and 'ethnic groups' (1995: 11-26), the latter encompassing voluntary immigrants, and suggests that ethnic groups waived their rights to live and work in their own cultures when they chose to leave their original culture. In order to elaborate upon these arguments it is necessary to consider the precise definition of 'societal culture' and explain the distinction between 'national minorities' and 'ethnic groups'.[13]

Kymlicka readily admits that expressions such as 'cultural community' and 'cultural structure' are extremely hard to define (1989: 166) and so clearly sets out the cultural structure that is relevant to his argument. He is not concerned with isolating the character of a community at any one moment in time, so that any changes to this community would be considered a loss of culture. His focus is upon culture as a context of choice, with such a structure persisting even if its members should decide to modify the character of the culture, should it no longer find those ways worthwhile (1989: 166-77). Kymlicka defines his focus as 'societal culture' (1995: 76). Societal culture (1995: 76):

> [P]rovides its members with meaningful ways of life across the full range of human activities, including social, educational, religious, recreational, and economic life, encompassing both public and private spheres.

13 For an explanation of 'culture' see Kymlicka (1989: 166-67), and for a definition of 'societal culture' see Kymlicka (1995: 76-80).

Societal cultures involve more than just "shared memories or values" and must include "common institutions and practices" (1995: 76). The creation of societal cultures is intimately linked to modernisation, since modern nation-states have evolved through this process of building a shared culture.

Kymlicka makes it clear that immigrant groups do not possess societal cultures when they arrive in their host country (1995: 78):

> Some immigrants might hope to re-create these practices in their entirety in their new country. But that is effectively impossible without significant government support, which is rarely if ever provided.

Nevertheless, immigrants are no longer expected to assimilate in the host country; they are expected to integrate. By using the term 'integration' Kymlicka endeavours to convey that there has been a rejection of the model of anglo-conformity in favour of recognition that immigrants have the right to maintain their ethnic heritage in the private sphere. Whilst there are aspects of this ethnic heritage that survive, this will not result in the re-creation of a societal culture. Instead it merely contributes "new options and perspectives to the larger anglophone culture, making it richer and more diverse" (1995: 78-79). Societal cultures are the domain of national minorities and even national majorities, not ethnic groups. For Kymlicka, in today's world the only cultures that can hope to "survive and develop" are societal cultures because of the significant "pressures towards the creation of a single common culture in each country" (1995: 80). Ethnic groups, as he calls them, cannot expect to be provided with the resources necessary to recreate their own societal cultures; and for a diversity of cultures to survive amongst the homogenising tendencies inherent in the nation-state process they must be societal cultures.

Let me explain a little further what I believe Kymlicka is arguing here. He believes that immigrants have societal cultures, but that they have left them behind in their country of origin. He suggests that this societal culture does not organically replicate itself in the host country because of the tendencies of the nation-state process; behind the idea of a nation-state are concepts such as cohesion, stability and security and in order to engender these characteristics the nation-state process involves the creation of a uniform and homogenous societal culture. In the face of this nation-state process, immigrants will require, *inter alia*, state resources to go about recreating their own societal culture in the host country. It is through his distinction between 'national minorities' and 'ethnic groups' that he explains why immigrants should not receive such state support, and why they are not entitled to recreate their societal cultures.

Kymlicka's second move involves this distinction between 'national minorities' and 'ethnic groups'. National minorities are found in multination states where cultural diversity is the consequence of the incorporation of previously self-governing, territorially concentrated cultures into a larger state. As an example of a national minority Kymlicka (1995: 11) points to American Indians living in the United States. In contrast, ethnic groups are found in polyethnic states, where cultural diversity is a consequence of familial and individual immigration (1995: 16). As an example of ethnic groups Kymlicka (1995: 17) points to the immigrants from Britain's former colonies that were accepted by Britain after the Second World War. It is perfectly possible (and likely) that a country is both multinational and polyethnic (1995: 17).

Kymlicka states that ethnic groups "wish to integrate into the larger society, and to be accepted as full members of it" (1995: 11), whereas the needs and desires of national minorities are very different and reflect their particular histories. His understanding of the nature of familial and individual immigration is elaborated when he seeks to answer the question (1995: 95):

> If people have a deep bond with their own culture ... [as he argues] should we not allow immigrants to re-create their own societal cultures (and thereby effectively become a national minority)?

In response he explains that immigrants can be separated from colonists because the latter arrive with the intention and deliberate policy of the systematic creation of a new country in the image of the old one they have left behind. Immigrants, on the other hand, arrive on the basis of an individual or familial choice to leave their society and join another existing society. Whilst the possibility of allowing immigrants to settle together, even allowing them to have their own homelands, and providing the resources necessary for them to re-create a societal culture is a legitimate policy that would certainly not be inherently unjust, nor is it unjust not to provide these sorts of resources and not to give immigrants the legal status necessary to become national minorities. To expect immigrants to integrate is not unjust because (1995: 95-96):

> [M]ost immigrants (as distinct from refugees) choose to leave their own culture ... they know when they come that their success, and that of their children, depends on integrating into the institutions of English-speaking society.

Kymlicka explains that people have the right to live and work in their own culture, but this is a right that can be waived, and "immigration is one way of waiving one's right" (1995: 96).

However, this does not mean that voluntary immigrants forfeit all of their rights relating to the expression of their identity. In this regard Kymlicka refers to Parekh (1990) and clarifies that integration is a two-way process requiring larger society to adapt itself to immigrants and immigrants to adapt to larger society (1995: 96). This form of mutual integration would require efforts to fight prejudice and discrimination, which means not only legislating against discrimination but also changing perceptions of immigrants in, for example, school textbooks, government documents and the media; in essence, such efforts can be seen as an attempt to shed ethnocentric assumptions and attitudes. Integration may need to go further than this, and require "some modification of the institutions of the dominant culture in the form of group-specific polyethnic rights", one of the examples given being the exemption Sikhs have from motorcycle helmet laws on account of their turbans (1995: 96-97). Ethnic groups are not, however, entitled to any form of self-government rights. Self-government rights are defined as including "some form of political autonomy or territorial jurisdiction, so as to ensure the full and free development of…cultures" in accordance with the best interests of those people (1995: 27).

Prior to considering why these arguments are flawed, it is worth noting that Kymlicka's distinction between national minorities and ethnic groups has been mirrored by judicial interpretation of anti-discrimination legislation in Britain. The Race Relations Act 1976 (RRA) prohibits direct and indirect discrimination on "racial grounds",[14] which is defined to cover "colour, race, nationality, or ethnic or national origins".[15] The courts have held that English people come under the head of national origins and not ethnic origins.[16] In terms of the anti-discrimination claim before the court very little turns on this distinction. However, it serves to highlight the difficulties with this national/ethnic dichotomy in Britain. The key principle of belonging for the English is their national origins, whereas other groups, such as the Jews and Sikhs,[17] are identified by their ethnic origins.[18]

This seemingly harmless separation between national and ethnic elements masks a potentially malevolent form of thinking. Although Jews

14 Race Relations Act 1976, s. 1(1).

15 Race Relations Act 1976, s. 3(1).

16 See *Northern Joint Police Board v Power* [1997] IRLR 610 and *BBC Scotland v Souster* [2001] IRLR 150.

17 Both groups have been identified as having ethnic origins for the purposes of the RRA: see *Seide v Gillette Industries Ltd* [1980] IRLR 427 for the Jews, and *Mandla (Sewa Singh) and Another v Dowell Lee and Another* [1983] 2 AC 548 for the Sikhs.

18 I am taking on the terms of the RRA and using 'national origin' here as a categorisation which is distinct from 'nationality'.

have had a permanent and acknowledged presence in Britain since the late 17th century, they do not have national origins in this country. Those groups who cannot show an exclusive territorial connection with one country seem to be unable to fall within this bracket.[19] As Kymlicka's work confirms, territorial connections lead to a stronger claim of belonging and thus result in stronger rights, such as self-government rights. Jews are an especially good example of why this national/ethnic separation is therefore malevolent; global movements of peoples (excluding those that moved with empire expansion in mind) have tended to be prompted by disadvantage of some sort, whether this was an economic disadvantage or outright persecution. Ethnic groups are, therefore, penalised twice, first by the disadvantage they suffer and, second by the thinning of the rights they can claim as a consequence of this territorial movement. It is regrettable that Kymlicka takes on this national/ethnic dichotomy without enquiring into the underlying malevolent thinking that informs the distinction.

The national/ethnic distinction that Kymlicka replicates is troubling, but more problematic is his reduction of the cultural rights of voluntary immigrants to virtually nothing. His exclusion of voluntary immigrants from any substantive cultural rights cannot be sustained for at least three reasons. First, his understanding of the cultural structures of immigrant groups is incongruent with social realities, at least as far as post-war migrants in Britain are concerned. Secondly, his account of the choice that migrants make and their intentions when they leave their country of origin is inconsistent with historical realities. Finally, both his declaration that voluntary immigrants ought never to recreate their societal cultures and that they waive their rights to their own culture cannot hold on a philosophical level when the British born children of immigrants are considered.

It is clear from the earlier consideration of Ballard's study that anthropologists in Britain have come to very different conclusions as concerns the cultural structures of diasporic minorities; they have not abandoned their cultures as Kymlicka suggests they should; instead they have reconstructed their own cultures "on their own terms" (Ballard 1994: 34). Moreover, Pearl and Menski (1998) and Shah-Kazemi (2001) both confirm that this reconstruction has now developed to such an extent that informal mechanisms for dispute resolution, such as Shariat Councils, have evolved in Britain. In Britain at least, voluntary immigrants are recreating societal cultures, complete with their own institutional structures.

19 Muslims have been unable to show either ethnic or national origins under the RRA because it is not possible for them to claim one common geographical origin or one common language: see *Tariq v Young* Case 247738/88 EOR Discrimination Case Law Digest No. 2.

Secondly, Kymlicka misunderstands the intentions of these post-war migrants when they made the choice to leave their country of origin. Literature in this field indicates that the philosophical argument that voluntary migrants chose to migrate and therefore waive their rights to their culture cannot hold: post-war migrants were encouraged to enter Britain to fill labour shortages following the Second World War and, not only were they not made aware of any conditions of integration prior to migration, based on their colonial experience they had no expectation of a clash of cultures or that they ought to assimilate.[20] Indeed, literature in this field confirms that Britain's post-war migrants did not expect to be accepted by the host society, they expected to be kept out, and nevertheless they made the choice to migrate. Aurora's (1967) sociological study of Indian immigrants in Britain is just one example of such literature. Consider also the contents of an appendix to Lord Ouseley's report on race relations in Bradford after the 2001 riots, extracted in a *Guardian* report (Wainwright 2001 cited in Shah 2005b: 60):

> Immigrants ... can and often do maintain key elements of their culture for generations, but in many other ways they accept the dominant, host culture. Colonists do not. They come into a country to displace the existing culture and establish their own. From colonist to immigrant is the dominant pattern historically. However, this process seems to have been thrown into reverse in Bradford.

I would argue that it is less that the process has been 'thrown into reverse', and more that the assumption that immigrants implicitly agreed to shed their own cultures, societal or otherwise, and assimilate into mainstream society does not accord with the reality of the immigrant experience. Moreover, given that Kymlicka (1995: 86) states that leaving one's culture is "analogous to the choice to take a vow of perpetual poverty and enter a religious order", any agreement to leave one's culture would have to be explicit and the choice ought to be well understood; tacit assumptions are simply insufficient given the gravity of the consequences of this choice.

20 For example, colonial India was administered in accordance with a *millet*-like personal law system, and Indians were well aware that the British retained their own cultures and institutions, and did not assimilate. See Derrett (1968: 39-41) for a definition of the personal law system in India. For details of the impact of colonial rule upon Hindu Law in India see Menski (2006a: 239-49). See Menski (2006a: 116-17) for an argument that legal pluralism is not a consequence of colonialism and modernity; there are examples of forms of such legal pluralism that pre-date colonial India and those plural legal systems introduced by Muslim rulers.

Finally, there are problems with Kymlicka's arguments on a philosophical level if the British born children of these voluntary immigrants are considered. Even if we accept that voluntary immigrants have no rights to recreate their own societal cultures, why should succeeding British born generations continue to bear the burden of their elders' choice for time immemorial? They have, after all, made no choices to leave the country that they were born in, or to leave their own culture. For how many generations must they live as a dispossessed culture? It seems that it must be conceded that there is a point, somewhere in the future, when ethnic groups have lived in a country for long enough for them to legitimately make the transition to become a national minority. If there is such a point, then Kymlicka's argument merely defers the recreation of societal cultures by immigrant groups and the transition from ethnic group to national minority.

Moreover, if voluntary immigrants waive their rights to their own cultures by choosing to move countries, and thus ought to stop insisting upon recreating their own societal cultures, Kymlicka must also show that their children and following generations also consent to this waiver of cultural rights. Whilst he recognises this problem in a small footnote (1995: 215, n.19) and admits that "the children of immigrants do not consent, and it is not clear that parents should be able to waive their children's rights", he goes on to fudge the issue by suggesting that the strength of their cultural rights (which I ought to add, cannot now be distinguished from the strength of the cultural rights of a national minority) means that governments ought to endeavour to make the children of immigrants "feel 'at home'" (1995: 216, n.19). However, he equates 'feeling at home' to ensuring that these children integrate into mainstream society. Thus, he provides no greater rights for the children of immigrants than the polyethnic rights he provides for voluntary immigrants who have waived some of their cultural rights. In effect then, it is as if immigrant parents have waived the cultural rights of their children on their behalf.

In summation, I have demonstrated that Kymlicka's argument excluding ethnic groups, as he terms them, from anything more than the polyethnic rights he describes is weak on a philosophical level, and unconstructive given the social and historical realities that persist in Britain.[21] I would like

21 In a Symposium on Multicultural Citizenship (1997) Joseph H. Carens, Iris Marion Young, Bhikhu Parekh and Rainer Forst provide critiques of Kymlicka's theory. Whilst each author goes into far more depth than has been possible here and considers the totality of Kymlicka's theory, at some point, and in varied ways, they all find his exclusion of ethnic groups from some cultural rights problematic. Kymlicka provides a reply to these critiques (Kymlicka 1997), and this reply paper becomes a chapter in one of his books (Kymlicka 2001: 49-66); the crux of his response to the critique of this exclusion of ethnic

to take this claim further and venture an explanation for Kymlicka's exclusion of ethnic groups; he makes this exclusionary move as a side-effect of his wish to ensure that ethnic groups cannot make territorial claims. He fears that, if allowed, ethnic groups will seek to create segregated societal cultures at odds, and perhaps even in conflict with mainstream cultures.[22] While this may be a legitimate fear, far sounder philosophical arguments than those he provides are necessary in order to sustain the claim that they have waived the bulk of their cultural rights, given that he has so convincingly argued that cultures provide meaning to our lives and that each of us has strong and deep bonds to our own cultures such that a life without them would be an impoverished one.[23] Indeed, the enormity of constructing such philosophical arguments is a testament to the strength of the normative foundations he constructs as to the importance and value of our own cultures.

1.2 Dominant Legal Responses to the Challenges of Cultural Diversity

I have established that Kymlicka does not provide compelling arguments that weaken the strength of the core normative argument in support of cultural diversity as it applies to Afro-Asian diasporas in Britain. In the final part of this chapter, I return to consider the two examples of dominant legal responses to cultural diversity that were extracted before I had set out our core normative argument. I am now able to evaluate these responses in light of the normative foundations Kymlicka provides. With these normative foundations, I approach these responses from within a framework that accepts, first, that cultures give meaning and value to our lives and, second, that we have strong bonds with our own cultures, and that justice therefore demands that minority cultures not be allowed to disintegrate.

In evaluating Pearl in light of my normative position, a subtle impact can be detected. He shows much sensitivity to the arguments that sustain our normative position: he indicates that migrants have not just discarded

groups is that hard choices have to be made in a liberal democracy, and this exclusion is just one of those hard choices.

22 This very concern is reflected in much post-7/7 media consideration of multiculturalism in Britain. Trevor Phillips, Chair of the Commission for Racial Equality made a speech on 22 September 2005 at the Manchester Council for Community Relations where he declared that Britain was "sleepwalking into segregation". See http://www.cre.gov.uk/Default.aspx.LocID-0hgnew07s.RefLocID-0hg00900c002.Lang-EN.htm.

23 This question strays into areas which are more accurately considered with the proper role of the state. However, Kymlicka does not explicitly address this issue.

their family customs; that their customs are deeply ingrained into their way of life; and that English law cannot just cast aside these customs. However, the suggestion that these alien customs can only be recognised "in so far as they do not fall below minimum standards of public policy" is discordant with the notion of culture as outlined by our normative position, since implicit in this statement is the suggestion that someone else can dictate to an individual the boundaries of their culture. As I have shown, this has not and cannot be the case. Indeed, the consequences of denying individual agency were made clear in the example of the girls who had rejected a forced marriage but wished to remain in contact with their parents. Pearl's failure to take the normative step has an impact upon the strength of his arguments and his suggestions, although he shows some understanding of realities amongst British Afro-Asian diasporas. By juxtaposing this extract of Pearl's work and a normative position, I have illustrated that normative foundations are vital to the cogency and practical utility of legal responses to cultural diversity. Furthermore, a clear normative position has enabled me to question the justice of Pearl's seemingly liberal response.

Viewed from the perspective of the normative base I have set out above, Poulter provides a striking illustration of the impact of normative foundations upon legal responses. It should be initially stated that Poulter does not set out any normative bases to explain why he considers that there must be some legal recognition of ethnic minority customs (as he phrases it) in any of his works. This, I believe, is a missing step which has a significant impact upon the strength and justice of his claims.

If I look specifically at the passage extracted above and measure Poulter's analysis of the questions raised by diversity against our normative foundations that our own cultures are vital to our lives, he stumbles with his very first question. He considers the issue to be a simple choice between two different cultures. However, our normative position, which I can support with sociological and anthropological accounts, makes it clear that there can be no simple choice between cultures in the way that individuals may choose between a white and a blue shirt. Instead, it is evident that British South Asians are engaging in adaptive strategies which involve the reconstruction and renegotiation of their own cultures. Moreover, I have explained that this reconstruction takes place *on their own terms*; Poulter completely fails to appreciate this dimension of individual agency in his analysis of the challenges of diversity. For him it is choice to be made, and that choice must be made by English law and those who decide upon British political objectives; Afro-Asian diasporic individuals are merely passive recipients of these choices.

Poulter suggests that assimilation is a viable possibility, though our normative foundations clearly show that living without our own cultures means living an impoverished existence. For Poulter there are no questions relating to the quality of life a nation-state may wish to promote amongst its citizens, instead, the reasons that it might be advisable for those who make the choices to allow some ethnic minority customs to persist are, foremost, commonsense and practicality, but also religious tolerance, racial harmony and individual liberty.

Poulter's failure to take this normative step and enquire why culture, religion and even individual liberty are worth promoting means that his arguments lack solid foundations. In turn, this lack of sound normative foundations has a direct impact on the practical utility of his suggestions; if it is not possible to understand and defend why a particular position should be taken, it is not robust enough to be considered as a serious option. Moreover, in using my normative position it has been possible for me to raise fundamental questions about the justice of Poulter's suggestions.

I believe Poulter himself intuitively felt this need for a stronger normative position upon which to base his conclusions about the limits to which diverse cultures can be accommodated in one nation-state. This led him to borrow and lean on the norms behind human rights, and justify his conclusions by making the challenges of diversity a question of how to balance competing rights (see Poulter 1998). However, by using this method he fails to do the groundwork that I am arguing for here. His conclusions and claims remain identical to those that he makes in his earlier works, it is merely the format of the argument that changes. Where it was once that the Muslim divorce offended against core English values, he is now able to identify that civil liberties and fundamental rights constitute these core values.[24]

Whilst it is unfortunate that Poulter appears to be reasoning backwards here,[25] my concern is that he leans on the normative background to human rights in a way that does not place justice as his primary aim. When rights are used in any legal context, these rights invoke a normative argument that has already occurred. By claiming the right to life I invoke the spirit of infinite amounts of normative reasoning that led to the conclusion that this right is a fundamental human right. By entering into a dialogue about the correct interpretation of the right to life, for example by questioning whether life starts at conception or birth, I engage with this normative reasoning. The problem with using the normative foundations of human rights to resolve the quandaries of cultural diversity is that they

24 Compare Poulter (1986: v-vi) and Poulter (1998: 22-26, 391).

25 What I mean by 'reasoning backwards' is that looking across Poulter's work in this way, it seems as if he has arrived at his conclusions and then proceeded to fit the human rights arguments into these conclusions, when the correct order would be to consider and weigh the value of the competing rights and draw conclusions at the end of this process.

were not reasoned out with a concern for the specificities of the cultural diversity that Poulter looks at. In this way his writing fails to concern itself with the justice of that specific situation of cultural diversity.

Let me illustrate the claim that failing to take the step of constructing a normative argument displaces the pursuit of justice in a more explicit manner. The conclusions that Kymlicka and Poulter reach on the rights of diasporic minorities to their own cultures are broadly similar; both argue for limits to the rights they can claim to their own cultures and both place these limits in about the same place by arguing that they should stop when the cohesiveness of the nation is threatened. Kymlicka expresses this limit by arguing that ethnic groups cannot have self-government rights, whereas Poulter writes of the importance of not eroding shared core values. Ultimately they both argue that it is just to allow Sikhs the turban exemption (Poulter 1998: 277-332, Kymlicka 1995: 96-97), but that separate regulatory systems based upon cultural differences would be to go too far (Poulter 1998: 195-236, Kymlicka 1995: 26-33, 95-100). Although both Kymlicka and Poulter reach a similar endpoint, the manner in which it has been possible for me to analyse their responses is markedly different; I have been able to question the very pursuit of justice in Poulter's conclusions, but I have only been able to *assess* the justice of Kymlicka's conclusions. My criticisms of Kymlicka's response to voluntary immigrants only comes down to a disagreement of degrees. I have been able to pick small holes in the substantive content of some of his conclusions by using our normative foundations; I have not been able to suggest that he has side-lined the pursuit of justice in his response to plural societies precisely because he clearly sets out his normative foundations. In contrast, Poulter's lack of normative foundations has enabled me to attack his arguments at their very core and do the necessary work to claim that his conclusions are ill-founded and side-line the requirements of justice.

Failing to take the step of constructing normative foundations displaces the pursuit of justice when making legal responses to cultural diversity, making it a periphery concern. Why does the pursuit of justice matter to such responses? I could defer here to broad claims that law, in each and every situation it acts in, ought to be pursuing justice, but I can put forward a more urgent and situation-specific argument. All of the responses to cultural diversity that I have considered here, but especially those of Pearl and Poulter, illustrate how the law can be used as a tool to outlaw and exclude certain cultures. In a post-7/7 Britain we are acutely aware of the potentially devastating impact of excluding particular groups.[26] With

26 See, for example, Ignatieff (2003: 6-7) who argues that the humiliation, resentment and lack of sense of belonging caused by mainstream British society rejecting minority cultures makes British subjects willing recruits to terrorist

this in mind, it is vital that we are able to explain why laws that exclude are made in the pursuit of justice. In fact, if we are able to explain such laws as a by-product of justice, it may even be possible to dampen the exclusionary impact that they have.[27] It is for these urgent, pressing and weighty reasons that I argue that legal responses to cultural diversity must take the vital step of setting out their normative foundations.

In this chapter I have endeavoured to demonstrate the value of clarifying one's normative position to the pursuit of justice in responses to cultural diversity. It is vital to be clear, however, about what I am not suggesting with my arguments. I do not claim that it is inappropriate for lawyers to suggest that there are limits to that behaviour which is deemed acceptable; I am not making a relativist's argument which suggests that all kinds of behaviour should be tolerated in the name of culture. In fact, I make no suggestions at all as to how the law and lawyers can resolve and meet the challenges of cultural diversity. My claim is that as lawyers, before we can even begin to think about these questions, we need to be clearer about their normative foundations. If those are sound, both the questions and responses raised by cultural diversity may become clearer.

organisations such as Al Qaeda who hijack religious ideologies and claim to speak on behalf of the humiliation of the rejected. This argument is based upon the norms elaborated by those who write about the 'politics of recognition'. The main proponents of the politics of recognition are Charles Taylor (1994), Axel Honneth (1992, 1995), James Tully (1995) and Iris Marion Young (1990, 2002), although Young and Tully do not use the terminology of recognition.

27 I am implicitly making reference here to arguments about how an understanding of the reasons behind the claims of other participants in a dialogue adds something to the process of dialogue in the public sphere that makes consensus in the face of conflicting claims more likely. See, for example, Rawls (1993), Habermas (1993, 1996, 1998) and Fraser (2003).

Chapter 2 Immigration, Diversity and Integration: The Limits of EU Law

Valsamis Mitsilegas

2.1 Introduction – The Uncertainties of Integration in Europe

The issue of 'integration' has become an increasingly contested and important topic in European politics in recent years. A number of European governments have adopted a series of measures aimed at ensuring the integration into their societies of individuals and/or groups perceived not to fit in. An example of this strategy has been the introduction of 'citizenship tests' for the purposes of naturalisation in a number of countries, including the United Kingdom. However, while in principle there seems to be a general political consensus that 'integration' is a worthy objective, what is meant by the term remains unclear. The *degree and nature* of integration are unclear: does integration mean assimilation, or multiculturalism? Is it to be perceived in terms of rights, or in identity terms? The rekindling of the integration debate in Europe was triggered largely by violent incidents and terrorist attacks, which have brought questions of identity and belonging prominently to the fore. However, these questions – while leading to a proliferation of calls for 'integration' of perceived outsiders – have also blurred further the picture regarding the *ratione personae* scope of integration: are integration measures targeted at 'immigrants' inside the territory of a country, or also at those wishing to enter the territory? Is the term 'immigrant' applicable only to third country nationals, or also to citizens of European countries with an immigrant/ethnic minority background? The debate in the UK after the 7/7 London bombings has been indicative of this confusion.

Dealing with the issue of integration at the EU level adds another layer of complexity. Integration elements have been featuring increasingly on the EU immigration strategy, and have been proliferating in the light of the centrality of the issue in the domestic politics in a number

Prakash Shah (ed.), Law and Ethnic Plurality: Socio-Legal Perspectives. *pp. 31-45.*
 ISBN 978 90 04 16245 7.

of Member States. Both the Commission and the Council have emphasised the importance of integration, perhaps with a slightly different focus. However, as far as common EU principles or standards are concerned, the uncertainties surrounding the scope and content of integration measures are compounded by the new dimensions of concepts such as citizenship and identity at EU level (and the extent to which these can be disassociated from the national level). Further complexity is added by the constitutional limits to the Union's powers to act on these issues. These uncertainties and complexities will inform my analysis of the development of an EU legal and policy framework on integration. By examining both Treaty provisions and secondary Community law, the chapter aims to paint a detailed picture of this framework, while highlighting the limits that EU law imposes on national and European integration agendas.

2.2 The Emerging EU Framework on Integration

Integration considerations started becoming visible at Tampere. The opening part of the 1999 European Council Conclusions includes an express reference to the development of a common approach to ensure the integration of those third country nationals who are lawfully resident in the Union.[1] A more detailed mandate is included in the chapter on the 'fair treatment of third country nationals', where it is stated that a more vigorous integration policy should aim at granting these individuals *rights and obligations comparable to those of EU citizens* and should enhance non-discrimination in economic, social and cultural life and develop measures against racism and xenophobia (point 18). A common approach is thus advocated specifically regarding third country nationals who are lawfully resident in the EU (and not for those wishing to enter the EU or nationals of Member States). Integration is viewed as a two-way process, with third country nationals having rights and obligations, and the granting of rights and non-discrimination. The Conclusions also stress the importance of political rights in the integration process by further stating that the legal status of third country nationals should be approximated to that of Member States' nationals and that offering the opportunity to the former to obtain the nationality of the EU Member State where they reside should be encouraged (point 21).

The follow-up to Tampere has not been particularly impressive in the field of economic migration and the rights of third country nationals. However, the few legally binding instruments adopted – in particular the Directive on the rights of third country nationals who are long-term

1 http://europa.eu.int/council/off/conclu/oct99/oct99_en.htm: Point 4.

legally resident in a Member State[2] and the Directive on family reunion[3] – could contribute *inter alia* to fostering integration. Important 'horizontal' Community law measures with a potential impact on integration policy are anti-discrimination measures, in particular the Race Directive.[4] However, integration has not been the primary focus or subject-matter of either of these measures. It reappears in a central position in 2003 in the Commission Communication on 'immigration, integration and employment' (COM (2003) 336 final). According to the Commission, integration "should be understood as *a two-way process* based on mutual rights and corresponding obligations of *legally resident third country nationals*" (p. 17). However, later on in the same document the Commission also addresses the integration of second and third generation immigrants, who may be EU citizens (p. 25). In addition to the Tampere-inspired 'two-way' approach, the Commission stresses the need for a so-called 'holistic approach' which takes into account "not only the economic and social aspects of integration but also issues relating to cultural and religious diversity, citizenship, participation and political rights" (p. 18). Key elements to 'holistic integration policies' include integration into the labour market, education and language skills, housing, health and social services, the social and cultural environment and civic rights (pp. 20-22). In the context of civic and political rights, the Commission reiterates the Tampere objective of legally resident third country nationals being offered the opportunity to obtain the nationality of their country of residence – however, the Commission adds that acquiring nationality need not be the ultimate aim of the integration process (p. 22).[5]

The Commission's Communication led to a call by the June 2003 European Council in Thessaloniki for the development of common basic EU principles on integration.[6] This call was reiterated in the Hague Programme, Tampere's successor, which contained specific programmatic ele-

2 Council Directive 2003/109/EC, OJ L16, 23.1.2004, p. 44.

3 Council Directive 2003/86/EC, OJ L251, 3.10.2003, p. 12.

4 Council Directive 2000/43/EC implementing the principle of equal treatment between persons irrespective of racial or ethnic origin, OJ L180, 19.7.2000, p. 22.

5 On the debate on whether the acquisition of citizenship is the endpoint, or reward, of a successful integration process, or rather a means towards the achievement of this aim, see Kymlicka (2003).

6 Conclusion 31. The Council also invited the Commission to present an Annual Report on Migration and Integration in Europe. Two such Reports have been produced thus far: COM (2004) 508 final, Brussels 16 July 2004; and SEC (2006) 892, Brussels 30 June 2006.

ments developing the EU Justice and Home Affairs agenda to 2009.[7] The Hague Programme sketched a number of basic principles on integration, which were further developed by the Justice and Home Affairs Council in their conclusions on 'immigrant integration policy in the EU'.[8] The Justice and Home Affairs Ministers take up the point of the Commission that integration policy must engage the local, regional and national institutions, but, unlike the Commission, do not refer to the EU level.[9] The Council stresses that the development and implementation of integration policy is *the primary responsibility of individual Member States* rather than of the Union as a whole, adding that the precise integration measures a society chooses to implement *should be determined by individual Member States* (points 3 and 5 respectively). However, the Council deems the development of common basic principles as essential in the light of Member States' shared interest. The aim of these principles is to be a 'simple, non-binding thoughtful guide' and – in a manner reminiscent of other EU 'open method of co-ordination' initiatives[10] – to serve as a basis for dialogue between Member States (point 8). The Council thus makes clear the limits of EU competence in the field, stressing that integration-specific EU action will take the form of strictly non-legally binding supporting principles.

The principles themselves are noteworthy. The catalogue begins with the statement that integration is a "dynamic, two-way process of *mutual accommodation* by all *immigrants and residents* of Member States" (point 9). The 'two-way process' mantra is reiterated, but the reference to 'rights and obligations' in previous policy documents has been replaced by the looser term 'mutual accommodation'. As regards the scope of integration measures, reference is made to *immigrants* and *residents* – terms which may be broader than the reference in earlier documents to 'third country nationals lawfully resident in the EU'. The annex developing these principles further strengthens this expansive interpretation by avoiding references to third country nationals and referring to "immigrants and their descendants" (p. 19). The reference to the 'two-way process' juxtaposing immigrants on the one hand and – as is stated in the annex – 'national citizens' on the other, as well as the emphasis on 'mutual' accommodation and 'mutual' rights and responsibilities are also striking. Rather than promoting integration, they seem to imply a continuous dichotomy between 'Us'

7 The Hague Programme: Strengthening Freedom, Security and Justice in the European Union, OJ C53/1, 3.3.2005, at p. 4.

8 Justice and Home Affairs Council of 19 November 2004, Council doc. 14615/04 (Presse 321), pp. 15-24.

9 Point 3 of Conclusions, and the Commission's 2003 Communication p. 23.

10 Of the abundant literature on the open method of co-ordination, see in particular, Szysczcak (2006).

and 'Them', with both parties called upon to foster integration on the basis of mutual obligations. This strategy may be seen as an example of what Balibar calls the 'stigmatisation' of the foreigner, where national citizens can be persuaded that their rights exist if they see that the rights of foreigners are inferior, precarious, or conditioned on repeated manifestations of allegiance (Balibar 2004: 37).

This Us/Them perspective is also prominent in a number of other common principles, which emphasise integration in identity terms. The Council stresses unequivocally that "integration implies respect for the basic values of the Union" (point 10). To the question of what these values actually include, the annex to the principles refers to the 'provisions and values' of the EU Treaties including respect for the principles of liberty, democracy, respect for human rights and the rule of law and respect for the EU Charter of fundamental rights and the concepts it enshrines (p. 19). The annex explains that "everybody resident in the EU must *adapt* and *adhere closely to* the basic values of the EU as well as to Member States laws", adding that "views and opinions that are not compatible with such basic values might hinder the successful integration of immigrants into their new host society and might adversely influence the society as a whole" (ibid.). The emphasis on adherence to the common 'EU' values – notwithstanding the broad character and contested nature of these values – by Member States may seem as leaning more towards an assimilationist model of integration.[11] The emphasis on the *laws* of Member States moreover may be seen as implying the illegality of certain practices by targets of integration. The underlying objective seems to be the acknowledgment and compliance of the constitutive values of European societies. This conclusion can also be drawn from the principle calling for respect of cultural and religious diversity – this must be safeguarded "unless practices conflict with other inviolable European rights or with national law" (point 16). In the case of a clash, according to the annex, coercive measures can also be used by Member States (p. 23). The influence of those Member States expressing anxieties about integration and introducing national integration programmes or conditions is clearly visible in this context.[12] This influence is also evident in a different principle, which states that "basic knowledge of the host society's language, history, and institutions is indispensable to integration" (point 12). Again the change of wording from earlier documents – from country of residence to 'host' society – is noteworthy, and could be seen as implying that individuals who are seen as targets of integration programmes are merely guests having to comply with conditions.

11 For a typology of assimilation, see *inter alia* Brubaker (2001).

12 For an overview of recent programmes on integration by Member States, see S. Carrera (2006) and Suessmuth and Weidenfeld (2005).

The emphasis on the identity aspects of integration co-exists with the application of integration principles to a wide range of other policies and aspects of life, presumably reflecting the emergence of a 'holistic' approach to integration. Thus the principles acknowledge that *employment* is a key part of the integration process (point 11), efforts in *education* are critical *for immigrants and their descendants* (point 13) and access for immigrants to institutions on a basis equal to national citizens in a non-discriminatory way is a critical foundation for better integration (point 14) – with the annex recognising that "the prospect of acquiring Member State *citizenship* can be an important incentive for integration" (p. 22) (although, as the Commission's 2003 Communication stated, acquiring citizenship need not be the ultimate aim of integration) . It is also acknowledged that participation of immigrants in the democratic process, especially at the local level, supports their integration (point 17). The principles also refer to the need for frequent interaction between 'immigrants and Member State citizens' via mechanisms such as shared forums and *intercultural dialogue*. They also call for the mainstreaming of integration policies in all relevant policy portfolios and levels of government and public services (point 18).

The Common Basic Principles on integration have been greatly influential in the development of policy and thinking by the EU institutions. In the 2005 Commission Communication on a 'common agenda on integration', the basic principles served as headings to set out objectives and benchmarks for action at the national and at the EU level (COM (2005) 389 final). The Common Basic Principles, and the follow-up work by the Commission, feature prominently in the Justice and Home Affairs Council Conclusions on a 'common agenda on integration' in December 2005.[13] Integration thus remained prominent in the EU's policy agenda, with the London bombings in July 2005 contributing to this attention. The bombings may have also attenuated the identity aspect of integration policies, while also further 'securitising' the integration debate. A prime example of this shift at EU level has been the Commission Communication on terrorist recruitment of September 2005 (COM (2005) 313 final). The Communication includes a detailed analysis of factors which, according to the Commission, contribute to radicalisation. Emphasis is placed in this context on "not feeling accepted in society, feeling discriminated against and the resulting unwillingness even to try to identify with the values of the society in which one is living" (p. 12). This is linked with the root causes of radicalisation, which include the fragmentation of feelings of belonging and identity and confusion with regard to personal allegiances (p. 14). This emphasis on identity and belonging and its link with societal values is

13 Council doc. 14390/05 (Presse 296), pp. 36-38. The importance of the network of national contact points on integration is particularly highlighted.

strongly reminiscent of the discourse in the Common Basic Principles on integration – only in this context is failure to integrate linked with the concrete danger of committing terrorist offences. Given this emphasis, it is not surprising that a large part of the Communication is devoted to "integration, intercultural dialogue and dialogue with religions", where the view is expressed that "integration policies – which are stand-alone policies having their own specific goals – could have positive ancillary effects on preventing violent radicalisation" (p. 6).

A multi-level, multi-faceted EU policy on integration is thus rapidly being developed.[14] It covers all aspects of the immigrant experience in their society of residence – from access to employment, to cultural integration, to the acquisition of citizenship/naturalisation.[15] But while this process would seem to be addressed to *third country nationals* only, the framing of integration in identity terms has resulted in a more general – and at the same time vague – terminology at EU level. Rather than using the standard EU law term of 'third-country nationals', the relevant documents widely use the term 'immigrant', with references being made also to the descendants of migrants or second and third generation migrants – which indicates that integration is also addressed to citizens of the EU and implies that these would belong to minority groups. This general *ratione personae* scope of EU integration policy raises important constitutional questions for the EU, in particular regarding its competence to legislate or regulate such matters.

These questions proliferate in the light of the diversity of areas influenced by integration policies and the diversity of means under which integration could be achieved: employment, education, citizenship and cultural diversity are expressly mentioned in the General Principles on integration, while security and counter-terrorism are implied in the radicalisation context. Moreover, some of the policies involve the explicit granting of legal rights, while others involve a 'softer' approach. However, the extent and degree of powers of the EU in these fields – and on integration policies per se – are uneven and contested. Moreover, even if EU competence in these areas is ascertained, the recognition that action in some cases may be best achieved at the local level raises important issues of subsidiarity. The limits of EU law in developing common integration policies will be further demonstrated in the next two parts.

14 This development has already attracted detailed academic commentary: see the special issues of the *European Journal of Migration and Law* and the *Journal of Common Market Studies* , both in 2005 (vol. 7/2 and vol. 43/4 respectively).

15 For an interesting classification of the various phases of migration (extending beyond the processes described in this chapter), see Benhabib (2004: 136).

2.3 Integration Aspects in the EU Treaties

Although the Treaties do not currently include express legal bases for the adoption of specific EC/EU integration measures, it could be argued that more general provisions could allow for such powers. Moreover, as shown above, integration objectives can be found in a number of other national and Union principles (such as equality and non-discrimination) and policies (including education, culture, employment and citizenship) and are increasingly linked with debates on multiculturalism and identity. This part will examine the possibilities and limits of the EU Treaty framework regarding both the adoption of integration measures per se and the content and scope of integration policy in the light of the Treaty framework on a number of the related policies mentioned above – with the emphasis being upon issues of identity and diversity in the EU.

2.3.1 Immigration

One might expect that the part of the EC Treaty dealing specifically with immigration (i.e. the so-called 'Title IV') would provide more opportunities and tools to develop common standards on integration. However, the Treaty currently does not contain an express legal basis for the adoption of EC measures on integration, even in the case of third country nationals. Of course, such measures are not excluded by the Treaty: Article 63(3)(a) provides the legal basis for the adoption of Community measures on, *inter alia*, conditions of entry and residence of third country nationals in the EU, while Article 63(4) calls for measures defining the rights and conditions under which nationals of third countries who are legally resident in a Member State may reside in other Member States. Both these provisions are broad enough to be used by the Commission and Member States in the Council as legal basis for specific integration measures.[16] However, agreement on such a possibility has not been reached. This has been demonstrated by the negotiations on the recently adopted Decision transferring decision-making on irregular migration and border controls to the 'Community method' from 1 January 2005: in the initial draft, the measure involved transfer of integration-related measures to this form of decision-making, while the finally adopted text only contains a vague preambular clause stating that "incentive measures to support acts of Member States on the integration of legally resident third country nationals might be adopted by the Council acting in accordance with the appropriate legal basis".[17] This is a rather cryptic clause, which could be read in principle as

16 Of course these provisions have provided the legal basis for a series of measures dealing with the rights of third country nationals with a direct impact on integration – these will be analysed in the following section.

17 Decision 2004/927/EC, OJ L396, 31.12.2004, p. 45, recital 10.

not excluding EC competence on integration currently, provided action is only supporting and Member States agree on the existence of an appropriate legal basis in the EC Treaty. The compromise reached reiterates Member States' reluctance to allow for extensive EU action in the field, and can be seen to imply that, even if competence can be ascertained, EU action may not be necessary or desirable. The Constitutional Treaty would make things somewhat clearer by introducing an express legal basis for measures on the integration of third country nationals – however EU action would be merely supporting and consist of incentive measures, while harmonisation is explicitly excluded.[18]

2.3.2 *Citizenship*

The acquisition of civic rights and ultimately naturalisation feature prominently in the emerging EU integration policy. Although the EU documents do not state it explicitly, naturalisation can be perceived as the 'crown' of a successful integration process (Groenendijk 2004: 113; on naturalisation in general see Kostakopoulou 2006). This view to some extent reflects the recent tightening of naturalisation conditions in a number of EU Member States, where passing integration tests (on language or culture) is a condition of naturalisation. However, any EU attempts to dictate to Member States either an obligation to grant citizenship to third country nationals who are deemed to have been successfully integrated, or the conditions which must be met for citizenship to be granted meet the barrier of the citizenship provisions of the EC Treaty (currently Article 17 TEC). Citizenship of the EU leads, according to the Treaty, to a series of political rights and it has been evoked by the Court of Justice in Luxembourg to enhance the rights of EU nationals.[19] However, as is clear from the Treaty, EU citizenship complements, and does not replace, national citizenship. Moreover, EU citizenship is granted only to those holding the nationality of an EU Member State – thus third country nationals legally resident in the EU are not EU citizens according to the Treaty. For the purposes of integration policies, this means that the granting of any political rights to third country nationals under integration policies is a power residing with Member States; and that the conditions that a third country national has to fulfil in order to become an EU citizen are similarly set out exclusively by Member States according to their domestic law and procedure.

18 Article III-267(4).

19 From the voluminous literature on EU citizenship, see in particular Shaw 1998; on the exclusionary potential of EU citizenship, and its emphasis on identity, see Balibar (2004: 65).

2.3.3 Culture, Identity and Diversity

Access to education and respect for cultural and religious diversity are central to the EU integration policy. Moreover, EU documents in the field increasingly frame the integration debate in identity terms. This framework raises the general question of what kind of identity is the Union promoting and how much space there is for cultural diversity in EU law. These questions become more prominent in the light of the recent trend to 'securitise' integration and call for allegiance to the basic societal values of Member States. The existence and content of an EU identity based on EU values is significant in this context.

Insights on this subject may be provided by the EC Treaty provisions on education (Articles 149-150 TEC) and culture (Article 151 TEC) – both very relevant in the context of integration. Community action in both fields at most supports and supplements Member States' action – thus Community powers are quite limited. The wording of these provisions merits closer examination. Article 149(1) on education calls for EC action "while fully respecting the responsibility of the Member States for the content of teaching and the organisation of education systems *and their cultural and linguistic diversity*" (emphasis added).[20] On the other hand, Article 151(1) states that the Community "shall contribute to the flowering of the cultures of the Member States while respecting their national and regional diversity and at the same time bringing the common cultural heritage to the fore". The fourth paragraph of this Article further states that the Community must take cultural aspects into account in other policies "in order to respect and promote the diversity of its cultures".

It thus seems that, in negotiating the relationship between national and European identity on the grounds of culture and education, the Treaty stresses the fact that – while some common 'European' elements exist and can be brought into the fore – this can be done only by supplementing Member State action and it is *national* cultures and *national* identity that take precedence (Mitsilegas 1998). The wording of the provisions implies that the focus is the diversity *of* national cultures in the EU and not diversity *within* national cultures. The zeal to protect national identity is also reflected in Article 6 of the Treaty on EU, where references to the values upon which the EU is founded (including human rights) are followed by an explicit reference, in Article 6(3), to the fact that 'the Union shall respect the national identities of its Member States' and the absence in the current

20 On the EC education policy in a human rights context, see Ch. Wallace and Jo Shaw, *Education, Multiculturalism and the EU Charter of Rights*, Constitutionalism Web-Paper ConWEB No. 5/2002, http://les1.man.ac.uk/conweb.

Treaties of an express reference to minority protection.[21] While the Treaty wording on all these occasions is inherently unclear (what is included in 'identities' and 'cultures' of Member States?), the purpose of the provisions appears to be to protect the dominant culture/identity in Member States, without necessarily extending to the protection of minority or immigrant cultures. In terms of immigrant integration, this approach may serve to reinforce the message that integration is primarily a matter for Member States, and that clauses asserting the need for compliance with domestic societal values must be safeguarded.

2.4 Integration Aspects in Secondary EC Legislation

Notwithstanding the reluctance of Member States to recognise a specific Community competence on integration measures in the current Treaties, integration considerations and provisions do appear in secondary Community law determining rights for third country nationals and Community citizens. Measures on third country nationals even include specific integration clauses. While this may seem at first sight at odds with Member States' reservations, it can be explained by the fact that these clauses involve *conditions* of integration that must be met by a third country national for the enjoyment of Community law rights, conditions which will be determined *by Member States*. However, as will be demonstrated below, Community law places limits on national discretion in this context.

2.4.1 Legislation on Third-Country Nationals

An important measure giving rights to third country nationals, and thus with a significant potential impact on their integration, is the 2003 Directive concerning the status of third-country nationals who are long-term residents in Member States. The Directive grants these individuals equal treatment as regards *inter alia* access to employment, education, social security, housing and freedom of association – all elements of the developing EU integration policy. However, the Directive stops short of granting equal treatment as regards electoral rights, with the Commission arguing that there is no explicit EC competence in this regard (Shaw 2003: 496-98). The importance of the integration of third-country nationals is recognised in the Preamble of the Directive, which states that integration is "a key element in promoting economic and social cohesion, a fundamental objective of the Community shared by the Treaty" (recital 4). Integration thus here

21 This is notwithstanding the fact that minority protection is a criterion determining accession to the EU. The Constitutional Treaty includes minority protection as one of the values of the Union (see article I-2). See B. de Witte 2004. On minority protection in the specific context of EU integration policy, see G. N. Toggenburg 2005; see also R. Cholewinski, same issue.

appears as *a means* of achieving broader Treaty objectives. However, concerns by Member States and the parallel development of restrictive integration policies at national level have led to a number of countries arguing for making the granting of rights to long-term legally resident third-country nationals subject to the fulfilment of integration measures and/or conditions. The compromise reached was that Member States *may* require third-country nationals to comply with *integration conditions* (a stricter requirement than mere 'integration measures') in accordance with *national law* in order to grant them long-term resident status (Article 5(2)). Third-country nationals who have acquired such status may be subject to further *integration measures* as a condition of residence in another EU Member State (Article 15(3)). The imposition of integration conditions in this context has been criticised as confirming an assimilationist policy and as being contrary to international minority rights standards (Toggenburg 2005: 731, Peers 2004: 155).

Another measure of fundamental importance for integration is the family reunion Directive. Its Preamble explicitly recognises the importance of family reunion to integration: it helps to create 'sociocultural stability' facilitating integration, which serves to promote the Community objective of economic and social cohesion (recital 4); integration of family members should thus be promoted and they should be granted a status independent of that of the sponsor (recital 15). However, as in the long-term residence Directive, Member States pushed for the inclusion of potential limits to rights on the basis of integration requirements. Member States thus may require compliance with *integration measures* in accordance with national law in order to allow the exercise of the right to family reunion (Article 7(2); see Groenendijk 2006). Another restriction is the derogation to the two-year lawful residence of the sponsor (which Member States may require for the exercise of the right), according to which Member States may provide for a waiting period of a maximum of three years where their legislation in force on the date of the adoption of the Directive takes into account national reception capacity (Article 8). However, perhaps the greatest restrictions – which are also linked to integration requirements and considerations – involve the very scope of the Directive. Article 4, which defines 'family members' for the purposes of the Directive, allows Member States to derogate from the provisions on minors. Where a child is aged over 12 years and arrives independently from the rest of its family, Member States may, before authorising entry and residence, verify whether the minor meets *a condition for integration* provided by existing legislation (Article 4(1) in fine). In an even more sweeping derogation, Member States may also request that applications for family reunion of minors have to be submitted before the age of 15 (Article 4(6)). According to the Preamble, the possibility of limiting the right to family reunion of children over the age of 12, whose primary residence is not with the sponsor, is intended to reflect *the children's capacity for integration* at early ages and will ensure that they acquire the necessary education and language skills in school (recital 12; see Groenendijk 2004).

The restrictions to the right to family reunion have been criticised on the grounds that they violate the fundamental right to family life, with the European Parliament challenging the Directive on such grounds focusing on Articles 4(1) and (6) and Article 8. The judgment of the European Court of Justice in Case C-540/03 *Parliament v Council* is extremely important. It is the first case where the Court makes express reference to the EU Charter of Fundamental Rights (para. 58 of judgment). However, the Court found that the Directive's provisions are not *per se* contrary to the right to family life. Article 4(1) in fine partially preserves a margin of appreciation for Member States, which is no different from the margin accorded to them from Strasbourg (para. 62). Most importantly, the Court found that a condition for integration is not in itself contrary to the right to respect family life in Article 8 ECHR, as this right does not necessarily oblige Member States to authorise family reunion (para. 66). Balancing this ruling, the Court referred to the fact that integration constitutes a general objective of the Directive (para. 69) and placed Member States' implementation of the Article 4(1) restriction within the framework and limits of Community law. According to the Court, "the fact that the concept of integration is not defined cannot be interpreted as authorising the Member States to employ that concept in a manner contrary to the general principles of Community law, in particular fundamental rights" (para. 70). Member States are thus bound by these principles – according to the Court, article 4(1) in fine cannot be interpreted as authorising Member States, expressly or impliedly, to adopt implementing provisions that would be contrary to the right to respect family life (para. 71). The Court thus upheld integration conditions and Member State discretion in principle, but placed these firmly within the limits of Community law.[22]

2.4.2 Legislation on Union Citizens

One would not expect to see provisions on integration in legislation related to the rights of Union citizens and their family members. Their rights are at the heart of Community law, have been affirmed by primary and secondary legislation and ECJ case-law, and extended by the concept of Union citizenship. However, integration-related provisions can be encountered in a major legal instrument consolidating existing provisions and case-law, the

22 See also paragraphs 84-90 of the judgment in relation to Article 4(6) and paragraphs 97-109 in relation to Article 8. In both cases the Court found that the Directive's provisions are compatible with fundamental rights.

2004 Directive on the rights of EU citizens and their family members to move and reside freely within the territory of the Member States.[23] In line with the spirit and content of free movement rights and Union citizenship, the focus and role of integration here is markedly different to the measures on third country nationals. According to the Preamble, "in order to be a genuine vehicle for integration into the society of the host Member State in which the Union citizen resides, the right of permanent residence, once obtained, should not be subject to any conditions" (recital 18). Permanent residence is thus viewed as a means of achieving greater integration. From the other side of this coin, the Preamble states that expulsion of Union citizens and their family members should be limited and proportionate to the degree of integration of the persons concerned – the greater their degree of integration, the greater the degree of protection against expulsion should be (recitals 23 and 24). This principle is reflected in the Directive's provision on protection against expulsion, where it is stated that Member States must take into account the length of residence and 'social and cultural integration' before taking an expulsion decision (Article 28(1); see also Groenendijk 2004). Integration thus becomes here a *protective factor* against expulsion and enhancing the security of residence.

2.5 Conclusion – Features and Limits of Integration in the EU Legal Framework

In the development of EU law and policy in the field, integration is seen as having a number of *diverse roles*: integration can be *a Union objective* as regards third country nationals; it can also be *a means* of achieving Community or Union objectives (such as economic and social cohesion or fighting terrorism); it has been presented as *a condition* for granting rights under Community law; on the other hand, it has also been used as a *protective concept* enhancing security of residence. These different roles may seem at odds with, or even contradictory, to each other. They co-exist however, in the light of the different categories of individuals who are targeted by it: integration in Union law is relevant to both foreigners and citizens; it is addressed to: third country nationals outside EU territory wishing to enter; third country nationals resident in the EU; third country nationals who are family members of Union citizens exercising Community law rights; Union citizens exercising Community law rights; and even Union citizens resident in their country of nationality. This variety of integration targets is inextricably linked not only with the different roles of integration policy, but also with the different aspects of law and policy it is linked with: these range from horizontal issues of equality and non-discrimination, to

23 Directive 2004/38/EC of the European Parliament and of the Council, OJ L229, 29.6.2004, p. 35.

employment, education, cultural diversity, citizenship and naturalisation, the 'war on terror' and the protection of fundamental rights.

Which of these elements are more relevant in developing an EU concept of integration is a matter which is inextricably linked with the interaction between Union law and national law on integration. Developments in recent years have demonstrated that Member States are reluctant to cede sovereignty in integration-related matters, and have proceeded on a domestic level to make the acquisition of rights more difficult by framing integration as an issue of identity and security. Member States have also managed to export this restrictive integration agenda into the secondary EC law on third country nationals. However, by entering the realm of the Community legal order – which is based on a series of principles including equality, non-discrimination and the respect for fundamental rights – Member States may see this security/identity agenda on integration diluted by a rights approach based on these principles. While Community/Union law at present has considerable limits in developing specific standards of integration, it can also impose specific rights-based limits on Member State action in integration-related fields. The role of the Court of Justice is crucial in this context. While in the family reunion case the Court accepted in principle Member States' restrictive agendas, it made clear that fundamental rights must be observed. In the implementation by Member States of integration standards in the context of Community law, the Court will be watching.

Chapter 3 Changes in Drugs Policy and Practice: Implications for the Black Community

Anita Kalunta-Crumpton

Drug misuse constitutes one of the main problematic issues in the UK, attracting fast and seemingly ongoing changes in policies. Despite the fact that certain drugs – currently classed as illegal – have been known to mankind for thousands of years, discussions and debates on the contemporary drug problem often project a distorted picture of its history and invariably assign limited insights into the contexts of its emergence. In like manner, current drugs policies did not develop in a vacuum; rather they can be traced back through a long history of discursive and practical attitudes towards drugs. Whatever forms and contexts that drugs policy changes have taken, they have at least in theory been justified as imperative to the control of drug demand and drug supply. An examination of the historical transition in policy related to drug demand and drug supply is imperative in order to put into perspective the practical implications of drugs policy for the black community. As will be demonstrated in subsequent sections, respective policy and practice approaches to drug demand and supply have continually adopted differing positions in relation to the black community.[1] Whilst black people have continued to remain highly prominent in the legislative and law enforcement attack on drugs supply, they have in contrast remained relatively marginalized in the strategy towards drug treatment and drug prevention.

1 Whilst acknowledging that there is not just one 'Black community' in Britain but rather a plurality of people of African and African Caribbean descent, in this chapter I use the term Black to signal the fact that we are in the realm of a particular racialised discourse and praxis which tends to mark out 'Black' people for singular treatment.

Prakash Shah (ed.), Law and Ethnic Plurality: Socio-Legal Perspectives. *pp. 47-67.*
 ISBN 978 90 04 16245 7.

3.1 The Black Community in the Drugs Discourses of the 19th and 20th Centuries

Despite the strong association between drugs and the black community in contemporary Britain, there was a time in history when black people were invisible in discursive and policy responses to drug use and drug supply. Even though black people already had a presence in the UK as far back as the 16th century (Fryer 1984), they remained absent from popular reactions to the drug scene even at a time of growing concerns over working class use of opiate towards the latter part of the 19th century. 'Race' at the time was signified in expressed concerns about Chinese 'opium dens', the spread of Chinese opium smoking into white middle-class groups, and calls by the anti-opium movement to stop what was considered an 'alien vice' (Berridge 1988). Nevertheless, it seemed that class was a more prominent concern. There was a demarcation in perceptions between white middle- and white working-class opium consumption. In contrast to the 'bad habit' thesis that had justified middle-class opiate use and addiction, working-class opiate addiction was viewed and interpreted as a 'problem' and a 'vice'. Thus blame was placed on availability and the ease with which drugs could be procured for recreational purposes; the solution was focused on the need to curtail supplies. While working-class drug consumption influenced drug prohibition policies, drug use amongst their middle-class counterparts influenced drug treatment policies. To a significant extent, the recreational use of opium by the working-class influenced the passing of the 1868 Pharmacy Act (Berridge and Edwards 1981), which placed restrictions on opiate sales through a pharmacy. On the other hand, the 'disease' theory developed by the medical profession in the late 19th century to explain alcoholism was applied principally to explain middle-class addiction to opium and its perception as a problem of habituation. This view called for treatment via maintenance prescribing and gradual withdrawal.

Moving into the early 20th century, the black community continued to remain non-existent in discussions about drugs. However this was to change in the post-war years following the influx of Caribbean immigrants into Britain in the late 1940s and in the 1950s. The black community was gradually becoming deeply intertwined with class in explanations surrounding the use of a 'new' type of drug – cannabis. Britain had her first experience of large numbers of people smoking cannabis following post-war black immigration (Plant 1987). Cannabis had already come under legislative controls under the 1925 Dangerous Drugs Act (Dorn et al 1992). The sanctions on cannabis, as with other drugs legislation passed between 1920 and 1964, were meant to meet international demands.

Despite the criminalisation of cannabis, prosecutions for drug offences between 1929 and 1948 mainly involved heroin and cocaine, which may imply that cannabis attracted relatively less attention during this period

(Stimson and Oppenheimer 1982). The government, satisfied that cannabis was neither extensively used nor caused grievous harm, was able to claim in its 1932 report to the League of Nations that 'the illicit use of and traffic in the drug appears to be confined to Arab and Indian seamen'; and in 1935 the government also stated that "such cases of illicit import of drugs as were discovered were individual attempts on the part of seamen, mainly Orientals, to bring in small quantities for the use of compatriots in the United Kingdom" (Spear 1969: 249). But in 1946, the black community was clearly recognised in the government's annual report on drugs which observed that "it is known that the traffic in Indian Hemp is practically confined to two negro groups in London and those attempting to import the drugs have generally been coloured seamen" (ibid.).

Towards the latter part of the 1940s and into the 1950s the use of cannabis increased (Willis 1973), a transition which was reflected in the rapid rise in the numbers of prosecutions and convictions for cannabis offences. For example, from 1946 to 1959, there were 1,269 prosecutions for cannabis offences as against 93 between 1929 and 1945 (Stimson and Oppenheimer 1982). Where the black community is located in the numbers of the prosecutions, particularly in the post-war period, is not apparent, but what is clear is that they were prominent in influential discursive representations of cannabis in the post-war era. Although cannabis was commonly used by Jazz musicians and delinquent youths from various social backgrounds in the 1950s (Glatt 1974), and had been used for recreational and medical purposes before and during the 19th century, it was in the early 1950s that the Home Office appeared to realise that "cannabis was a drug with a certain amount of appeal" to the 'indigenous population' (Spear 1969: 249). However, the association between cannabis and non-white people had begun to be established in the media. According to *The Times* (2 July 1955), cannabis was "largely confined to Africans, Asiatics and West Indians...".

The spotlight on cannabis in the 1950s pushed heroin and cocaine to the backstage; heroin and cocaine addiction was relatively uncommon and so were offences relating to both drugs. However, this was also a period when addiction was largely confined to professionals and middle-class non-therapeutic addicts (Willis 1973). But during the late 1960s and 1970s, serious concerns were voiced about the emergence of younger (white) addicts whose drug use was viewed as subcultural, hedonistic and non-therapeutic (MacGregor 1989). Thus, the early and mid-20th century popular impression of the use of addictive drugs as an exclusive privilege enjoyed by middle-aged and middle-class therapeutic or non-therapeutic addicts began to change as soon as addiction was seen significantly to affect other social groups. The new pattern of drug consumption, according to MacGregor (1989: 170) involved increasing numbers of pleasure-seeking young people and, according to Jamieson et al (1984: 6), also involved "less respectable characters, more often members of the underclass and petty criminal underworld" who obtained "their drugs from other addicts" and for whom "the grip of the medical profession over their care began to loosen". A notable contribution to the increase in illicit drug use among young people was availability of drugs via the black market, prescriptions or theft. About one-third of the registered heroin addicts were in their teens and a significant number of them came from the working-class (King 1969). The use of other drugs such as amphetamines and cocaine was on the increase during the 1960s.

The striking change that took place in the nature of the drug scene from the 1960s called for a new government response which was to bring an end to the 'British system' in the late 1960s. Restrictions were thereafter placed on the drug prescribing powers of the medical profession. Notwithstanding the increasing numbers of heroin users in the late 1960s and in the 1970s, heroin use attracted both statutory and non-statutory intervention offering treatment, rehabilitation, counselling and advisory services to both drug addicts and users (Dorn and South 1987). Furthermore, heroin did not witness as many prosecutions and convictions as would have been expected. In 1968 for instance, only 73 were prosecuted and convicted for heroin offences whereas there were 2240 registered and 2232 non-therapeutic heroin addicts known to the Home Office (Stimson and Oppenheimer 1982).

Whilst the treatment response to drug use maintained the heroin addict as its major focus, concerns mounted around the use of cannabis, amphetamines, glue sniffing and alcohol drinking. Unlike heroin, the post-war period of disquiet about cannabis use was not about health concerns and its ramifications on the black community. Rather the emphasis placed on the spread of cannabis into the indigenous population unveiled resentment towards the black community for the supposed threat that their involvement in cannabis use and trafficking posed to the white community. For one, there were discursive representations of cannabis dealing as the main area of concern in the political and media arenas (Howe 1973, Gilroy 1987). The connection made between black people and cannabis was fundamentally understood in its criminal form while also being contextualised in relation to structural patterns of social exclusion suffered by the black community. Juxtaposed to this was a relatively severe law enforcement response, resulting in a rapid increase in the prosecutions and convictions for cannabis offences. There were 3071 prosecutions and convictions for cannabis offences in 1968 (Stimson and Oppenheimer 1982), far outnumbering recorded heroin offences in the same year. By this time, the Dangerous Drugs (Prevention of Misuse) Act 1964, the Dangerous Drugs Act 1965 and the Dangerous Drugs Act 1967 were pieces of legislation in place to deter drug offences through increased penalties. Police powers to control drugs had been increased under the Dangerous Drugs (Prevention of Misuse) Act 1964, and consequently the police acquired the authority to arrest without a warrant a person who was committing or was 'reasonably suspected' of having committed a drug offence (Deedes 1970). Police could also search premises if there was evidence that a drug offence was being committed (Plant 1987). Further powers were granted to the police under the Dangerous Drugs Act 1965 (Deedes 1970, Plant 1987).

In the 1960s it was common for the police to conduct drug raids in black communities (Roach Family Support Committee 1989). By the 1970s, black localities had become popularly noted for drug dealing. Writing about Rastafarianism and criminality, Dodd (1978: 600) referred to "the emergence of a black street sub-culture in the working class slums" in which "there is meaning in music, there is meaning in ganja and there is meaning in crime". Cashmore and Troyna (1982: 12) drew attention to the characterisation of Rastafarianism as a "mafia-style organisation dealing in prostitution and dope…". Unemployed West Indians, according to Rex (1982: 65), were believed to "live by pimping, by cheating and thieving, and by peddling 'ganja'…". Such typifications of black people and drug dealing were illustrated in law enforcement practice amounting to the concentration of policing, police drug raids and arrests in deprived inner-city areas where most black people resided. Humphrey and John (1971: 36) observe how these drug laws were allegedly utilised by the police to discriminate against the black community:

> In Moss Side the police had upset the blacks by making a drive on illicit drugs and using their powers under the Dangerous Drugs Act 1965 to stop and search people in the street or at house parties. Black people felt that they were being singled out for these searches and some retaliated leading to charges of assault on the police.

In Handsworth, similar feelings were voiced in the black community:

> Youths and their parents complain…of men being put against the walls of the police station and searched, at the same time being asked 'where are the drugs, you dirty black bastard?', 'you don't work, you scum'… (ibid. 7).

Many black people interviewed by Humphrey and John (ibid.) in Handsworth reported that in some cases black people were planted with drugs and dangerous weapons. Humphrey (1972) also cites cases of alleged police drug planting. The passing of the Dangerous Drugs Act 1967 further exacerbated the subjection of the black community to systematic police harassment (Humphrey 1972), which seemingly continued under the Misuse of

Drugs Act 1971 (consolidating previous drug offence legislative measures and since forming the basis of Britain's drug controls) as well as by subsequent legislation.

3.2 The 1980s Heroin Epidemic: Drug Demand

> The 'whiteness' of Britain's heroin epidemic was so much taken for granted…that social researchers almost invariably did not even bother to use any system of ethnic monitoring when studying local populations (Pearson and Patel 1998: 199).

The 1980s not only witnessed a marked increase in heroin use but also its spread in various parts of the country (Haw 1985, Parker et al 1986). Consequently the drug problem came to the top of Britain's social concerns agenda. The 1980s drug problem, as Gay (1989: 8) observed, became an epidemic that "was no longer confined to certain localities or defined groups" because "the problem could clearly affect any family anywhere". However, the heroin outbreaks of the 1980s were concentrated in deprived urban areas in parts of the country such as London, Manchester, Glasgow, Edinburgh and Merseyside. The rapid engagement of young people in illicit heroin use was of particular concern at public and official level. In the two decades prior to this, heroin use was part of a hippie lifestyle involving users in their 20s and 30s. At the time, the majority of UK heroin users were based in London (Stimson and Oppenheimer 1982). In contrast, Pearson (1987: 4) stated that the "new heroin users are more likely to be young men and women in their teens and early twenties". Those new and young heroin users mostly resided in deprived localities, were undereducated, unemployed and had to supplement welfare benefits with acquisitive crime and drug dealing in order to fund their drug habits. For females, reliance on prostitution was another source of generating income for drugs.

The 1980s saw the development and growth in drug treatment and rehabilitation services, as well as a new approach to addressing the threat of HIV and other blood transmitting diseases. The prevalence of HIV infection was rapidly increasing among injecting drug users through the sharing of injecting equipment. This problem was clearly recognised by the Advisory Council on the Misuse of Drugs (ACMD) in its reports *Aids and Drug Misuse* published in 1988 and 1989. Consequently, the development and promotion of initiatives such as needle/syringe-exchange schemes, outreach work and the provision of information on HIV/AIDS, safer injecting and sexual practices formed a fundamental part of the tasks undertaken by drug treatment services. Underlining this strategy was the crucial need to minimise the health-related harm caused by drug misuse to the users and the even greater potential threat that the HIV virus posed to the wider society.

But in all the debates and questions surrounding the nature of the heroin epidemic, its cause/s and how best to address the problem in terms of policy and practice, ethnicity was insignificant. The centre of interest in discourse, research, policy and practice was the white population and 'white' heroin use. Whilst the concerns instigated a transformation of political and research interests into the epidemiology of heroin use, there was no focus upon any influence that the heroin epidemic might have had on visible minority ethnic groups at both individual and community levels. Even when class reared its head once again as an integral part of the discursive and evidential typification of drug users, ethnicity remained unnoticed.

Although theoretical explanations linking drug use to socio-economic deprivation were popular in academic, official and public discourses, the obvious indications that drug use does not necessarily reflect marginalised socio-economic experiences were not ignored. In the 1980s, correlations were drawn between middle-class areas and drug use, and low rates of drug use and areas of high levels of deprivation (Pearson et al 1987). By referring to the place of the black community in the heroin epidemic, Pearson (1992: 286) has reasoned that the causal link between drug use and socio-economic deprivation is not that straightforward:

> It was noticeable, for example, that the heroin epidemic mainly affected white working-class communities in the North of England and Scotland, as well as many areas of working-class London; and that in spite of the higher levels of unemployment, educational disadvantage, housing deprivation, etc., experienced by Britain's black communities, black people were considerably underrepresented among known heroin users.

Why black people were and are still underrepresented in the numbers of known heroin users has been a subject of debate since the 1980s. In any case their relative absence – for whatever reasons – in concerns expressed in the 1980s about the heroin epidemic invariably meant that drug treatment policies of this period catered to the needs of the growing number of heroin addicts who were known to be mainly white.

3.3 The 1980s Heroin Epidemic: Drug Supply

Political debates as to the cause of the 1980s heroin epidemic alluded to the plentiful supply and greater availability of modestly priced heroin in many cities and towns. The primary focus of drugs policy on the treatment model of maintenance prescribing – ranging from long-term to short-term treatment practices – was to witness a paradigm shift in the mid-1980s towards law enforcement. Although law enforcement had long been a part of drugs control strategy, its role had not been as central as it became in the 1980s. It was during this period that the notion of drug 'dealing' or 'pushing' transformed into drug 'trafficking' to mirror the increased seriousness attached to drugs supply (Dorn et al 1992). It was also in the 1980s that drug trafficking became racialised (ibid.). The treatment and harm-reduction drug policy models which accompanied the increase and spread in heroin use, and the arrival of and escalation in HIV/AIDS became secondary to the law enforcement approach. This distinction clearly reveals itself in the five-pronged approach outlined in the government's UK-wide drug strategy, *Tackling Drug Misuse* (Home Office 1985):

1. Reducing supplies from abroad;
2. Tightening controls on drugs produced and prescribed here;
3. Making policing even more effective;
4. Strengthening deterrence;
5. Improving prevention, treatment and rehabilitation.

The supply-oriented policy measures had been preceded, or at least placed alongside, political and media discourses which successfully constructed the drug trafficker as one of UK's no. 1 public enemies. Drug traffickers were viewed in the same light as terrorists by the government and law enforcement officials (Green 1991). Dorn and South (1987: 122) described the 1980s Conservative government's representation of drug traffickers as "serious criminals akin to terrorists, and drug users...as helpless victims reduced to moronic garbage". At both local and national levels, the press played a prominent role in giving drug trafficking activity prime exposure by presenting a criminal and deadly image of the drug trafficker, alerting the public to the supposed dangerous existence of drug trafficking, and furthermore reporting on an ongoing war on it. Such discourses popularised drug trafficking as an imported phenomenon, locating its roots – both in terms of drug production and distribution – in foreign countries and nationalities. Thus heroin, cocaine and cannabis acquired foreigner status.

Illicit drugs such as LSD and amphetamines, whilst illegally produced in the UK and abroad, are like other drugs such as barbiturates, "mainly obtained by diversion from the licit market in this country" (Home Office 1985: 4). However, the concerns about drugs supply in the 1980s rendered LSD, amphetamines and similar drugs insignificant against the manifest discursive, policy and practical prioritisation of certain class 'A' drugs and, to a significant extent, cannabis. Related to this, portrayals of the whole process through which these prioritised drugs find their way to the UK market represented accusations against non-western countries. These included the externalisation of transit points for drugs heading for the UK with reference to, for example, countries and nationalities in Africa and the Caribbean. Following the top priority gained by drug trafficking in the 1980s war on drugs, both international and domestic levels of drugs control narratives familiarised and constantly reminded us of the trafficking role of Jamaican 'yardies', Nigerian drug couriers, Colombian cartels, inner-city black males and so forth. Whilst drugs supply was externalised as a foreign invention principally piloted by non-whites, demand was internalised inasmuch as drug addiction was evidenced as a phenomenon threatening the UK white population. This distinction drawn between drugs supply and drug use is noted by Green (1991: 21) as she argues that the "constructed drugs 'crisis' is seen as a principally imported crisis – imported by West Africans, Asians or South Americans, fuelled by Third World supplies rather than domestic demand." Domestically, the racial demarcation in the supply of and demand for drugs was also evident, as exemplified in Gilman's (2000: 205) account of the 1980s heroin markets in Greater Manchester:

> Predominantly white users now bought their heroin from black strangers. These strangers did not use heroin; they did not like heroin and saw it as a 'dirty' drug that was used by 'dirty' white junkies who had no self-respect and therefore deserved no respect.

The discursive externalisation of drug trafficking was to be translated into drugs control policy and practice. The 'alien threat' characterisation of drug trafficking justified stringent law enforcement and repressive punitive measures against certain groups of people. Publicised calls from politicians and government officials were made for the enactment of stringent punitive measures on drug trafficking, including the death penalty. Subsequently there came the Controlled Drugs (Penalties) Act 1985 and the Drug Trafficking Offences Act 1986. The former increased the penalty for trafficking in a class 'A' drug from 14 years prison sentence to life imprisonment while the latter introduced the powers of asset confiscation. Thus courts acquired powers to confiscate drug traffickers' assets, believed to be their profits from drug trafficking. Default of payment or refusal to comply with a confiscation order incurred an additional prison sentence commensurate with the assessed value of the proceeds from drug trafficking. The implications of these stringent measures for black people were demonstrated in official prison statistics for drug offences for which they were not only over-represented but were also serving long sentences (Home Office 1986, also see Kalunta-Crumpton 1999 for a descriptive account of the impact of the confiscation order on black drug offenders). This was more evident in the female prison population where the highest proportion of black people received under sentence was for drug offences (Home Office 1986). Since the 1980s, the disproportionate presence of black people in UK prison establishments has been significantly influenced by the high numbers of foreign nationals – from West Africa and the Caribbean – charged or convicted for importing illegal drugs (Green 1991, Harper and Murphy 1999).

The overhaul of drugs law enforcement in the 1980s also reached the police forces. During this period drugs policing witnessed a new organisational structure, based largely on the recommendations of the Broome Report 1985. Three broad levels of drugs policing were devised (see Advisory Council on the Misuse of Drugs (ACMD) 1994, Dorn et al 1992). They consisted of: (1) regional crime squads to focus on major drug trafficking business involving a network of importers and distributors at both national and international levels; (2) force drug squads to address mid-level traffickers in the drug distribution chain; and (3) divisional-level enforcement involving the policing of localities by police officers in the normal course of their duty.

Out of these three forms of drugs policing, it was the divisional level that attracted emphasis as a vital pattern of drugs law enforcement due to its demand and harm reduction approach to drug misuse. Policing drugs at this level has involved the concentration of street-level police surveillance, and police stop and search practices in specific areas such as council estates, public houses, rented flats and streets. Top-level drugs policing has been known to be problematic (Dorn et al 1992) amidst complexities involved in intercepting drug traffickers at the upper reaches of the drugs economy, thereby rendering this level of policing limited in its cost effectiveness. Although this does not imply ineffectiveness at the higher levels of police operational response to drugs, it does highlight at least one reason why divisional-level policing in the 1980s and beyond remained prominent in the domestic war on drug trafficking via its focus on drug traffickers, buyers and users in select, usually deprived inner-city areas, with the aim of disrupting low-level drug transactions and in turn reducing the availability of, and demand for, drugs. This grade of drug trafficking has since received widespread publicity, not only through the prominence accorded to it by way of stringent law enforcement measures, but also via the media which in their prime and sensational exposure of drug trafficking activities in inner-city neighbourhoods, accompanied by the image of the deadly drug trafficker, constructed and perpetuated a connection between drug trafficking and race. Black men were defined as the drug traffickers and represented in the image of professionals in drug trafficking activities. Representations of gun-related violence following the arrival of crack cocaine in the later part of the 1980s, accompanied the black community/drug trafficking public discourse. Black men in effect remained key targets in drugs policing practices. Indeed as Cashmore and McLaughlin (1991: 11) describe:

> Throughout the 1970s and the 1980s the concern about black youth and their supposed 'heritage of violence' as 'muggers', 'drug barons', 'steamers', 'Yardies' and 'posses' has been handled in such a way as to engender public support for police strategies, especially as most of the stereotypes

have been uncritically accepted and, at times, supported by politicians and the mass media.

Over-policing operations, including military-style tactics in drug raids and surveillance, in black residential areas had long been justified in the name of divisional-level policing. The consequences have included violent encounters between the police and the black community as instanced in the 1985 urban disorder in Handsworth (Birmingham) and Broadwater Farm Estate (London). Nevertheless, it was a form of drugs policing considered necessary, warranting its survival beyond the 1980s.

3.4 The Black Community, Drug Demand and Supply Policies from the 1990s

The 1990s were a decade of drugs policy transitions with regard to illicit drug use, principally in the multi-agency ideals underpinning the contemporary approach to drug use. The multi-agency approach to drug use was set in motion by the government publication, *Tackling Drugs Together: A Strategy for England 1995-8* (Home Office 1995). The idea was to fit together the three strands of present UK drugs policy – treatment, prevention and law enforcement – in a coordinated approach to illicit drug use. This strategic mechanism was based on the principles of both national and local partnerships involving agencies and local communities in tackling drug misuse.

Until the 21st century, the identification of ethnicity in responses and national policy relating to drug treatment and drug prevention were seemingly non-existent or very minimal. For example, the Home Office publications, *Tackling Drug Misuse: A Summary of the Government's Strategy* (Home Office 1985) and *Tackling Drugs Together: A Strategy for England 1995-8* (Home Office 1995) failed to recognise racial and ethnic diversity in drug prevention and drug treatment strategies. In 1998, the government's 10-year national drugs strategy, *Tackling Drugs to Build a Better Britain: The Government's Ten Year Strategy for Tackling Drug Misuse* was published (Home Office 1998). Whilst the strategy placed emphasis on the three strands – treatment, prevention and law enforcement – as the way forward for action as far as drug misuse was concerned, the strategy acknowledged race and ethnicity in a generic context. However, this acknowledgement was merely limited to reiterating what was already known about the reluctance of problem drug users from minority ethnic groups to access white-run mainstream drug services, and recommending that racial equality be practiced in service provision and delivery.

3.5 Drug Treatment through the Criminal Justice System

Although it has been acknowledged that minority ethnic problem drug users are underrepresented as clients of drug services, studies have drawn attention to the continued link between black drug use and the criminal justice system. Mirza et al (1991a) noted that the majority of drug users known to criminal justice agencies were black people who were most likely to be arrested for a drug offence. Relating such arrests to crack cocaine, Mirza et al (1991b) observed that while such police action presented crack and cocaine use as a black problem, white people made up the vast majority of users of these drugs. Whilst contacts between cocaine/crack users and drug treatment agencies have been relatively uncommon, their presence is significantly felt in the criminal justice system. According to the National Treatment Agency for substance misuse (NTA 2002a), a snapshot of drug users in treatment in Britain in the mid-1990s showed that black people made up approximately half of the cocaine clients. Furthermore, the NTA (2002b: 5) cites arrest and conviction as "among the crises which could prompt crack misusers to seek help and make crack misusers visible to services".

Drug treatment and testing orders (DTTO), introduced under the Crime and Disorder Act 1998, was first made available to the courts in England and Wales in October 2000. Its primary aim was to break the drug/crime cycle with regard to offenders charged for acquisitive crime. In this respect the DTTO required courts to conduct a regular review of an offender's progress and provides for compulsory regular drug testing for offenders (Turnbull et al 2000). Since April 2005, the DTTO has been embraced within a generic community order. This order, allowed under the Criminal Justice Act 2003, empowers courts to impose any of a wide range of drug rehabilitation requirements (of which DTTO conditions form a part) with one or more community sentences. An evaluation of the DTTO by Turnbull et al (2000) provides some insights into its usefulness at least to the extent that drug using offenders who pass through the criminal justice process can be successfully coerced into drug treatment. There is also evidence of reductions in drug use and drug-related criminal activity. This mark of success is however tempered with the high levels of DTTO breach (Hough et al 2003, National Audit Office 2004). Although the implications of the DTTO for black problem drug users seemed promising (Kalunta-Crumpton 2003a), the extent to which this group of problem drug users remained in treatment through to completion was a worrying situation given that the drug with which they are most associated – crack – has no medical treatment substitute as methadone is for heroin. As such black and minority ethnic problem drug users were more likely to be in breach of the DTTO (Sangster et al 2001). The threat of imprisonment as a consequence was therefore probable.

Arrest referrals and the drug treatment and testing order (DTTO) are two major schemes that signalled the involvement of criminal justice agencies in drug treatment – a product of the multi-agency strategy established in the 1990s. All police forces in England and Wales have arrest referral schemes, which aim to refer identified problem drug users at the point of arrest to treatment agencies with the view to breaking the relationship between drug use and acquisitive crime. Here, police officers work in partnership with drug treatment services and Drug Action Teams (DATs) to this effect (Home Office 2002a). Arrest referrals have their own advantages in addressing drug treatment. According to findings by the Drugs Prevention Advisory Service (DPAS), the schemes can make a positive impact on drug use and offending (Edmunds et al 1999). Furthermore, the success of arrest referral schemes in targeting problem drug using offenders, particularly crack/cocaine and opiate users, is shown in a DPAS publication based on data from the national arrest referral monitoring system (Sondhi et al 2002). However, the publication also notes that black problem drug using offenders and young male crack using offenders are among groups of problem drug users that fail to engage in drug treatment following an arrest referral.

There are also huge gaps in service provision and delivery within the prison establishment in meeting the demands of certain drug types and the treatment needs of certain groups of prisoners. Like the police and court services, the prison system witnessed policy developments in the 1990s as part of the multi-agency approach towards drug treatment via the criminal justice system. Since the publication in 1998 of the government's 10-year national drugs strategy (Home Office 1998), drug treatment programmes in prison have included the CARAT programme involving the provision of counselling, assessment, referral, advice and through-care services to prisoners. Such facilities are aimed at addressing problematic drug use in prison with a view to reducing drug use and reoffending after release. However, it has been observed that the majority of prisoners who use drugs do not have access to the treatment services they need (The Federation 2002). Prisoners with co-morbidity problems of mental health and drug/alcohol addiction are amongst those most affected. Whilst black people have continued to be disproportionately represented in the prison population, their treatment needs in prison have been traditionally overshadowed by the research and policy focus on the drug of most concern – heroin. In a Home Office report (2003a) on *The Substance Misuse Treatment Needs of Minority Prisoner Groups*, crack was identified as a drug on which both male and female minority ethnic prisoners, particularly black prisoners, were most often dependent, unlike their white counterparts, whose dependence was mostly on opiates. However, the treatment needs of crack users in prison are yet to be adequately met. Some of the difficulties which preclude appropriate treatment services for black prisoners were also noted in the report (Home Office 2003a: 2):

> It was noted rehabilitation services were not necessarily attracting ethnic minority men into treatment. Practitioners interviewed felt this may in part be due to a lack of ethnic minority practitioners and a perceived lack of cultural understanding from white staff.

It adds (ibid.: 3):

> A further point concerns approaches to detoxification and treatment of crack users. Practitioners saw the management of crack misuse as less straightforward than the treatment of opiate dependence. Unlike cases involving opiates, no substitute medication is available to manage the symptoms of withdrawal from crack.

Evidently crack occupies a 'special' position in the treatment agenda for a number of reasons. In the absence of a 'substitute medication', the report claims, alcohol is commonly used by problem crack users as "a sedative to soothe the 'come down' effects of the drug". This is a problem observed with regard to crack using prisoners whose dependence on crack is significantly accompanied by damaging amounts of alcohol consumption, particularly with the minority ethnic male prisoners. Furthermore, there was also the issue of 'psychotic and manic experiences' as a serious health ramification of drug use found especially amongst crack/alcohol using prisoners. Deliberate self-harm was a symptom of drug dependence specific to female prisoners of black and mixed race origins.

Improvements in the area of drug treatment via the criminal justice route are expected following the introduction of the Drug Interventions Programme (DIP) in April 2003. According to the Home Office (2004a: 17), this programme "takes advantage of every opportunity in the Criminal Justice System to direct drug-misusing offenders out of crime and into treatment". This includes providing through-care (for those drug misusers passing through the criminal justice system and beyond) and after-care (following sentence/treatment completion) services to drug misusers. Under the DIP – which is in operation in 66 areas with the highest rates of drug-related crime – there is evidence of an increase in the numbers of drug users entering drug treatment (Home Office 2004a). Another notable policy development in the area of criminal justice is the Drugs Act 2005. This Act makes provisions for drug offenders to be tested on arrest rather than on charge, and for those who test positive to undergo an assessment by a drugs worker. These developments are meant to increase opportunities to access 'hard-to-reach' groups of problem drug users, but the extent to which they have made a positive impact on black problem drug users is yet to be determined.

3.6 Drug Prevention

In relation to drug prevention, the black community (and other visible minority ethnic communities) is relatively insignificant in prevention work despite the 'new emphasis' placed on prevention as a vital strategic approach to the drug problem. In the *Updated Drug Strategy 2002*, the key purpose of prevention is clarified:

> Success for the Drug Strategy means preventing today's young people from becoming tomorrow's problematic drug users.... That is why prevention and early intervention with young people, before problems escalate, is the only way to make a long-term difference (Home Office 2002a: 14-15).

Prevention was part of the government's drugs control policy of the 1980s, but it occupied a secondary position to the law enforcement approach that was top priority on the agenda. The government's drug strategy publication, *Tackling Drug Misuse* (Home Office 1985), made the order of priority clear – law enforcement efforts toward the control of drug trafficking were the central focus. Whilst the strategy had planned for the development and proliferation of drug prevention measures through health education and information campaigns, local community action and the training of professional groups who come into contact with drug users, controlling drug supply via law enforcement was also integrated in principle as part of drug prevention strategy. The argument behind the connection between prevention and law enforcement was that by restricting the availability of drugs, opportunities for experimentation and continued drug use are invariably restricted. However, in the early 1990s drugs policy attitudes towards promoting prevention in its own right began to gain in importance and in 1995 and 1998 the government's drug strategies as represented in *Tackling Drugs Together* and *Tackling Drugs to Build a Better Britain* made the emphasis on prevention more explicit.

Drug prevention programmes have included drugs education projects for young people and those in vulnerable groups such as the homeless; drugs awareness sessions and prevention work with parents of young people; and supporting local community development and coordination of drug prevention strategies. Despite what seemed to be a growing practice, drug prevention initiatives have encountered difficulties in reaching minority ethnic groups. In the Home Office paper entitled *Dealing with Diversity*, it was clearly stated that minority ethnic groups were "not being reached adequately by drug preventive services and health promotional facilities"

(Johnson and Carroll 1995: 13). With particular reference to the black and Asian communities, these findings were attributed to factors which, on the one hand, preclude minority ethnic group use of services and, on the other hand, pose problems for service providers in reaching clientele from minority ethnic groups. For the former, factors restricting access to services include language barriers, distrust of white agencies, inaccessible service provision, and the lack of black and Asian imagery in drug prevention and health promotion materials and locations. In the latter scenario of service provision, barriers include lack of multi-cultural working and ethnically diverse staff composition, service staff ignorance of minority ethnic community issues, lack of resources for positive outreach work, and difficulties in accessing ethnic minority communities (Johnson and Carroll 1995). The acknowledged gap in issues of racial and cultural diversity in prevention work was viewed as an obstacle, which can only be tackled if the often culturally homogenous structuring of drug prevention services begins to embrace fully the demands of diversity.

Some of these barriers to collaborative drugs prevention work in minority ethnic communities, especially black and Asian communities, have been recognised by the Home Office Drugs Prevention Advisory Service (DPAS). In its publication, *Delivering Drug Services to Black and Minority Ethnic Communities* (Sangster et al 2001) recommendations were mapped out on how best to tackle some of the problems that emerge from work with drug users from minority ethnic communities.

3.7 Tackling Drug Supply via Law Enforcement

The Home Office (2002b) publication *Tackling Crack: A National Plan* marked the recognition of crack misuse at governmental level, even though the presence of crack misuse, often associated with the black community, was known since the late 1980s. This publication was the product of a national crack conference held in 2002 and embodies a national action plan for tackling crack. According to the publication, the relatively recent approach towards crack stems from a recognition that crack use is steadily increasing across the UK and its link to acquisitive crime, violent crime and sex work renders it a serious threat to community order, particularly in London. It demonstrates an overt recognition that the relative neglect of crack has also meant that there have been gaps in treatment service provision for crack users, unlike their heroin using counterparts who are predominantly white and whose drug using needs have shaped the development of mainstream services. Thus the publication reflects an agenda that has drug treatment and prevention as some of its main objectives, and meeting the "needs of ethnic minority users…more effectively" (Home Office 2002b: 4) as one of its anticipated results. The specific reference to minority ethnic users in this sense is linked to observations that African-

Caribbeans tend to use crack as a primary drug and are less likely to use heroin either on its own or alongside crack. Primary crack users as opposed to secondary crack users are more likely to attract the more acute forms of problems associated with crack use. Invariably crack use and its problems are more likely to have a damaging impact on African-Caribbean communities, which according to the Home Office (2002b: 10) are "more likely to be located in the poorest and most deprived inner city neighbourhoods where crack houses tend to be found" (also see Home Office 2003b).

Whilst *Tackling Crack: A National Plan* takes on board the need to address treatment and preventive measures on crack cocaine, law enforcement significantly features as an integral part of the plan to tackle the increasing use of crack via a focus on crack dealing and markets. In the executive summary of the National Crack Action Plan, the African-Caribbean community is identified as a group disproportionately affected by crack markets that mostly operate in deprived localities. Law enforcement strategy in this respect has intensively focused on increasing arrests and convictions for crack trafficking, and closing crack houses particularly in areas named as high crack areas, many of which are also high crime areas (NTA 2003). Key drugs law enforcement achievements outlined in the government's drug strategy progress report of 2004 have included the closure of approximately 150 crack houses between January and September 2004, a practice effected under new powers given to the police in the Anti-Social Behaviour Act 2003. This piece of legislation allows the police "to close crack houses within 48 hours", to seize assets and firearms (aimed at tackling gun crime, part of which is associated with drug trafficking), and to target drug dealers. Following the introduction of the Drugs Act 2005, the Anti-Social Behaviour Act 2003 has been amended to enhance police powers to enter premises (using reasonable force where necessary) including crack houses for the purpose of serving a closure notice. As part of the police attack on drug trafficking, 'Operation Crackdown' (a three-month joint campaign by the Home Office and the Association of Chief Police Officers) was launched in 2005 to target class 'A' drug dealers and drug-related gun crime, and to close crack houses (Turning Point 2005). According to the Home Office (2005), the operation "saw police close more than 170 crack houses, take over £13.4 million of drugs off the streets, arrest more than 3,400 Class A drug suppliers, and seize cash assets worth more than £3 million".

Increased powers given to law enforcement agencies under the Drugs Act 2005 include allowing courts to remand in police custody for up to a further 192 hours those who swallow packaged drugs in order to increase the likelihood of recovering the evidence; and requiring a court or jury to assume intent to supply where an accused is found in possession of a certain quantity of a controlled drug. Thus far it is known that the number of drug offenders that appear before the court has been on the increase and that the courts impose harsh sentences of immediate imprisonment on the majority of class 'A' drug traffickers (Home Office 2005). It is also known that there is a disproportionate representation of black people in the prison establishment for drug offences (Home Office 1993, 1999, 2000, 2004b), mirroring the intensifying law enforcement attack on drugs.

As with policy developments on drug trafficking in the 1980s, the 1990s and beyond continued to see emphasis placed on deterrence through stringent legislative attack. For example, Section 2 of the Crime (Sentences) Act 1997 introduced mandatory sentences of a minimum of seven years for repeat drug trafficking offenders involved in a class 'A' drug. Asset confiscation constitutes another important preventive measure against drug trafficking. The Criminal Justice (International Cooperation) Act 1990 authorised the forfeiture of drug trafficking money being exported from or imported into the UK, and, the Drug Trafficking Act 1994 (DTA) consolidated the Drug Trafficking Offences Act 1986 (DTOA) and the confiscation provisions of the Criminal Justice Act 1993. Under the DTA, a convicted drug trafficker serves a default prison sentence where s/he fails to comply with the confiscation order but unlike the DTOA, this sentence runs consecutively with the term of imprisonment for drug trafficking. In the past, failure to surrender proceeds of drug trafficking was punished by a default prison sentence which thereafter erased the confiscation order. This practice changed under the DTA which not only removes a confiscation order as a determining factor in the court's sentencing decision but also stipulates that a confiscation order still stands even after a prison sentence has been served. The DTA also allows HM Customs or police officers to seize drug trafficking money being imported into or exported out of the UK. Targeting assets as a deterrent measure against drug trafficking continued into the 21st century. New legislation, the Proceeds of Crime Act 2002, has attracted weightier law enforcement operations. The establishment of an Assets Recovery Agency under this Act gives law enforcement agencies greater powers of asset confiscation, which moves beyond powers of criminal confiscation to incorporate powers of civil recovery.

In line with such changes in drug trafficking legislation, the targeting of drug trafficking and traffickers culminated in tougher law enforcement response. Simultaneously, black people (both foreign and British nationals) continued to be drawn into the criminal justice system for drug offences, particularly drug trafficking for which their involvement is often shown at the lower end of the drugs trade. Studies have drawn attention to the low-level drug trafficking role of drug importers often arrested by HM Customs and Excise (Green 1991). According to Green (1998), the majority of drug seizures by HM Customs and Excise involve relatively small amounts of drugs; cannabis comprises most of the seizures, and often the seizures are from individual air passengers from the Third World rather than air freight. Green (1998) also argues that drug traffickers who appear in court are often at the lower end of the drugs trade; this category – unlike "major drug traffickers" who "have few problems protecting and concealing their assets" – have confiscation orders "routinely applied against" them (ibid.: 168; also see Kalunta-Crumpton 1999).

Similarly drugs policing continued to feature at the lowest levels of drug trafficking activities. Such police activities have been geared toward detecting retail drug markets and, despite their implications for ethnic minorities, are deemed justifiable. In a report by the Advisory Council on the Misuse of Drugs (1994: 3-4), the divisional-level drugs policing strategy and what seems to be its inevitable consequence on black people are justified thus:

> An important element of street level policing is the tactic of stop and search of individuals suspected of involvement in drug offences. A significant amount of activity involving drugs is concentrated in our inner cities, where ethnic minorities are also heavily represented. In turn, this can result in apparently disproportionate numbers of ethnic minorities being stopped and searched compared with the general population.

Notwithstanding the ethnic and class implications of the emphasis on low-level drugs policing, it is a strategy that has not only remained prominent but has subordinated upper- and mid-level drug trafficking in the police operational response to drugs. Efforts to disrupt low-level drug trafficking have continued to be strengthened, more evidently in the area of crack cocaine. Since the late 1980s policing crack has been a central aspect of drugs policing in the black community. At a time when the crack presence in the UK was nowhere near the United States crack experience, the government, law enforcement and the media joined forces in exaggerating its potentially dangerous combination of guns and violence to mean an imminent threat to law and order within and beyond the black community. The sensational reportage of the dangers of crack intertwined with a new police focus on tracking crack dealers, particularly 'yardies'. Through Operation Lucy set up by the Metropolitan Police in 1988 and later replaced by Operation Dalehouse, the Metropolitan Police created its own Crack Intelligence Coordinating Unit to gather intelligence on crack. Although Operation Dalehouse, as a specialist unit for crack, came to an end in 1992, crack supply was still targeted within the general operational framework of drugs policing. This was to change with the resurrected specialist police interest in crack. According to Sudbury (2002: 66) "the Metropolitan Police received £800,000 in 2000 to carry out Operation Crackdown". This operation targeted "low-level dealers of crack and class 'A' drugs on council estates in boroughs with large black populations. The operation led to surveillance of 700 properties, over 80 raids and 1000 arrests" (ibid.). In 2000 when Operation Trident, an elite unit set up in 1998 to focus on all gun crime in London (*The Guardian*, 1 August 2000, Evans 2002), redirected its focus to wholly concentrate on the so-called drug-related black-on-black killings, it thereby served as another reminder that the police specialist interest in the 'yardies' and crack was not over. According to Evans (2002), Lambeth, Southwark, Hackney, Haringey, Brent and Newham make up the six 'hotspot' localities of Operation Trident and, in 2001, Operation Trident resulted in 441 arrests following an increase in the same year in the number of shooting incidents and murders.

The continued emphasis on street-level drugs policing of class 'A' drugs into the 21st century is further illustrated in one of the most significant law enforcement policy developments of the century: the reclassification of cannabis from a class 'B' to a class 'C' drug and the increase in the penalty for trafficking in a class 'C' drug from 5 to 14 years. As stated in the *Updated Drug Strategy 2002*, a central reason for this change was "…to free up the considerable amount of police time currently spent in dealing with minor cannabis possession offences" with a view to "supporting the wider strategy objective of refocusing efforts – including enforcement action – on the drugs that cause the most harm, i.e. heroin and cocaine" (Home Office 2002a: 36). The *Updated Drug Strategy* 2002 cites the impact of the London borough of Lambeth Cannabis Warning Pilot Scheme, introduced and run by the Metropolitan Police July 2001, on the overall drugs law enforcement in Lambeth. The scheme, which had the objective of diverting police attention to more serious crime, including a focus on class 'A' drugs, involved the use of on-street police warnings in cases where small quantities of cannabis were possessed for personal consumption. The outcome of the scheme showed, alongside police time saving and reduced arrest rates for cannabis possession, an increase in police law enforcement efforts and arrests in connection with trafficking in class 'A' drugs.

In the pursuance of law enforcement policies and practices such as those illustrated above, those most affected – the black community – suffer the greatest punitive consequences. By June 2002 the percentage of black people imprisoned for drug offences had soared to 30 per cent, from 18 per cent in June 1998 (Kalunta-Crumpton 2003b). Clearly they are a stark indication of the prominent position that the black community has come to occupy as clients of the criminal justice system for drug offences, and in particular drug trafficking.

3.8 Conclusion

The black community is highly visible in policy and practical responses to drugs supply. In contrast, they are relatively invisible in responses to drug treatment and drug prevention. Crack use – often associated with the black community – has since 2001 become more widespread than heroin use (Home Office 2005). In spite of this changing trend in patterns of drug use, heroin use remains the primary focus of drug treatment service provision and delivery, resulting in a greater number of heroin users (NTA 2005) and a lesser number of crack users accessing treatment (Turning Point 2005). Whilst this is not to claim that opiate use is unfamiliar to problem drug users from the black community (see Kalunta-Crumpton 2003a), it does highlight the recurring concern about the underrepresentation of black (and other visible minority ethnic) problem drug users in treatment services. The concern fundamentally points to the structure of mainstream service provision and delivery: statutory agencies are run by whites for white clientele; they are not often ethnically representative in terms of staffing; and they do not often operate culturally competent, responsive and sensitive programmes to address the needs of problem drug users from minority ethnic groups. These limitations in drug treatment are found in drug prevention strategy where the needs of black and minority ethnic communities have not been sufficiently addressed.

Many years of concern over Britain's drug problem have expressed themselves in a drugs policy through which drugs supply is primarily targeted via law enforcement. This response results in a clearly marked difference in the ethnic composition of those most likely to be arrested, convicted and imprisoned for drug trafficking offences (Kalunta-Crumpton 1999). But whilst the drugs war has catapulted many black people of British and non-British nationalities into the prison system, it is difficult to argue that this penal response has made a significant impact on the drug problem. A key reason for this is that the drug trafficking role of black people is hardly capable of sustaining the drug demand in the UK, principally because this ethnic group occupies the lower levels of the drugs distribution chain, which often operates at street level. In contrast, their white counterparts are located at the top end of the drugs economy as suppliers and distributors with access to the lucrative parts of the drug trade (Ruggiero and South 1995). Yet this category – favoured by drug treatment and drug prevention policies and practices – is relatively sidelined in the war on drug trafficking.

Chapter 4 Common Law and Common Sense: Juries, Justice and the Challenge of Ethnic Plurality

Roger Ballard

In Common Law systems, juries fulfil a crucial role as assessors of the evidence presented by the contending parties to legal proceedings, and consequently act as finders of fact. In the first place the jury is the source of that vital yardstick 'the reasonable man': the instrument through which a relevantly contextualised assessment of things done or said can be confidently and, at least in principle, reliably implemented. Secondly and just as importantly, the jury is and always has been a bastion against overweening authority (including, where necessary, that of judges), and ultimately the over-mighty power of Kings. That is precisely why the right to trial by a jury of one's peers is a key component of the *Magna Carta*.

From a thirteenth century perspective, the socio-political structure of contemporary England would be wholly unrecognisable. Not only has a parliament of commoners comprehensively superseded the powers of the Crown, but all aspects of the administration of justice are now handled within the context of a centralised bureaucracy. At the same time the role of the jury has been substantially constrained. Whilst still central to the trial process in the most serious criminal cases, it has long since been abandoned in the civil courts. Even in those cases where the presence of a jury is retained as a finder of fact, its powers have been significantly clipped in favour of a professional judiciary, whilst both its role and its mode of recruitment have been comprehensively transformed. As a leading member of the English bar put it in a contribution to the *Harvard Law Review* a century ago:

> The function of the jury continued for a long time to be very different from that of the jury of the present day. The jurymen were still mere recognitors, giving their verdict solely on their own knowledge of the

Prakash Shah (ed.), Law and Ethnic Plurality: Socio-Legal Perspectives. *pp. 69-105.*
 ISBN 978 90 04 16245 7.

> facts, or from tradition, and not upon evidence produced before them; and this was the reason why they were always chosen from the hundred or vicinage in which the question arose. On the other hand, jurymen in the present day are triers of the issue; they base their decision upon the evidence, whether oral or written, brought before them. But the ancient jurymen were not impanelled to examine into the credibility of evidence; the question was not discussed before them; they, the jurymen, were the witnesses themselves, and the verdict was, in reality, the examination of these witnesses, who of their own knowledge gave their evidence concerning the facts in dispute to the best of their belief (Stephens 1896: 157–58).

The transformation could hardly have been more dramatic. Where personal knowledge of the litigants and of the context within which they operated was once a positive recommendation for recruitment to a jury, it is now a ground for disbarment from that role; and where once it was taken for granted that jury members would be recruited from within the community to which the litigants belonged (and specifically from amongst their peers if the Crown was directly involved in the proceedings), contemporary practice has moved in the opposite direction. Contemporary juries are drawn at random from the population at large.

4.1 Common Sense in Medieval England

A vision of 'common sense' has always been an integral feature of the English tradition of Common Law. Over and above the commonplace observation that a central feature of this mode of legal practice is that judicial decisions are primarily based on considerations of tradition, custom, and precedent, rather than being spelled out with reference to an explicit statutory code, a central feature of the whole edifice is the role allocated to the jury as finders of fact. The basis on which they are expected to do so is quite explicit. When a judge concludes his summing up to the jury – having thus far simply fulfilled the role of referee in an adversarial contest between the prosecution and the defence – he invariably goes on to distinguish between his own role as an advisor to members of the jury on matters of law, and their role as finders of fact. Having done so he then goes on to urge them to assess the details of the evidence laid before them in the light of their own *common sense* understandings as they go about the process of reaching a verdict.

As with *Magna Carta* reiterated, a central role of the jury was to provide what we would currently identify as a democratic bastion against the overweening power of the state; a further contemporary function is to restrain the wiles of expensive lawyers employed by wealthy litigants to deploy casuistic tricks in an effort to extricate their clients from awkward circumstances. But, if the jury are to fulfil their role effectively, one crucial prerequisite must of necessity be in place. The jury's resources of common sense – no less at an individual than at a collective level – must be sufficiently wide and deep to enable its members to place and understand the evidence with which it has been presented to them within an appropriate context. Only then will they be in a position to make informed and sensible judgements about its significance. It was precisely in an effort to ensure that such findings of fact would be made using an appropriate yardstick, rather than one which had been carefully constructed to the Crown's convenience, that the *Magna Carta* gave the King's subjects a right to be tried not just by a jury, but by a jury of their peers.

In medieval England the normative procedure followed in the vast majority of low-profile cases was to recruit jurors from within the local hundred; from that perspective the provisions of the *Magna Carta* simply reaffirmed that when great magnates found themselves arraigned before the King's Justices, they would likewise be entitled to trial before a jury of their peers, rather than by royal/judicial fiat. Whilst this further reinforced the view that triers of fact were both expected and entitled to utilise 'common sense' as the basis on which they reached their verdict, it simultaneously accepted that this common sense was *not* common to the entire gamut of the King's subjects.

In medieval times our contemporary concept of national homogeneity was unknown. Whilst it went without saying that all the inhabitants of King's realm were his subjects, and consequently stood in a common condition of fealty to their ruler, it was equally self evident that they were far from being a homogeneous mass. Not only was fealty articulated through a feudal hierarchy, such that the population was divided into a series of clearly differentiated ranks, but the broad mass of the population lived within innumerable local communities, whose members were in turn skilled in a wide variety of occupations – all with their own distinctive customs and 'mysteries'. In the midst of such a social order, common sense was manifestly *plural* rather than singular in character, and hence specific to a multitude of differing bodies of people. The conventions of jury recruitment took direct cognisance of this condition of differentiation, and so produced juries congruent with the plural character of the social order. This had a further consequence – at least with respect to developments which were yet to come: there was no need for expert witnesses. Juries were recruited in such a way that their members' common sense was grounded in extensive prior knowledge of the litigants and their daily *modus operandi*. Hence they were *ipso facto* expert to the issues at stake in the proceedings, as well as to the precise circumstances in which the events in question occurred. In this respect the system of justice-delivery was well suited to cope with the plural character of medieval England's socio-cultural order.

4.2 Common Sense and Ethnic Plurality in Contemporary Britain

During the course of the past eight centuries the English tradition of common law has undergone all manner of transformations, as has the character of the society whose members' doings it seeks to order and regulate. Firstly all the various components of the British social order are – or are at least envisioned as being – far more socially and ideologically interconnected than was the case in medieval England. Likewise their doings are subject to much more comprehensive and centralised forms of organisation and control than anyone could have imagined way back in the thirteenth century. In our current circumstances, the notion that British society is ordered around a single set of socio-cultural understandings, such that its members can safely be regarded as forming a more or less homogeneous whole, seems far from unreasonable. Hence the proposition that there is a single nationally applicable vision of 'common sense' to which everyone would in broad terms be prepared to subscribe appears, at least on the face of it, to be as sensible as it is realistic.

Indeed it is precisely on the basis of such a set of assumptions that the concept of 'the man on the Clapham omnibus' came to the fore in legal usage. Initially constructed as a descriptive representation of a reasonably educated, intelligent and thoroughly ordinary average citizen, it followed that the notion of such a person could be deployed as the model of a 'reasonable man' against whose opinions a defendant's conduct might be equitably adjudged (*McQuire v Western Morning News* [1903] 2 KB 100). To be sure the phrase deployed to identify such a person – 'the man on the Clapham omnibus' – sounds distinctly anachronistic in the context of twenty-first century discourse. Nevertheless the notion that certain matters do indeed fall within the realm of common knowledge, and that there is indeed a set of common behavioural yardsticks on which all sensible members of the population at large can be expected to agree, remains a largely unquestioned feature of contemporary legal discourse.

This view was explicitly confirmed in a series of cases heard during the course of the 1970s and 1980s, in which counsel for Afro-Caribbean defendants sought to use their right of peremptory challenge in effort to ensure that juries trying their clients' cases had some degree of racial and ethnic balance. As it happened Lord Denning had recently heard an appeal launched by two policemen facing criminal charges, and had sought to have the jury vetted to ensure that it did not include anyone who had been successfully prosecuted by the police, and might consequently wish to get their own back. Denning rejected their argument with his customary clarity:

> Our philosophy is that the jury should be selected at random, from a panel of persons who are nominated at random. We believe that 12 persons selected at random are likely to be a cross-section of the people as

> a whole and thus represent the view of the common man. (*R v. Crown Court at Sheffield, ex parte Brownlow* [1980] Q.B. 530)

Shortly afterwards Lord Lane LCJ also found himself addressing the issue of jury selection, but this time with respect to arguments as to whether in cases involving minority defendants, the jury should consist partly or wholly of members of that same ethnic group. Framing his analysis in terms of potential bias rather than the potential availability of special knowledge or awareness, he quoted his colleague's argument with approval before saying that English law:

> had never been held to include discretion to discharge a competent juror or jurors in an attempt to secure a jury drawn from a particular section of the community or otherwise to influence the overall composition of the jury. For this latter purpose the law provides that 'fairness' is achieved by the principle of random selection. (*R v Royston James Ford* (1989) 89 Cr App 280)

Two points are worth noting here. By focussing on potential bias, rather than potential knowledge, and hence on the legitimacy of selectively discharging otherwise competent jurors, the Lord Chief Justice was able to overlook English law's long history of selecting expert juries; however in defending that position he also found it expedient to quote the Master of the Rolls' judgement – expressed in a very different context – highlighting the intrinsic fairness of random selection. However the core premises which underpin these arguments are not hard to discern. Firstly the population at large can safely be regarded as being 'unstructured' in a statistical sense – or in other words patterns of differentiation within it are individual rather than structural in character; secondly that by selecting a jury at random, its members can reasonably be expected to provide a fair approximation of the (broadly homogenous) views, knowledge and experience of the population at large.

Yet, just how sound are these 'commonsense' premises? An examination of the character of twenty-first century passengers on the Clapham omnibus would provide an effective answer to that question. Any such inspection would of course immediately highlight a salient feature of contemporary Britain: that its urban population, and most especially the urban population of the capital, is now markedly ethnically diverse. Hence the outcome of such an inspection would almost certainly reveal that only a small minority of the passengers were of indigenous ancestry; everyone else would turn out either to be recent immigrants, or failing that the offspring of such parents. British society is now significantly ethnically plural

– and growing more so by the day. This chapter seeks to explore the consequences of our contemporary condition of plurality.

4.3 Expert Witnesses and their Role

In view of all this, can Lord Lane's *dictum* be left standing with any safety? Some fundamental issues of principle are at stake here. If justice is to be done in a society which is *de facto* ethnically diverse, should legal proceedings take cognisance of that condition of plurality? If so, how can that best be achieved? In medieval England plurality was not a significant problem. Besides playing a much more salient role in the fact-finding process, juries were selected in such a way that their members were able – and indeed expected – to draw on their own context-specific expertise. But as the social order became ever more diverse, the role of the jury was steadily reduced. The power of judges to order and control legal proceedings grew steadily greater, with the result – amongst other things – that juries lost their investigative powers, and their role was restricted to the assessment of the evidence laid before them during the course of the proceedings. Moreover as the social order became more complex there was an ever-increasing prospect that a regularly assembled jury would lack the specialist knowledge required to make an equitable assessment of the evidence laid before them. One obvious solution to this was to make a deliberate effort to recruit an expert jury. As the inestimable Learned Hand (1901: 41-42) noted:

> The custom was not only known but exceedingly common in the city of London throughout the fourteenth century in trade disputes .... The mayor then summoned a jury of men of that trade, and their verdict decided whether the defendant had offended the trade regulations, and upon it the mayor gave sentence... The special jury continued as an institution of England. So we find in 1645 that the court summoned a jury of merchants to try merchants' affairs "because it was conceived they might have better Knowledge of the Matters in Difference which were to be tried, than others could, who were not of that Profession."

However as time passed the practice of recruiting 'expert juries' in this sense gradually slipped into abeyance, to be replaced by the introduction of a new form of evidence into the proceedings: that provided by witnesses who had not necessarily observed the events in question at first hand, but rather those whose expert knowledge and experience was such that they were in a position to advise the court on technical matters which it was reasonable to suppose would otherwise lie beyond the knowledge and experience of lay jurymen. The key case in this respect was a dispute over the cause of the silting up of the harbour at Wells-next-the-Sea heard in 1782, in which Lord Justice Mansfield allowed an expert witness to be called to give evidence with respect to technical issues, having ruled that:

> The general opinion of scientific men upon proven facts may be given in evidence by men of science within their own science. (*Folkes v Chard* (1782) 3 Doug KB 157)

Whilst current practice with respect to the introduction of expert evidence in English law can be traced back to that landmark decision, case law has led to the precise role and status of experts within legal proceedings being steadily more tightly specified. In doing so two issues have been of perennial concern. Firstly as to whether the experts called before the court really were experts, especially when they turned out to disagree with one another; and secondly a fear that experts were beginning to play such a salient role in the proceedings that they became finders of fact in their own right, thereby potentially sidelining the whole judicial process (Jones 1994; Redmayne 2001).

Nevertheless the courts have found it quite impossible to do without experts, or even to limit the subjects which experts called before them might be invited to address. Only two restrictions have been imposed: firstly that their evidence must focus on issues germane to the proceedings, and which also lie outside the knowledge and experience of ordinary people. Lord Justice Lawton summed up this position when he ruled that:

> Expert evidence is only admissible if the evidence of the particular expert is significantly probative of issues which the triers of fact would, left with the established facts and their own knowledge, be unable to determine because they are outside ordinary human experience. (*R v Turner* [1975] 2 QB 834)

Nevertheless his objective in staking out this position was not to extend the issues which experts might address, but rather to limit them. Considering the admissibility of psychiatric evidence in a case where the issue at stake was provocation, Lawton LJ ruled that in this particular context the issues which the psychiatrist sought to address lay "well within human experience", and hence was inadmissible. As he went on to elaborate,

> An expert's opinion is admissible to furnish the court with scientific information which is likely to be outside the experience and knowledge of a judge or jury. If on the proven facts a judge or jury can form their own conclusions without help, then the opinion of an expert is unnecessary. In such a case if it is given dressed up in scientific jargon it may make judgment more difficult. The fact that an expert witness has impressive

> scientific qualifications does not by that fact alone make his opinion on matters of human nature and behaviour within the limits of normality any more helpful than that of the jurors themselves; but there is a danger that they may think it does (ibid.: 841).

4.4 My own Initiation into the Provision of Expert Evidence

Many years ago I was asked to come to court to give evidence in a case in which a Sikh father had killed his daughter in a fit of rage having discovered that she was having an affair, and had entered a plea of guilty to manslaughter. As I recall, I received no written instructions, and so had not prepared a written report in advance; and when counsel asked that I be called to give expert evidence, the Judge promptly ruled that such evidence was inadmissible. Much has changed since then. As the years passed I began to receive a steadily mounting stream of requests from solicitors to provide expert reports about one aspect or another of the distinctive lifestyles of South Asian settlers in Britain, for use in all manner of legal proceedings in which their clients had found themselves involved. By fits and starts I began to learn how best to respond to their requests, and to ensure that I was properly instructed.

As this occurred I found that I had been led into fulfilling a more or less unprecedented role: the provision of expert anthropological evidence illuminating one aspect or another of the everyday lifestyles of South Asian settlers in Britain and their UK-based offspring. As information about my availability spread by word of mouth, the frequency with which I received instructions began to grow exponentially. I have by now prepared around 400 reports in cases spread across all manner of proceedings in the civil, criminal, family and asylum and immigration courts. Although a number of other anthropologists have also begun to dip their toes into this pool, there are nevertheless good grounds for believing that at present there is no one more experienced than myself when it comes to the preparation of expert anthropological evidence for use in mainline English legal processes, as opposed to the narrow world of asylum and immigration tribunals. However my entry into this career path was in no sense pre-planned: I have arrived at my current position simply as a result of receiving a steadily rising flow of instructions. My central objective in this chapter is consequently to step back and take stock of the position in which I have found myself, and in doing so to take the opportunity to reflect critically on my experience of fulfilling what appears to be a largely unprecedented role.

4.5 On Becoming an Expert Anthropologist

When I was first blundered my way into this field I was profoundly inexpert in legal terms. Besides having no legal qualifications, I soon found that there were no obvious precedents around which to build my practice.

Moreover at that stage I was unaware that anthropological evidence differs significantly in character from that provided to the courts by fellow professionals in the human sciences such as psychologists and psychiatrists, and even more so from that offered to the courts by the usual run of forensic scientists. I consequently found myself embarking on a fairly steep learning curve with respect to the limitations and expectations of English Law, together with the arcane mysteries of court proceedings. As a result I now have a great deal of experience of acting as an expert – as opposed to an academic – anthropologist. Whether I can claim as much competence in the former role as I can in the latter will be for the readers of this chapter to decide.

As I settled into my role, I soon realised that whilst lawyers had gone to great lengths to establish the parameters within which experts in general were expected to operate, the role is nevertheless surrounded by all manner of contradictions. Hence, for example, the current rules make it quite clear that the expert's duty is to provide an objective professional analysis to the court, and most emphatically not to seek to advance the interests of the party by whom one has been instructed. However I soon began to realise that as soon as one appears in court to give evidence in person – as opposed to preparing a written report – this ideal is promptly undermined by the adversarial structure of proceedings. Having stepped into the witness box one is examined, cross-examined and re-examined just like any other witness. In no way is one's opinion treated as objective: cross-examiners routinely assume that the expert's position is partial to the interests of those instructing him – as is indeed bound to be the case. His evidence would not have been disclosed, nor would he have been called to give evidence in person, unless his conclusions did indeed serve the purposes of those instructing him. Like it or not, experts find themselves caught up in the tactical battles waged between the contending parties.

In the midst of such battles any suggestion that one is fulfilling the role of an objective servant of the court begins to feel entirely fictitious: rather one becomes a bagatelle in a complex tactical game, which becomes yet more surreal when the judge himself gets drawn into the fray. To make sense of the arcane debates which developed about the admissibility of my expertise (but from which I was excluded except in one case where the judge decided to hold a *voire dire*), I decided that I had no alternative but to do some serious legal homework.

4.6 The Status and Admissibility of Expert Evidence

Although an expert who appears in court has the status of a witness, one is nevertheless a witness of an unusual kind. Unlike a witness of fact, the expert will not normally have witnessed the things said or done with his own eyes. Rather the expert's role is to produce an expertly informed commentary on the evidence which has been set before the court by other first-hand witnesses. In other circumstances, evidence of this kind would be excluded as hearsay. However in the expert's case this rule is of necessity set to one side. Without such an exception the expert would not be in a position to express an opinion on the facts of the case, for to do so would be to trespass on the role of the jury. Nevertheless in doing so experts in general, and anthropological experts in particular, come perilously close to superseding the role of the jury as finders of fact. Hence whilst there are in principle no limits to the matters outside "ordinary human experience" counsel may invite an expert to address, clear limits have been set as to how far one can go in addressing them. As Lord President Cooper put it:

> Expert witnesses, however skilled or eminent, can give no more than evidence. They cannot usurp the function of the jury or Judge sitting as a jury, any more than a technical assessor can substitute his advice for the judgment of the court. Their duty is to furnish the Judge or jury with the necessary scientific criteria for testing the accuracy of their conclusions, so as to enable the application of their criteria to the facts proved in evidence. The scientific opinion, if intelligible, convincing and tested becomes a factor (and often an important factor) for consideration along with the whole other evidence in the case, but the decision is for the Judge and jury. (*Davie v Magistrates of Edinburgh* [1953] SC 34)

Yet, despite confidence with which such formulations may be expressed from the bench, all sorts of complications and contradictions begin to emerge when efforts are made to put them into practice. Indeed, as Learned Hand noted in an incisive commentary penned over a century ago, there are several senses in which the adversarial system renders the role of the expert witness thoroughly anomalous – and sometimes impossibly so. With this in mind it is worth summarising the core of his arguments:

> The real question that arises is how to put at the disposal of the jury the knowledge of experts in the decision of the issue.... it is not as a witness of facts at all that his position is peculiar; it is because as an expert witness he is allowed to testify to his conclusion from the facts, which he has either himself observed or which are in evidence from the testimony of others. His position is only peculiar in that a common witness is forbidden to testify to conclusions. ... the history of ... expert witnesses ... [is] simply the history of the exception in his favor to the rule that witnesses shall testify only to facts and not to inferences (Hand 1901: 43-44).

But as he promptly goes on to note, this precipitates contradictions between the role of the jury and that of the expert. Hence although "it is the jury that should form the opinion, make the conclusion and say truly – *vere dicere* – as to the facts, whilst the witness merely says what he knows" (p. 44), this careful distinction collapses as soon as one goes on to subject the interpretative role of the expert to detailed examination. Noting that the expert does not comprehensively usurp the role of the jury, for its members retain the capacity to reject the expert's testimony if they so choose, Hand nevertheless firmly reminds his readers that even though the jury may have the last word, "the important thing and the only important thing to notice is that the expert has taken the jury's place if they believe him" (p. 52).

Likewise Hand goes on to put his finger on precisely the dilemma which I myself experienced as soon as I stepped into the witness box:

> When an expert is on the stand what are the methods resorted to? Quite the same as when it is a witness. He is first examined in chief by the side which calls him. Assuming he has no direct evidence of facts to give, he must be plied with hypothetical questions, at as great length and in as great detail as seems necessary ... Assume that the expert has testified to a certain number of propositions expressing such general truths; he is then handed over to the opposite side for cross-examination.
>
> There are two and only two possible efforts which the cross-examiner will make. First, he may seek to bring out other general propositions favorable to his contention; second, he may seek to shake the validity of those already testified to. Similarly when it comes the turn of the opposite side to submit evidence, it has the same two possible objects, to introduce evidence showing the invalidity of what the opposite experts have said, or to bring out other general truths favorable to them.
>
> The trouble with all this is that it is setting the jury to decide, where doctors disagree. The whole object of the expert is to tell the jury, not facts, as we have seen, but general truths derived from his specialized experience. But how can the jury judge between two statements each founded upon an experience confessedly foreign in kind to their own? It is just because they are incompetent for such a task that the expert is necessary at all (pp. 53-54).

Although Learned Hand went on to argue that if justice is adequately to be done in circumstances of this kind, it would make good sense to refer the matters in dispute to a board of experts acting as an advisory tribunal, whose conclusions would in due course be forwarded to the trial jury as expert evidence, that is not a solution which judges or lawyers have found in any way attractive, not least because it would lead to the establishment of tribunals that would be beyond their immediate control, such that they would be capable – at least in their view – of causing all manner of chaos. In these circumstances some judges have sought refuge in the proposition that far from being the objective experts they claim to be, such persons are merely hired guns, only too willing to advance the interests of whoever is providing them with their fees. This was precisely the position taken by Sir George Jessel MR in a case heard towards the end of the nineteenth century. On the grounds that dissention amongst self-professed men of science could only be caused by financially-driven partisanship, he adopted a stance of extreme scepticism:

> Undoubtedly there is a natural bias to do something serviceable for those who employ you and adequately remunerate you. It is very natural, and it is so effectual that we constantly see persons, instead of considering themselves witnesses, rather considering themselves as the paid agents of the person who employs them. (*Abinger v Ashton* (1873) L.R. 17 Eq. 374)

4.7 The Status of Anthropological Expertise

Much has changed since Learned Hand grappled so illuminatingly with these issues a century ago. The scope of scientific understanding has increased by leaps and bounds, and along with this there has been a growing public awareness of the necessarily tentative nature of scientific hypotheses. Hence however much the courts might wish to be provided with an incontestable, scientifically justified account of the truth of the matter, experts invariably offer an *interpretation* of the evidence laid before them. In these circumstances differences of opinion between experts do not invalidate the exercise, but are an integral part of it – and best resolved by means of informed debate amongst those who know what they are talking about. If, however, the courts turn their back on allowing such debates to take place on expert rather than on legal terms, inexpert juries will find themselves placed in the invidious position of being required to choose between doctors who disagree. How, then, are they to resolve the issues? Much of the chaos precipitated by the way paediatric expertise was handled in recent cases where infant deaths were alleged to have been caused by 'shaken baby syndrome' and/or by 'Munchausen's Syndrome by Proxy' appears to have been precipitated by the courts' poor handling of the expert evidence laid before the jury.

The presence of plurality raises a yet more complex set of issues, not least because it raises a further set of questions as to how far, and in what sense, it is legitimate to identify social anthropologists as 'men of science' in the sense understood by lawyers. We must of course be careful of anachronisms here. As Jones (1994) shows in great detail, the rapid development of the role of the expert witness that followed Lord Mansfield's decision in *Folkes v Chard* took place on the back of a wave of nineteenth century enthusiasm for the wonders of science and technology. Not only do all the early legal sources consequently reflect nineteenth century understandings of the term 'science', but contemporary scientists' definitions of what their science is about frequently differs radically from those advanced by their forbears. That is certainly true of anthropology. To this also must be added the fact that few if any of the lawyers who become engaged in courtroom debates about the role and status of expert witnesses have had any training in the sciences, let alone the social sciences. This causes particularly acute problems with respect to the issues which concern us here. Even if most (but not all) lawyers and judges are now aware that anthropology is a discipline whose exponents are involved in a much wider range of activities than 'measuring heads', few can go much further than identifying the discipline of Social Anthropology as having something to do with the study of cultural practices. But whose cultural practices? And in any event, what sort of phenomenon do the courts, let alone contemporary anthropologists, have in mind when they use the term culture?

In my experience the vast majority of lawyers rely on popular understandings of what culture and ethnicity are all about, and use them to identify the kind of issues which it is reasonable to expect an anthropological expert to address. My experience suggests that anthropologists are routinely assumed to be primarily concerned with cultural alterity, and hence with the cultural practices of non-European people. A central consequence of this vision – which, to tell the truth, the anthropological profession has as yet done remarkably little to mount a public challenge – is that 'our' behaviour (in other words, the behaviour of members of the indigenous majority) is regularly assumed to be normal and hence a-cultural, with the result that it is only behaviour of non-assimilated members of Britain's non-European minorities which is significantly conditioned by 'culture'.

Secondly, and equally erroneously, it is routinely assumed that culture is a static and determinate set of rules which govern the behaviour of such persons, and that the mindless application of these rules can consequently precipitate all manner of pathological outcomes. Examples of such outcomes include forced marriages, exorcisms and honour killings, which are in turn held to arise when young people who have been exposed to more advanced notions of personal freedom as a result of their British upbringing seek to liberate themselves from the oppressive and authoritarian cultural restrictions imposed on them by their parents.

Whilst there is undoubtedly a grain of truth in such stereotypic understandings, the real world invariably turns out to be a great deal more complex. Hence the contents of my reports invariably come as an eye-opener to those instructing me, not least because they include detailed analyses of inter-personal relations within the extended families within which a disaster of one kind or another has occurred, and show that whilst cultural factors invariably condition behaviour, they rarely *determine* it. Moreover my reports regularly highlight the complex and sophisticated ways in which members of the younger generation navigate their way into and out of a range of differently ordered socio-cultural arenas, including those dominated by the native English; and as I sketch out these manoeuvres, it soon becomes apparent that those with the requisite navigational skills constantly re-order their behaviour as they move through a varied range of cultural contexts, further illuminating my point that culture *conditions* behaviour.

It goes without saying that all sorts of thoroughly familiar inter-personal contradictions can arise in the midst of all this, some of which sometimes get entirely out of hand. Domestic violence – up to and including homicide – is a universal phenomenon. Nevertheless the precise dynamics of the processes which lead to such outcomes is invariably far distant from the naïve visions of 'adjustment problems' and 'culture conflict' from which most external observers – including those instructing me – all too readily assume will lie at the heart of such 'ethnic cases'. For those seeking meaningful explanations of otherwise bizarre behaviour, such an analysis can be a godsend, although one that immediately poses a challenge as to how to present such matters to the jury. By contrast those with a pre-formed opinion about the significance of the events in question, and who have consequently commissioned an expert report to confirm a hypothesis to which they are already committed – as has often been the case when I have been instructed by the prosecution – invariably find such a response most disconcerting.

4.8 Issues of Admissibility

However, the preparation of a report in response to a solicitor's instruction is one thing; ensuring that it is accepted as admissible as expert evidence and put before the court is quite another. There are several potential hitches along the way. In the first place counsel may well come to the conclusion that it would not be advisable to place the report before the court, either because he takes the view that doing so would not be tactically advantageous, or because he fears that the judge may regard it as inadmissible; secondly, even if the report crosses that hurdle, the judge may indeed rule that its contents are such that it cannot be accepted as admissible. As I have gradually come to realize, in the eyes of many lawyers anthropological evidence often sails very close to the wind in terms of admissibility. We need to consider why.

As we have seen, judges have taken great care to guard the boundary between the role of the expert as a commentator on, and potential illuminator of, the evidence placed before the court, and their own and the jury's role as finders of fact. As Lord President Cooper put it in his *dicta* quoted earlier, the expert may not usurp the function of the jury or of a judge sitting as a jury. But whilst there are obvious strategic reasons why judges should be so keen to sustain this distinction, it is far less clear as to how far this can be sustained in practice without compromising the prospect of delivering justice on an equitable basis in the context of an increasingly plural society. A case study will serve to underline the point.

4.9 Regina v Jameel Akhtar

Jameel Akhtar found himself in court, charged with conspiring to import 20 kilograms of heroin into the UK. Ironically enough, the consignment of heroin in question had actually been imported into the UK by Customs and Excise in a process known as 'controlled delivery'. As such it was one of a whole series of operations designed, at least in principle, to enable Customs Officers to identify and prosecute major importers of Class A drugs into the UK. The case presented by Customs – who at that stage were still entitled to bring prosecutions themselves, rather than routing them through the Crown Prosecution Service – ran as follows:

> A Drugs Liaison Officer attached to the British High Commission in Islamabad reported that a Participating Informer with the code-name 'Mark' reported that he had been asked to act as a 'mule' by transporting a consignment of heroin to the UK. In return for a substantial reward, 'Mark' agreed to allow the DLO to tape-record a series of telephone conversations between himself and the supplier in Pakistan, and to notify the DLO as to when and where he would take delivery of the consignment, so enabling the DLO to surreptiously observe the hand-over.
>
> Some days later Mark handed over the consignment to the DLO at the High Commission in Islamabad, where the consignment was weighed and sampled before being flown to the UK, as was Mark. On arrival in the UK 'Mark' was set up in a ready-prepared Customs safe house in Birmingham, along with the consignment of heroin. From there 'Mark' made a number of telephone calls to the defendant (which were again recorded by Customs and Excise), as a result of which Jameel eventually agreed to meet 'Mark' in the car-park in Birmingham New Street station.
>
> When they met in the station car-park, 'Mark' opened the boot of his car, and handed a hold-all to the defendant. At this point a party of Customs Officers who had concealed themselves behind neighbouring vehicles stepped forward and arrested the recipient, accusing him of importing the consignment of 20kg which was found in the holdall. On being questioned Jameel vigorously denied having anything to do with the importation of drugs, and insisted that 'Mark' was merely a friend of a friend who had phoned him up to seek his assistance in starting up a business in herbal medicines. He did not open the holdall after it had

> been handed to him by 'Mark', and as far as he was concerned all it contained was samples of herbal medicine.

In the face of the evidence pressed forward by the prosecution, Jameel's explanation appeared, at least at first glance, to be exceedingly lame. Even his own solicitors, themselves of South Asian origin, were unconvinced by it, although they nevertheless put it forward in his defence as professional etiquette required. But quite by chance an eager young pupil came up with a lucky break: having been instructed by his pupil-master to find out whether there was anything significant about the number 420 in South Asian contexts, by sheer good fortune he put a call through to me. I promptly informed him that the phrase *char sau bis* (420 in Urdu) was a routinely used term for a cheat or a confidence trickster, and derived from Section 420 of the Indian Penal Code, which deals with Cheating and dishonestly inducing the delivery of property. Our discussion of the issues soon went far beyond the issue of *char sau bis*, which had allegedly been used as a code-word, and after further negotiations with counsel himself, I was instructed to act as an expert. I was consequently given access to all the evidence advanced by the prosecution.

The further I delved into the material, the more suspicious I became about the role which the Participating Informer had allegedly played in the whole operation. I had several grounds for doing so. According to 'Mark', his role was merely that of a passive bystander who had been drawn in by happenstance to act as an intermediary between a wholesale supplier of heroin in the North West Frontier Province and a recipient resident in the UK. Yet despite his nominal status as a mere mule, 'Mark's' evidence suggested that the supplier, Abdullah Khan, had expected him to extract a substantial payment from Jameel before handing over the consignment; but despite much nagging, Jameel showed little interest in closing the deal which he allegedly made by making such a payment. In the end 'Mark' settled for much less than he had demanded: £500. Yet having failed to persuade the customer to pay up, whilst also allowing a 20kg consignment of heroin which had been entrusted to him to be seized by Customs, there was no sign that Abdullah Khan was particularly troubled when 'Mark' subsequently returned to Pakistan. Something very fishy appeared to have been going on.

With this and a number of other concerns in mind, I turned to the key component of the evidence which Customs had put forward to substantiate their case: tape-recordings of 'Mark's' conversations with Jameel, Abdullah, and several of Abdullah's and his own associates in Pakistan. All those conversations had been conducted in Urdu and subsequently transcribed into English: it was those transcripts which the prosecution had set before the court as evidence. I promptly demanded access to the original tape-recordings. Whilst those recorded in Pakistan were of very little evidential substance, the contents of conversations between 'Mark' and Jameel following his arrival in the UK were a revelation.

Since the Pakistani social order is also strongly hierarchical in character, Urdu speech is full of all sorts of polite sentiments which immediately reveal the relative social status of the participants. Far from talking like the lowly servant of his boss, Mark consistently led the conversation, constantly told the alleged drug baron what he should do, even though his status was allegedly that of a mule. Moreover Jameel's responses to all this hardly seemed congruent with that of a major drugs-smuggler about to take delivery of a million pounds-worth of heroin. Far from being keen to check up on the quantity and quality of the consignment, and to make arrangements for its delivery, Jameel's responses suggested that he was largely unconcerned about the matter, with the result that he consistently but politely declined Mark's increasingly insistent demands for money. At the same time it was equally apparent that 'Mark' had conducted the conversations with great care. Not only did he lead the conversation, but conducted it in such a way as to elicit a whole series of polite expressions of acknowledgement (*ji, hãnji, bilkul* and so forth) from Jameel in response to a whole series of deeply incriminating statements he himself had made – and which were duly rendered as 'Yes', 'certainly', 'I agree' and so forth when the conversation was subsequently transcribed into English. All this led me to conclude that Mark had carefully constructed the conversation in such a way that Jameel would appear to entrap himself, on the expectation that once it had been transcribed into English neither his minders from Customs and Excise, nor the judge and jury before whom the transcription would eventually be laid as evidence would be sufficiently aware of Pakistani social and cultural conventions, let alone of Urdu linguistics, to be able to rumble what was going on.

On these grounds I concluded that there were strong indications that the whole operation might well have been a put-up job in which 'Mark' had deliberately ensnared a victim who might well have been an innocent victim of a complex and carefully ordered conspiracy. I also reached the conclusion that if the Customs Officers who had engaged 'Mark' as a PI were unaware of the games which their informant appeared to have been playing, they must have been remarkably gullible, naïve and short-sighted.

Having set out these arguments, analyses and conclusions in a detailed report,[2] I attended the trial, expecting to give my evidence in person. However, that was not to be. After an extended legal debate – from which I found myself excluded – the trial judge ruled that my report was inadmis-

2 A copy of this report can be found at www.art.man.ac.uk/casas/pdfpapers/akhtar.pdf.

sible. The proceedings went ahead. Jameel was duly found guilty, and sentenced to thirteen years imprisonment. Moreover, his defence team had no greater success when the matter was taken to the Court of Appeal, which roundly supported the trial judge's decision to exclude my report from the proceedings. The arguments put forward by Buxton LJ to justify his decision are worth quoting in full:

> It is difficult to summarise Dr Ballard's report and we will not seek to do so, save to say in very brief terms that first of all Dr Ballard sought to analyse the conversations between Mark and Mr Akhtar and to indicate how they fitted into the cultural background of those taking part, and how therefore that might reflect on the alleged credibility or content of those conversations; and also gave extensive evidence, or wished to do so, about cultural and social aspects of life and politics in Pakistan: the importance that would be attached to persons like the Khans, the dangers for a man like Mark of double crossing them as Mark, in effect, said he had done in this case, and the extent to which unfair practices took place in Pakistani politics, such as Mr Akhtar alleged had been his fate in this case.
>
> The judge was clear that none of it should be admitted.... The substance of the judge's ruling was that in so far as the evidence went to an issue in the case, it concerned issues that were for the jury to decide.
>
> Mr Enright [counsel for Akhtar] has stressed the different cultural background of the jurors in this case and those concerned in events in Pakistan. That is true, but juries in this country often find themselves trying cases of this sort, and with assistance from the judge, such as the jury certainly received in this case, they are able to do that perfectly fairly. None of the issues in this case are unusual.
>
> Again, as was pointed out in argument, it is not the prerogative of Pakistan or of any country for it to be the case that to cross an influential drugs dealer is something that is only done with caution and trepidation. Nor will it be surprising to people in any country that there may be political plots which lead to events such as Mr Akhtar alleged to have happened in this case. To that extent, therefore, the judge was quite right to think that the additional evidence of Dr Ballard would not add anything in substance; quite apart from the fact, and we emphasise the judge did not rely on this, that Dr Ballard's evidence, no doubt, would have been met by other evidence from other anthropologists or other universities, an accretion of evidence that would be wholly unjustified.
>
> We further say, however, for the avoidance of doubt, that insofar as Dr Ballard's evidence was going to be relied upon by the defence to seek to elucidate the truth or plausibility of what Mr Akhtar gave as the explanation of his various conversations with Mark, we consider it was

inadmissible in any event. *It was or would be evidence seeking to support the credibility or truth of another witness* [my italics]. This was nothing to do with the evidence of Mr Akhtar's psychology, state of mind or anything of that sort. It was evidence of cultural background which, in our judgement, would not be admissible in any event when the issue in the case was whether when they met on those occasions Mark and Akhtar had been discussing heroin or herbal remedies: a matter in our judgement not illuminated at all by any expert in any discipline whatsoever.

It was for the trial judge to decide whether Dr Ballard should be allowed to give evidence. He was entirely right in not admitting his evidence. (*R v Akhtar* Case No. 9701082/Z2, Court of Appeal Criminal Division, 10 March 1998)

In the light of the analysis set out earlier in this chapter, the grounds on which the Court of Appeal confirmed the trial judge's decision to exclude my evidence is quite clear. Whilst the learned judge was mistaken in suggesting that my report was primarily focussed on the behaviour of the defendant, for by far the greater part of its contents focussed on the activities of the PI Mark, he nevertheless concluded that in so far as my report provided an analytical commentary on the things said and done by another witness to the proceedings, I had strayed into territory in which the jury alone could legitimately operate. Hence my evidence was of necessity inadmissible.

However in so ruling, the learned judge also appears to have accorded the jury hearing this case – and other cases like it – with something close to superhuman powers. Hence even though counsel at the trial had sought to persuade the judge that the jurors might have difficulty in appreciating evidence which was set within a cultural and linguistic context with which it was most unlikely they would be in any way familiar (the case was in Worcester, a city with an insignificant South Asian population), Lord Justice Buxton strongly supported the trial judge's rejection of such arguments. Moreover he also took the opportunity to insert a further objection of his own, namely that if the appeal was to be allowed, there was a prospect that evidence of this kind "would have been met by other evidence from other anthropologists or other universities, an accretion of evidence that would be wholly unjustified."

But whilst his Lordship may have been echoing the fears of his predecessor Sir George Jessel, there can be no dispute that English juries do indeed regularly find themselves trying cases of this sort. Is it really the case, as the learned judge confidently went on to assert, that with assistance from the judge, such as the jury certainly received in this case, they are able to fulfil their task perfectly fairly?

4.10 The Issue Comes Back to the Court of Appeal

In the goodness of time this confidently-expressed opinion turned out to be erroneous. In 2005 this case, along with four other similar 'controlled delivery' cases came back to the Court of Appeal, where all the convictions were quashed (*R v Liaquat Ali and others* [2005] EWCA Crim 1783). Lengthy investigations conducted by the West Midlands Police and the Criminal Cases Review Commission (CCRC) generated a great deal of new evidence, which placed that evidence heard at Jameel's trial in an entirely new light. In the first place it emerged that 'Mark' was no mere bystander drawn into a conspiracy between Jameel and Abdullah by happenstance: on the contrary he had fulfilled the role of Participating Informer many times before, and he had been paid £12,000 (a princely sum in a Pakistani context) for his time and trouble in 'exposing' Jameel. Nor was the supplier unknown to Customs and Excise. On the very day when Jameel was arrested in Birmingham, there was a meeting between Abdullah Khan and two DLOs at the High Commission in Islamabad to discuss the implementation of two more Controlled Deliveries to the UK. What is more, in four Controlled Deliveries conducted during the previous year in which Abdullah had been the supplier and Mark the courier, the consignments had been seized by Customs Officers. There were also strong indications that the 'samples' extracted from the consignments by Customs Officers had in fact been in the kilogram range, and had subsequently 'disappeared'. As a result of all this (and much more besides) the Court of Appeal not only took the view that severe doubt consequently had to be cast on any evidence provided by Mark, but also roundly castigated Customs and Excise for its failure to make adequate disclosure of evidence in its possession during the course of the trial. Hence Lord Justice Hooper concluded that:

> Having reviewed the evidence in this case, the nature of the material that was not disclosed and the conduct of HM Customs and Excise, we are satisfied that Akhtar did not receive a fair trial. The undisclosed material could well have resulted in an acquittal. (*R v A* [2005] EWCA Crim 1788)

To put all this in context, it is worth noting that the Court reached similar conclusions with respect to all the 'controlled delivery' appeals which it was considering – although not before all those involved had served lengthy terms of imprisonment. Moreover, it did so primarily on the grounds that the Customs and Excise officials dealing with the appeal process, no less than those responsible for implementing the deliveries and following the cases through to trial, had systematically abused due process. This had further consequences. In an additional judgement delivered in 2005, the court set out a comprehensive critique of the obstructive manner in which

Customs and Excise had responded to those involved in the appeal process, leading to the conclusion that:

> In our view the respondent should have taken a proactive role with the Criminal Cases Review Commission. That overworked body should not have been expected to undertake over a period of 3 – 4 years the laborious and difficult task of untangling the evidence about Controlled Deliveries. The respondent should have done that and finished the task by about early 2001, thus saving the CCRC from spending so much time on these cases. It was the respondent's task, on the unusual facts of this case, to assess the safety of the convictions, not to allow another body to carry out the task for it.
>
> We have no doubt that the respondent has not conducted these appeals properly within the meaning of the Regulation. That has had two consequences. A huge amount of the time of this Court has been wasted – it has taken more than 20 hearings to dispose of these appeals. For that there is no remedy. The second consequence is that the legal aid fund has been significantly depleted when it ought not to have been. (*R v A* [2005] EWCA Crim 2598)

With this in mind, the court ordered Customs and Excise to pay 70 per cent of the appellants' costs, noting that this was merely a rough 'ball park' figure, and that if the figure was wrong, then it was too low rather than too high. It also specified the High Court Judge by whom the expected flood of claims from those who had been wrongly convicted should be heard. Nor was that all: on 7 April 2006 three of the Customs Officers involved in the Controlled Delivery programs were found guilty of a series of serious criminal offences, including collaborating with a drug smuggler on the run from justice, allowing at least 1.7kg of heroin to be sold in Leeds and Bradford, permitting heroin suppliers in Pakistan to receive a share of customs reward money funded by taxpayers as well as cash from street sales in Britain, and planning how to break rules covering informant handling and undercover smuggling operations.

Even so, it is not so much the seriousness of the system-failure to which these cases gave rise on which I want to focus here, but rather the reasons why the failure happened in the first place. With that in mind, two specific questions go to the heart of the original cases which were brought to trial. Firstly, how was it that what the Court of Appeal subsequently described as "a gentlemen's club of Drugs Suppliers and Participating Informers acting together and to the benefit of each other in Pakistan" managed so successfully to run rings round the Islamabad DLOs? Secondly, since it was subsequently discovered that those DLOs succumbed to the temptation to reach into the honey-pot themselves, how was it that during the course of repeated trials in criminal courts in the UK, counsel, judges, and juries failed to smell a rat, and to realise that the cases presented to them were merely put-up jobs based on severely flawed evidence? Could this happen again? With this in mind it is also worth noting that although the Court of Appeal has found that the reservations about 'Mark's' role which I set out in my report were in fact entirely sound,[3] Lord Justice Buxton's strictures about the inadmissibility of anthropological evidence remain untouched, at least in principle. It is hard to resist the view that if my evidence had not been excluded from the proceedings by the trial judge, there is an excellent prospect that Jameel Akhtar, as well as the victims of numerous parallel sting operations, would have avoided many years of wrongful imprisonment.

4.11 Wider Issues: The Implementation of Justice in Contexts of Ethnic Plurality

Although ethnic plurality is in no sense a novel phenomenon in either English or British contexts, its current salience may well be unprecedented. What cannot be denied is that given the scale of immigration during the past half-century, the social, cultural, linguistic and spatial distance of their countries of origin, together with the settlers' capacity to keep in touch with and to reproduce their own distinctive lifestyles in the aftermath of settlement, the courts now find themselves facing challenges of this kind with unprecedented frequency (Ballard 2006). As a result finders of fact – be they judges or juries – frequently find themselves expected to adjudicate in the proceedings where those involved routinely utilise a language other than English as a vehicle of communication. Moreover even when they have gained fluency in English, as is increasingly the case, settlers and their offspring frequently continue to order their inter-personal relationships in terms of premises and conventions which differ sharply from those routinely deployed by members of the indigenous majority. With such considerations in mind I would be the first to agree with Lord Justice Buxton that none of the issues raised in *Jameel Akhtar* were intrinsically unusual. But how far is the corollary which he so confidently goes on to assert – namely that with assistance from the judge, which they certainly received in this

3 Whilst my report was included in the documents considered by the Court of Appeal and the Criminal Cases Review Commission, there appear to have been two reasons why it was overlooked. On the one hand the CCRC appear to have deliberately avoided the problems associated with making a direct challenge to Lord Justice Buxton's ruling, given the complexity of the issues which were already on its plate; and secondly because the Court of Appeal decided for strategic reasons to focus primarily on the issue of due process.

case, juries are able to deal with the underlying cultural issues perfectly fairly – actually justified in practice?

In addressing such issues, it is self-evident that the capacity of lay juries to fulfil their role adequately will always be strongly conditioned by the effectiveness of the trial judge's instructions as to the basis on which they should set about their task; but no matter how clear those instructions may be, the jury's capacity to implement those instructions will be even more critically dependent on the quality of the evidence laid before them in the course of the proceedings, as well as the quality and character of the experiences and understandings on which the twelve jurors are in a position to draw in the course of reaching their verdict. However given the crucial role of *evidence* in this process, this raises a much wider range of issues than questions about whether – and in what format – anthropological insights should be made available to the jury. Similar questions also need to be asked with respect to all the other officers of the court – from the police officers who conducted the investigations which generated the evidence in the first place, through the solicitors and barristers (both for the prosecution or the defence) who considered the evidence and worked up a case, and finally the judges themselves. As things stand at present, how far are all these contributors to the judicial process adequately equipped to get to the bottom of actions and events conceived and implemented in linguistic and cultural contexts with which they themselves are unfamiliar?

With that in mind the core issue with which this chapter is concerned can be starkly formulated: was the sorry tale of the ease with which the courts were hoodwinked in the course of Customs' controlled delivery operations simply an exceptional one-off? Or were the underlying issues exposed in this particular case symptomatic of a much wider set of problems, and in that sense merely the tip of an iceberg? My experience is driving me inexorably towards the latter conclusion. But even though – or perhaps it would be better to say precisely because – members of the jury are the only non-professional participants in the whole process, they nevertheless have a crucial role to play as whistle-blowers. From a historical perspective speaking up on behalf of the common man in the face of the overweening power of the state has always been a central feature of the role of the jury. It is a role which is no less important today than it ever was, but can only be implemented if the jury is given adequate tools with which to work.

4.12 The Challenge of Plurality

Yet although the jury's role as purveyors of 'common sense' remains as central to the Common Law as it was when the Norman Conquest led to the consolidation of the English state under the purview of the Crown a full millennium ago, the organizational context within which juries now operate has changed almost beyond recognition. Firstly the powers of the

Crown have been transformed. Duke William and most of his immediate successors would doubtless have been astonished had they been informed of the success with which an initially merely advisory Parliament has by now managed to encroach on the personal powers of the monarchy, so much so that occupants of his throne have by now been reduced to little more than figureheads; nevertheless I have little doubt that the compilers of the Doomsday Book would have been astounded by the thoroughness with which officials based in the Palace of Whitehall have by now managed to extend their administrative tentacles into so many nooks and crannies of a far more populous and affluent United Kingdom. To be sure the state may now be democratically rather than autocratically constituted: but as Lord Bingham (2006) has recently reminded us, in the absence of the most careful scrutiny of the powers at its command, even the most nominally democratic governments can all too easily convince themselves of the righteousness of iniquitous policies and practices. That is why the constraints formally imposed by its subjects on the autocratic powers of the Crown in the *Magna Carta* remain as significant today as they were in the thirteenth century.

Moreover the dramatic changes in the character of the population over which the Crown now exercises its powers yet further reinforces the significance of those constraints. When Duke William successfully imposed his rule, it was taken for granted that juries would and should be drawn from members of the immediate community to which those in dispute with one another belonged, and that the more they knew about the litigants beforehand, the better. The jury's 'common sense' in this context did much more than underline its members' unanimity in reaching their verdict; it was also grounded in its members collective awareness of the customs and conventions of the locality, as well as of the background and personal characteristics of the litigants themselves. In such circumstances it followed that other than in terms of a common appreciation of the broad principles of English justice, there was nothing uniform or standardised about the grounds on which juries arrived at their verdicts. Rather each jury delivered a common-sense verdict on a contextually-grounded basis specific to the case in hand. The plural character of the wider social order within which those verdicts were articulated were simply taken for granted, and as such merely part of the scenery.

Since then much has changed. In the first place the delivery of justice has been brought under steadily greater central control: besides having been required to cede a substantial degree of autonomy to a professional judiciary, the twelve jurors' collective common sense is no longer held to be – nor expected or even allowed to be – rooted in a personal appreciation of the details of the specific context from which the litigants in the proceedings before them are drawn. Quite the contrary. In addition to being expected to disqualify themselves if they are personally acquainted with any of the litigants, jurors are recruited at random from amongst the population at large, such that they are 'likely to be a cross-section of the people as a whole and thus represent the view of the common man.'

In a world where sample surveys are regularly used as a dipstick to establish public opinion, the use of a random sample as a means of establishing the views of the common man may well appear to be a matter of common sense. Nevertheless there are good grounds for suggesting that where the object of the exercise is to select twelve persons to fulfil the role of finders of fact in a criminal trial, such a procedure must be regarded as intrinsically problematic, for reasons with which any statistician will be immediately familiar. The more the population from which the sample is drawn departs from a condition of homogeneity, the more difficult it becomes to claim that the one drawn is *representative* of the population as a whole. Moreover the smaller the size of the sample (and from a stochastic perspective 12 is an extremely small number), and the more salient and complex the diversities within the population in question are known to be, the larger those difficulties will loom.

Moreover even if statistically representative juries could be constructed, it certainly does not follow that this would be sufficient to deal with the specific issues at hand. The problem is best exposed by asking a simple question: of what are such juries expected to be representative? Of 'the common man' in the sense of the collective mean of the perceptions and understandings of the population at large? Or as a mode of jury selection which generates a reasonable (although in most circumstances only a remote) chance that at least one jury member will be familiar with the relevant cultural context? Moreover even if either of these outcomes was achieved, would that be a sufficient means of addressing the issues at hand? Does it make sense to expect the jury to use some kind of 'average' yardstick to assess the reasonableness or otherwise of behaviour articulated within the context of a plural society? I think not. And even if by some fortunate happenstance one member of the jury was familiar – or at least claimed to be familiar – with the cultural context within which the events in question were set, is it either reasonable, or even appropriate, to expect that the remainder of the jury will turn to, or that they will rely on that person's 'expert' understanding in reaching their verdict? Or is it more likely – given the sharpness of the contradictions surrounding ethnic plurality in contemporary Britain – that a sole dissenting voice of the minority juror would simply be overridden by the settled views of the dominant majority?

The dilemma is clear. Although experts now make ever more frequent appearances in the courts to testify on all manner of scientific, technical, professional, medical and psychiatric matters in cases where some of the issues at stake in the proceedings are deemed to be 'outside ordinary human experience', great uncertainty still surrounds the extent to which any of the issues associated with Britain's current condition of ethnic plurality can legitimately be so described. As a result the admissibility of expert evidence with respect to the specific character of the social, cultural, religious, familial and linguistic practices within minority communities, and on their likely impact on litigants' behaviour currently rests under a cloud of uncertainty. Hence the central paradox with which this chapter is concerned: whilst the social order which English Law seeks to regulate has grown steadily more plural, the ancient institutional means of providing a remedy against injustice in plural contexts has fallen into what appears to be irremediable abeyance.

4.13 Expert Anthropologists to the Rescue?

Now that expert juries have been comprehensively replaced by expert witnesses, it would seem reasonable – at least in principle – that those able to spell out the specific features of the relevant social, cultural, religious, familial and linguistic context would be routinely regarded as the most appropriate source of expert assistance to finders of fact (be they juries in criminal cases or judges in civil and family contexts) as and when that might seem appropriate. But as we have seen judges are often – although by no means always – reluctant to accept such evidence as admissible. The central reason for this, as I have gradually come to discern, is that the perspective on the available evidence which an anthropologist offers differs significantly from that offered by most other purveyors of expert opinion. As a result I have sailed straight into hitherto largely unexplored territory, no less in professional and intellectual than in ethical terms. Hence before closing this essay I would like to take the opportunity to reflect on some of the many dilemmas with which I have found myself confronting as a pioneer – at least in UK contexts – in this field.

As English Law stands at present, there is a strong presumption that expert evidence will normally be called with respect to scientific, technical and professional matters: hence accountants, architects, doctors and engineers of all kinds are routinely instructed to prepare expert reports, and there is rarely if ever any dispute about the prospective admissibility of such evidence. But although there are in principle no limits to the issues with respect to which litigants may seek to introduce expert evidence into the proceedings, if and when other parties challenge its admissibility judges often find themselves in something of a quandary. In the company of the doctors, engineers, and professional specialists in technical activities of one kind or another, the suggestion that an anthropologist is in a position to place the evidence in their appropriate *conceptual* context can all too easily appear to be wholly out of order: neither fish nor flesh nor good red herring. Lord Justice Buxton is by no means the only member of the bench who has been deeply sceptical as to whether expert evidence is in any way admissible. Hence even though I may be critical of the learned judge's conclusions, I would readily accept that the grounds on which, as well as the terms on which expert anthropological evidence might legitimately be set before the court does indeed require careful scrutiny.

4.14 Contradictions Inherent in the Role of the Expert Witness

It goes without saying that experts may not offer their opinions out of thin air: their role is to scrutinize, analyse and offer further comment on relevant components of the evidence set before the court, and to offer an objective opinion on its potential significance in the light of their expertise. Whilst experts appear in court as witnesses, they are nevertheless witnesses of a distinctive sort. They have rarely, if ever, witnessed any of the incidents in question at first hand: rather they are most usually invited to examine, and to offer their expert opinion on evidence which first hand witnesses have already provided. Experts are consequently exempted from the rule which excludes the introduction of hearsay evidence.

Nevertheless the commentary on the evidence which anthropologists find themselves offering is of a different character from that provided by the majority of other experts. Hence in sharp contrast to those who are called in to offer their opinion on physical and technical issues such as the silting up of harbours, the overloading of ships, finger-print matches, shaken babies or the precipitating cause of a fire, anthropologists find themselves addressing much more intangible issues. Hence my normal approach is set about locating the available evidence about things said and done in their appropriate social, cultural, familial and linguistic context, as a prelude to setting out a commentary on the likely significance of these events in the light of such considerations. From this perspective my central role is not just to contextualize the evidence, but in doing so warn the finders of fact of the pitfalls of ethnocentrism.

But in doing so I have become acutely aware that I am walking on a knife-edge. In putting the evidence through an ethnographic sieve, it follows that the operation I undertake in so doing runs closely parallel to aspects of the task which the finders of fact are expected to undertake. To be sure there are some significant differences. Whilst the filter through which members of the jury are expected to sift the evidence is their collective 'common sense', the sieve which I deploy as an anthropologist is my specialist knowledge of the relevant context-specific social, cultural, familial and linguistic conventions. Nevertheless the dangers here are precisely those identified by Lord Justice Buxton. If an expert anthropologist is permitted to perform a parallel exercise to the formal finders of fact, is there not a significant sense in which he or she will be usurping the role of the jury?

One way of answering that conundrum is to take shelter under Learned Hand's careful arguments. Having considered the role of the expert at great length, and having also noted that the credibility of any witness must also remain a question for the jury alone, he goes on to conclude that:

> Now the important thing to notice, and the only important thing to notice is that the expert has taken the jury's place if they believe him. It is of course not necessary for the jury to accept the expert's opinion, but were it not really of possible weight with them, it would not be relevant, and if of possible weight, it is only because it furnishes to them general propositions which it is ordinarily their function and theirs only to furnish to the conclusion which constitutes the verdict (Hand 1901: 52).

But although it consequently follows that any qualms an anthropologist may have on this score are not so much a function of his disciplinary perspective, but run in parallel with the contradictions which any other expert, regardless of discipline, is likely to encounter, this in no way attenuates the burden of responsibility that consequently falls on one's shoulders. Nor is this conundrum significantly lightened by Hand's important caveat: even if the judge rules that the evidence I proffer is admissible, my own credibility as a witness still rests with the jury. Like it or not I regularly find myself sorely tempted to act as an advocate of my own position; the further one progresses down this road the more the knife-edge of objectivity on which the expert must of necessity seek to balance sharpens, so much so that the satisfactory fulfilment of the role becomes much more of an art than a science. I find that the only way I can console myself when required to perform in this way is that justice and equity – which are likewise much more of an art than a science – would probably be the worse off if one did not attempt to implement this balancing act to the best of one's ability.

4.15 Contradictions Encountered before one even Reaches the Doors of Court

Nor is it just the role of the jury which anthropologists can find themselves usurping – or at least challenging. In considering the witness statements laid before me – whether they have been prepared by the police and defence in criminal cases, or by the solicitors for each party in civil cases – I regularly find that all sorts of pieces of information which I regard as crucial to a proper understanding of the issues in dispute are absent from the bundle of documents with which I have been presented. The most characteristic deficiency in South Asian cases is the absence of the material required to construct a detailed family tree, without which it is virtually impossible to begin to grasp the internal dynamics of the extended families of the litigants – and which in my experience are almost invariably a crucial factor in the underlying dispute, no matter whether the case is being heard in the criminal, civil, family or immigration court.

That such questions should remain unasked is hardly surprising. Corporate extended families and their associated kinship networks have never been a feature of the English cultural tradition. In the absence of suitably attuned investigative antennae, it is hardly surprising that solicitors and detectives have little notion of how best to lay out a family tree in a graphical format, let alone as to how to use such a diagram to explore potential and actual patterns of conflict and alliance between kinsfolk, and on that basis to explore the likely dynamics of interpersonal relationships within such an arena. Such an exercise is simply not a part of their standard investigative toolkit. In these circumstances I frequently find myself going back to those instructing me, and asking them to fill in potentially crucial details which did not appear in the witness statements presented to me. Hence in fulfilling my role as an expert I regularly find myself insisting that those instructing me should go back to their clients to pose a whole series of hitherto unasked questions and unexplored issues.

In doing so, I have gradually begun to realise that the responses I receive in so doing display some very significant variations, most particularly when the line of analysis I begin to pursue diverges significantly from their own assumptions about the core issues in the case. In my experience solicitors rarely if ever have qualms about seeking further instructions from their clients in response to my queries. If – as is most usually the case – my report throws new light on the issues, and enables them to argue their client's case more effectively than had hitherto been possible, my contribution is invariably welcome. But if my analysis blows large holes in the case they had hoped to advance, as most certainly sometimes happens, they simply shelve my report, since they have no duty to disclose it to their adversaries.

However I have gradually begun to appreciate that the Police and the Crown Prosecution Service – by whom I have so far been instructed a great deal less frequently than by defence – frequently find themselves in a much trickier position in such circumstances, not least because they have a duty – in sharp contrast to the defendants – to disclose all unused evidence to their opponents. Secondly, I invariably find that I only receive my instruction very late in the day, by which time all the evidence which the prosecution considers relevant to the proceedings has been gathered, committal proceedings have been completed and a skeleton argument – or at least a prosecution case summary – has been handed to the defence. Hence even though the instructions which I receive may be similarly worded to those I would receive from defence solicitors, the context in which they have been delivered is quite different. The Crown has already decided on – and indeed committed itself to – a specific line of argument. Indeed it may well be that the trial is only weeks away. In these circumstances what those instructing me are effectively looking for is expert confirmation of a line of analysis to which the prosecution is already committed.

Whilst I am sometimes able to fulfil those expectations, that is by no means always the case. Indeed just as happens in other contexts, I often find myself opening up new lines of enquiry which those instructing me have not hitherto considered. Hence I not infrequently find myself suggesting that the evidence available might be better interpreted in a manner wholly at odds with the line of analysis to which the prosecution has already committed itself. This can cause particularly severe consternation when – as in one case in which I was recently involved where very serious charges had been brought against three co-defendants – my analysis suggested two of those defendants were most unlikely to have been involved in the events which had led to the charges being brought. Whilst it went without saying that my report would be disclosed to the solicitors for the three defendants, the prosecution took the view that it was by then too late to change course with respect to the arguments they planned to present to the up-coming trial. Such experiences may well serve to explain why it is that my name has not been included on the register of experts maintained by the National Criminal Intelligence Service.

4.16 Experience in Court

My experience in court has also been riddled with similar contradictions. Despite Lord Justice Buxton's caveats, I found myself receiving a steadily increasing stream of instructions to prepare reports for use in an ever wider range of proceedings in the criminal, civil, family and immigration courts – with a wide variety of outcomes. On relatively rare occasions the admissibility has been challenged, sometimes successfully and sometimes not. Rather more frequently my reports have been discarded by those instructing me on tactical grounds, with the result that they effectively fell into abeyance, except in those cases where I had been instructed by the prosecution. That said, the vast majority of my reports overcame these initial hurdles, and were set before the court. Even so, we still have to consider the precise basis on which their contents were made available to the finders of fact.

It is, of course, by no means always a twelve-person jury which fulfils that role. In Magistrates courts, Tribunals of various kinds and in most forms of civil proceedings it is the bench which fulfils the role. However in a striking paradox, the only circumstances in which finders of fact normally have direct access to the text of an expert report is in the latter circumstance, where that role is most usually fulfilled by a judge. Juries – whose members are surely at least as much in need of direct access to their contents as are the learned occupants of the judicial bench – are invariably precluded from reading my reports. Instead they have to rely on what the expert has to say in the witness box. In the process of getting there one encounters all manner of additional shoals.

Despite the fact that the expert's central duty is to inform the court, rather than to advance the interests of those instructing him, the closer one approaches the doors of the courtroom the more the adversarial character of the proceedings begins to kick in. Hence as soon as the nominally independent and objective expert steps into court, he swiftly finds that he has been reduced to the position of a bagatelle in the game of thrust and counter-thrust between the contending parties. In my experience few holds are barred in this process.

In fact the implications of the adversarial nature of the proceedings begin to appear well before one approaches the courtroom door. Whilst Counsel rarely, if ever, query any aspects of their expert's conclusions (note the possessive), they not infrequently suggest that for tactical reasons significant components of the report are excised. Of course an expert is wholly within his rights if he refuses to do so; but it is equally within the rights of Counsel not to disclose the report if the expert refuses to make the suggested excisions. But even if the report is indeed disclosed and accepted as admissible, that is by no means the end of the road. If the contents of the report are accepted by the other side, the expert will not normally be called to give evidence in person: instead counsel will read out to the jury those parts of its contents which he considers most significant. If, however, the instructing party's opponents do not accept the report, the adversarial process kicks in once again. The expert will be called to give evidence in chief, and then be cross-examined and re-examined in the usual adversarial manner. My experience of being put through this process has left me with two very salient conclusions.

Firstly the notion that the expert is a servant of the court – rather than a hired gun wheeled in to advance the interest of those instructing him – is blown to the winds by the adversarial character of the proceedings. From the jury's perspective I have little doubt that the expert will be seen as a witness 'for' whichever party has instructed him. Secondly, and perhaps even more significantly, in no circumstances do the members of the jury actually get to see, read, and contemplate the actual contents of my report – which may well be thirty or forty pages long. Hence what actually informs their deliberations is not the report itself, but at best an account of its contents filtered through counsel's efforts to represent its main themes to them by reading out selected parts of its contents. If, however, the report is contested by the other side the jury's access to the expert's arguments, analyses and conclusions is even more limited. Restricted by the tactical manoeuvres of agile counsel competing with one another in the adversarial process of examination, cross-examination and re-examination, the long-suffering expert can only come to the conclusion that his efforts to provide the court with the benefits of his professional insights are entirely subordinated to demands of a strange ritual process which is alleged to be a highly effective means of getting to the truth of the matter.

4.17 Conclusion

By its very nature, plurality puts the skids under the commonplace assumption that our own taken for granted yardsticks can safely be regarded as being universally applicable. Those whose experience has hitherto been limited to life 'within the whale' may well take the view that they know their way around, and that the categories and concepts that they have encountered during the course of that experience are of universal applicability – little knowing that there are many other sea-creatures beyond the universe of their experience, each of which is structured in ways which often differ radically from the one which they themselves inhabit. This is not to suggest that each such universe is structured on an entirely different basis. Virtually all sea creatures have fins of one kind or another; most, but not all, have back-bones; others have external carapaces whilst yet others appear to be made entirely of jelly. Once one adopts an oceanic as opposed to a whale-based perspective, it becomes only too obvious that one size does not fit all.

Problems associated with the plural character of social and cultural universes which humans have constructed around themselves – or rather the problems with which one finds oneself confronted if and when one emerges from the belly of the whale – are by no means restricted to lawyers and the law. Those seeking to provide professional practice that brings them into contact with any kind of activity which is conditioned by our capacity to *create the conceptual foundations of our own existence*, as we humans routinely do as we go about our personal, domestic, familial, social, religious and linguistic business, can expect to encounter clients who put their lives together in terms of premises and practices which differ from their own. Sometimes those variations are relatively small, as for example those associated with differences of gender and social class within a single over-arching linguistic and socio-cultural order. However they are often far more substantial, either because the indigenous social order has long been deeply plural (as for example in the case of the Austro-Hungarian Empire) or because mass migration from the distant parts of the globe has sharply increased a pre-existing condition of mild plurality – as for example in the United Kingdom. From this perspective cultural plurality is in no sense 'outside ordinary human experience': indeed anthropological analysis suggests that in historical terms it is a core feature of human experience, albeit a phenomenon of which our awareness has steadily atrophied in the face of the unitarian perspective into which we have been socialised as a result of our contemporary commitment to modernity (Ballard 2007). In other words when it comes to their knowledge of the variety of conventions which humans use to order their lives, the scope of the 'ordinary human experience' with which both judges and juries are familiar is invariably far less universalistic in its reach than they routinely assume.

Whilst globalisation is shrinking the significance of distance, it is by no means undermining the plural character of the world in which we live. In historical terms successive inflows of immigrants from elsewhere in Western Europe have regularly introduced additional layers of plurality into Britain's established social order. In the past half-century, however, these processes have gone global. Not only have migrants been drawn in from much further afield, but linguistic, social, cultural and religious baggage which the settlers brought with them was far more distinctive than that imported by any of their predecessors. Moreover globalisation has also enabled settlers to keep far more closely in touch with their overseas roots than any of their predecessors. The ethnic colonies which settlers have formed have consequently remained strongly transnational in character – so yet further reinforcing the resilience of the additional vectors of plurality they have introduced into the pre-existent socio-cultural order. Whilst these new vectors are undoubtedly altering in character as adaptive processes kick in, they show little sign of diminishing significantly in strength. Plurality is here to stay.

Nevertheless the emergence of these additional dimensions of plurality has been, and remains, exceedingly contentious. As hostility to these developments has become steadily more salient amongst members of the indigenous majority – not just in Britain but across the length and breadth of Western Europe – the view that all public manifestations of ethnic diversity are *ipso facto* illegitimate has become increasingly widespread. In consequence this particular vector of plurality is currently strongly inegalitarian in character. In the face of all this I can see very little prospect of my new-found profession being significantly undermined in the immediately foreseeable future. Thus far, at least, accurate and sympathetic knowledge of the linguistic, social, cultural and religious baggage which non-European settlers brought with them to Britain – and into which they have done their best to socialise their offspring – have not spread far beyond the boundaries of the ethnic colonies which they have formed around themselves. Nor have there been any significant institutionally supported efforts to make analytical sense of the processes of culturally-creative readjustment which were going on within these thriving colonies, largely on the grounds that the significance of these necessarily ephemeral phenomena was strictly time limited. Hence little effort was made to bring the findings of those few scholars who have explored these developments to the attention of a wider audience. The consequences of this myopic stance are plain to see: the core agenda of the British educational system – the principal contemporary purveyor of both knowledge and the analytical frameworks required to make sense of it – remains largely untouched by these developments. To be sure most primary schools now make an effort to celebrate diversity: rival festivals to Christmas and Easter are now noted, and often more or less elaborately celebrated. Moreover such celebrations are frequently accompanied by primary-level – and hence inevitably stereotypical – accounts of what the underlying traditions stand for. But the further up the educational system one penetrates, the more such celebrations of multi-culturalism (for that is all they are) begin to evaporate, such that they are almost entirely absent from the agenda in higher educational contexts.

This has had several consequences, not least in the light of the steadily increasing maturity of the new minority settlements. Now that the British-born offspring of the original generation of migrants have not only reached adulthood, but also passed through the higher educational system in substantial numbers, fully qualified minority professionals are becoming increasingly commonplace, not least in legal contexts. In the course of gaining the necessary qualifications such students will have extensive contacts with their more indigenous counterparts – and of course vice-versa. Hence at one level experience of the new plurality is much more part of the scenery for rising generations than it was for their parents. Yet just how deep has mutual appreciation actually been?

Although most members of the rising generation of minority professionals have had far more contact with members of the indigenous majority that their parents ever did, their knowledge of, and insight into, the foundations of their own ancestral linguistic, social, cultural and religious heritage is often extremely limited. The reasons are plain to see. Although they have most usually been socialised into the popular dimensions of that heritage in domestic contexts, their awareness of that heritage, together with an insight into its conceptual foundations, is rarely if ever significantly reinforced during their passage through the educational system. Precisely because such matters are in no way represented in the academic syllabus, most minority students are at present exceedingly loath to raise their heads above the parapet with respect to all the issues associated with plurality. Their reasons for so doing vary enormously. Some do their best to put their ancestral heritage entirely behind them, and hence to assimilate in the way in which the majoritarian consensus requires. Others, perhaps the majority, sustain a positive appreciation of their heritage in personal and domestic circumstances, but nevertheless take the strategic decision to play down their alterity as much as possible whenever they find themselves in majoritarian company. Meanwhile those at the far end of the spectrum lead what can best be described as a split intellectual life: whilst making the best endeavours to gain the capacity to put on a skilled professional performance in whichever discipline they have chosen to specialise, they simultaneously maintain a private commitment to an alternative ideology – most usually grounded in a neo-fundamentalist reinterpretation of their ancestral religious heritage – from within which they condemn the ideological foundations of European intellectual traditions as being as hypocritical as they are misguided.

Unfortunately these developments remain largely subterranean. They do not appear on the conceptual radar of those who set the systematic agenda of the educational system with any greater salience than does the existence of plurality itself. One obvious consequence of this is that professional training courses of all kinds – including those offered in the vast majority of Departments of Law – are ill-equipped to provide their students with the basic ethnographic data, let alone the conceptual frameworks, with which to cope with the challenges of plurality highlighted in this volume. With such considerations in mind it is immediately apparent that the problems generated by our present methods of jury selection are not necessarily the most pressing of all the many issues we currently face. My own view is that until we regain the capacity to feel intellectually comfortable with the plural character of the world in which we live, and hence to *think plural*, we will make relatively little progress towards addressing the knotty issues in this sphere.

But just how might we best begin to move towards such an outcome? This chapter is a report from the coalface. As yet relatively few other UK-based anthropologists have followed me into the field of expert witnessing, and none have as yet become so deeply embroiled in it as I. But however much of a path-breaker I may be, I would hesitate before identifying myself as an expert expert. I am still in the midst of feeling my way through a novel sphere of activity, and the further I penetrate into the field, the more I have begun to realise that anyone who wishes to fulfil this role adequately needs to become as expert in law and legal procedures as in anthropology in order to do so. At this stage I readily acknowledge that I still have much to learn.

But by the same token that is not the only sphere where additional learning is urgently required. My experience also suggests that lawyers at all levels in the profession, whether drawn from majority or from minority backgrounds, still have much to learn about how all the knotty issues arising from our more salient condition of ethnic plurality can best be handled within the established procedural and conceptual frameworks of English law. However tempting it may be to evade the issues by brushing them under the carpet, the longer efforts to address these issues in a systematic way are postponed, the more seriously the English legal system's proud – but already damaged – reputation for delivering justice on an equitable basis to all comers will be further compromised. Nor will proposed legislative interventions with respect to ethnically specific phenomena such as 'Forced Marriage', 'Honour Killing', the Veil, People Smuggling, Hawala Value Transfers, Islamic fundamentalism and Terrorism necessarily make matters any easier for the courts, especially if the discussions and consultations associated with these developments, let alone the prosecution of such new-found offences, continues to sideline the potential contribution of anthropologically-informed insights and critiques.

In the midst of all this, I cannot avoid addressing one further set of criticisms with which any anthropological expert in this field will inevitably find himself confronted: namely that one is engaged in some form of special pleading. Such arguments take many forms, but two are particularly alarming. Firstly that one is seeking to place aspects of minority behaviour outside the scope of established legal rules and proceedings; and secondly that one is seeking to underpin and reinforce illiberal, authoritarian and generally patriarchal customs and practices still regretfully adhered to by many members of recently arrived and still largely unassimilated minority communities.

If either of those charges were sustainable, anthropological interventions in this field would be quite untenable. Precisely because this is so, anyone who does stray into this territory must pay careful attention if they are to avoid being waylaid – no less by accident than by design – into one or other of these pitfalls. In my view the firmest ground on which one can seek to stand is that of a servant of the court. From that perspective it follows that the core of one's role is to provide finders of fact with an insight into the conventions which are likely to have been deployed within the social and cultural context(s) within which the events in question took place, and their likely impact on the behaviour of those involved. This is most emphatically not a form of special pleading: rather it is to provide the court with an opportunity to consider which yardsticks it is most appropriate to deploy in making sense of the behaviour in question.

However fulfilling this role is not an easy task, especially in the adversarial context of an English courtroom. As Learned Hand rightly emphasises, however much the role of the expert may be formally defined as that of a servant of the court, that role is rendered entirely fictitious the moment one steps through the court-room door. Not only will instructing lawyers invariably have done their best to manoeuvre 'his' expert's evidence in such a way to maximise his strategic advantage before the trial has even begun, but counsel for the other side is equally likely to dismiss as special pleading all aspects of one's evidence that he regards as unhelpful to his cause.

In responding to such charges I must admit that I do very often have an agenda of my own – although I am rarely foolish enough to acknowledge it in the midst of adversarial cross-fire. Most usually I have two particularly salient objectives in mind. The first is to seek to do my best to ensure that no-one who has been drawn into the proceedings is found guilty of what I would describe as a 'cultural crime': namely of acting in ways which were entirely reasonable, appropriate and inoffensive in the particular context within which it occurs, but which can be represented as wholly unreasonable and inappropriate when viewed through the prism of external cultural yardsticks. At the same time one also needs to guard against falling into the pitfalls which lie at the opposite end of the spectrum. Hence whilst it is undoubtedly worth noting that homicidal revenge may in some traditions be regarded as an appropriate means of restoring one's seriously damaged honour, this certainly cannot be used to suggest that someone who has successfully done so should escape conviction for homicide. Set against this it is equally important to insist that by no means all homicides within South Asian families are necessarily honour killings in this sense, even if prosecutors all too often assume that this must inevitably have been the case. Such decisions can have quite disastrous consequences, some of which I hope to be at liberty to discuss at some point in the near future.

So just what is the role of the anthropological expert? At the end of the day I find myself coming down on Learned Hand's side of the fence: if one fulfils one's role as an expert judiciously, one does indeed at least supplant the role of the jury. That is precisely the burden of my comments in the paragraph above. But of course one does not – and indeed should not – wholly supplant the role of the jury; Learned Hand rightly adds the caveat *if they believe him* to his decisive comment. Nevertheless just what is an expert who fulfils his role judiciously up to? At the end of the day the lodestone which I have found myself following is that I should do my best to facilitate just and equitable outcomes, not least because I have also become ever more aware that in the absence of a capacity to 'think plural', the uncritical application of established European legal conventions can all too easily precipitate rank injustice. With this in mind it is worth remembering that *insaaf, justice*, is a value of no less significance in South Asian legal, religious and cultural traditions than it is in Common Law. If community cohesion is ever to mean anything less vacuous than it does at present, English law needs to return to its roots, and regain – and indeed to elaborate – the capacity to 'think plural' which it once enjoyed.

Chapter 5 Artistic Licence, Free Speech and Religious Sensibilities in a Multicultural Society

Ralph Grillo

5.1 Scenes from Multiculturalism

The governance of multicultural societies requires acknowledgement of the diverse values attached to, or associated with, different cultures and 'communities', and decisions about what kind of difference, and how much, to recognize, formally and informally, in private and public spheres. Sometimes differences may appear incompatible, as when secular liberal values, by and large predominant in Western Europe, are confronted by claims for recognition of special privileges for the values and sensibilities of religion. Such claims may *seem* – 'seem' is the right word – especially challenging when emanating from religions with theologies or adherents of extra-European origin. A key question is how multicultural societies should respond (e.g. through legislation and/or negotiation and dialogue) to such challenges.

In recent years there has been a number of episodes in Britain and other European countries apparently involving confrontations between artistic freedom and religious sensitivities, and through these we may catch glimpses of the more general question outlined above. They have been occurring with seemingly increasing frequency since the Rushdie affair of 1989. In Rotterdam in 2002, for example, Muslim activists objected to a theatre company mounting a production of the opera *Aisha and the Women of Medina* whose central character was a wife of the Prophet Mohammed (Meuleman 2001). The opera was withdrawn. In November 2004, the Dutch filmmaker, Theo van Gogh, was murdered by a Moroccan-Dutch Muslim who opposed van Gogh's film *Submission* about women and Islam. Based on a script by the Dutch-Somalian MP, Ayaan Hirsi Ali, *Submission* included images of a Muslim woman said to have been raped by a relative, and sequences in which women's bodies were covered in verses from the

Prakash Shah (ed.), Law and Ethnic Plurality: Socio-Legal Perspectives. *pp. 107-125.*
 ISBN 978 90 04 16245 7.

Koran, all thought to be highly offensive. Van Gogh himself was notorious for his opposition to organized religion, especially Islam (he referred to Muslims as "goat-fuckers"), and had supported the populist politician, Pim Fortuyn, himself assassinated in 2002. In 2005-6 cartoons, published in the conservative Danish newspaper, *Jyllands-Posten*, which *inter alia* portrayed the Prophet as a terrorist, evoked a world-wide Muslim response,[1] and in September 2006, a production in Berlin of Mozart's opera *Idomeneo* in which the director had inserted a scene including the severed head of the Prophet, was due to be cancelled following protests, but was eventually performed.

Although popularly associated with Islam such confrontations are by no means only about the Muslim religion: opposition to the filming, in 2006, of Monica Ali's novel *Brick Lane* (2003) by Bangladeshi residents of the London borough of Tower Hamlets was more to do with the novel's representation of their culture than with any critique of their faith. In any case, they are not confined to Muslims. In 2006 the Hindu Forum of Britain organized a successful protest against the exhibition at Asia House in London of the work of the "controversial Indian artist Maqbool Fida Husain, whose offensive paintings of Hindu Gods and Goddesses in sexual poses have caused outrage over the years amongst Hindus around the world",[2] and what became known as the *Behzti* affair (*infra*) involved British Sikhs. Nor do they involve only what are conventionally thought of as non-Western religions. In the UK in 2005 there was controversy over the televising of *Jerry Springer: The Opera* which offended certain Christians. Moreover, they are not restricted to religious minorities in Europe. In Egypt in 2004, for instance, Coptic (Christian) youths objected to the showing of an Egyptian film *I Love the Cinema*, criticized for its "scornful and insulting depiction of Coptic faith and culture",[3] and in India in 2005 there were protests against the alleged denigration of Sikhism in a Bollywood film, *Jo Bole So Nihal*.

The first part of this chapter analyses the circumstances surrounding one of these episodes, the *Behzti* affair of December 2004, placing it in its wider (local, national, international) contexts, and seeking clues as to how to interpret what was ostensibly a confrontation between the incompatible values of artistic licence and religious sensitivity. The chapter presents

1 There is a substantial literature on the Rushdie affair (Grewal 2006), and much has been written about the van Gogh murder (e.g. in English, Buruma 2005, 2006, Eyerman 2005). The response to the Danish cartoons, academic and non-academic, threatens, eventually, to be overwhelming.

2 http://www.hinduforum.org/Default.aspx?sID=45&cID=156&ctID=11&lID=0, accessed 18 July 2006.

3 http://www.copts.net/detail.asp?id=551, accessed 18 July 2006.

two sets of views about the affair: those of Sikh elders, who stressed the play's offence, and what Madeleine Bunting (*Guardian*, 14 September 2005) called the "muscular liberals", who stressed the rights of free speech. The idea that there were just two sides is, however, simplistic. There was a multiplicity of voices and opinions, and moreover the views of protagonists were not always what they seemed. The chapter then locates *Behzti* in the context of British multiculturalism, investigating the role of what are called 'faith communities' in contemporary society and government policy, and assesses the place of law in these conflicts of secular and religious value through an examination of the arguments surrounding what became the UK's Racial and Religious Hatred Act 2006. Finally, the chapter identifies certain similarities and differences between *Behzti* and other episodes, before concluding with a discussion of a possible convergence of views on the regulation of expressions of opinion about the culture of others when those opinions are likely to cause offence.

5.2 *Behzti*: For and Against

In December 2004, the Birmingham Rep, a highly respected regional theatre which prides itself on its role in a large, multi-ethnic city, decided to put on a play, *Behzti* ('Dishonour') by a British Sikh woman writer, Gurpreet Kaur Bhatti (2004).[4] Largely set in a Sikh temple (*gurdwara*), *Behzti* is a black comedy dealing with traumatic episodes in the past and present lives of the characters culminating in the rape of the heroine by one of the elders in the *gurdwara* and his eventual murder by her mother. Strong stuff, and the company was advised by the Director of Communications for the Diocese of Birmingham that it was likely to have a hostile reception. As a result, the management sought discussions with representatives of the local Sikh 'community' (inverted commas hereafter understood), but these did nothing to assuage Sikh objections that aspects of the play were deeply offensive to their faith. Protests were organized, and when these turned violent, with the theatre invaded by demonstrators, it was decided to end the play's run. This decision (and threats against the author) led to an immediate outcry in the local, national and international media, including the Internet, and a debate about what limits, if any, should be placed on freedom of speech, artistic licence and the right to give religious offence, which continued into 2005-6.

In the UK's 2001 census 4% of the population declared themselves 'Asian' or 'Asian-British'. Although the first generation (often elderly) continues to be important, many have now been born and brought up in Britain. Sikhism is a religion whose adherents came originally from Punjab, where the religion emerged in the 15th century, though its present form owes

4 See Grillo (2007) for a fuller account of the *Behzti* affair.

much to later developments (Ballard 1996). In fact, substantial numbers of British Sikhs were 'twice migrants' (Bhachu 1985) who came to the UK via East Africa where they had moved during the colonial period. The Census recorded some 336,000 Sikhs: about a third in the West Midlands metropolitan area, including Birmingham, and rather more in London and its environs. Many fared poorly in the recessions of the 1980s and early 1990s losing out in terms of manufacturing jobs and becoming more dependent on self-employment. Nonetheless, as with other British Asians, there are many young people entering the professions via higher education.

Although there are disputes about the fundamentals of Sikhism and about what constitutes Sikh identity, for most Sikhs central to the religion is the role of the original holy men (gurus) and reading and reflection on Sikh scripture, the Guru Granth Sahib. Religious participation is organized through *gurdwaras* (temples) and these are important as local centres for many community-based activities. In the UK, the elders of the *gurdwaras*, together with the networks of committees which link the temples in a particular locality, and a variety of national bodies (e.g. the British Sikh Consultative Forum) claim to represent Sikh views. Though its significance may be declining, caste and sectarian divisions permeate the organization of *gurdwaras*, family life, and marriage. Roger Ballard (1994: 88), writing about unity and disunity in the British Sikh population says of them:

> More graphically than any other comparable group, the Sikhs, with their distinctive combination of beard and turban, are a classic example of a group whose members have used physical and cultural symbols to construct an ethnic identity around themselves.

Devout Sikh men, it may be insisted, should grow their hair, wear a turban, and abstain from alcohol and meat, though many fail to follow all or some of those injunctions. There is evidence that some Sikhs are becoming more devout (especially as they grow older), and post-9/11 it is widely reported that Sikhs, like other Asians, feel insecure, fearful of being mistaken for bearded and turbaned terrorists.

Leading voices against *Behzti* were elders of the *gurdwaras* in the Birmingham area and other Sikhs prominent in public affairs including members of Birmingham City council. They had three main objections:

1. Use of Sikh hymns, in particular the *Aardas*, as background music to the rape scene, as specified in the play's stage directions (Bhatti 2004: 110). The *Aardas* has a particular significance in recalling the martyrdom of Sikhs at the hands of their religious opponents in India, and is central to the construction of Sikh identity. Its use in this context was thought deeply offensive.

2. Abuse of sacred symbols, for example, stage directions which called for the placing of a turban (sacred object) on a shoe rack; shoes and the dirt associated with them are believed polluting.
3. The setting of the play. Elders said that although they were not against the themes of rape and abuse of authority, the play misled audiences as to what happens in a *gurdwara*. They urged that the setting be changed to a community centre.

These objections were backed by leaders of other religious and interfaith groups.

The 'muscular liberals' centred their arguments around defence of the freedom of speech and artistic licence, and opposition to the use of violence. A widely circulated petition concluded:

> It is a legitimate function of art to provoke debate and sometimes to express controversial ideas. A genuinely free, pluralist society would celebrate this aspect of our culture. Those who use violent means to silence it must be vigorously opposed and challenged by all of us, whatever our faith, belief or opinions.

The theatre management, it was said, had consulted with the Sikhs and listened to their views, but rightly refused to bend to their demands. The Rushdie affair was much in people's minds and indeed Rushdie himself intervened in his capacity as President of PEN, the international writers' organization, arguing that in Britain there was an "*Anschluss* of liberal values in the face of resurgent religious demands ... we need to fight the battle for the Enlightenment all over again".[5]

On the surface, *Behzti*, like other affairs, is seemingly a consequence of the contemporary global resurgence of religious ideas, beliefs, practices, and institutions. Certainly, at some point the issues do involve conflict between religious and secular values, and this is a recurring feature of the contemporary world. But *Behzti* was in no way a simple confrontation between freedom of speech and religious sensibilities, rationality and faith, good and evil as it was sometimes represented. Indeed, the idea that there were two sides is misleading; there were many different shades of opinion, though some of these struggled to be heard. Moreover, if some among the play's defenders or critics were convinced of the righteousness of their cause, others had great difficulty in finding their way through the moral maze the affair presented. Among Sikhs, for example, there were many,

5 http://www.englishpen.org/events/recentevents/salmanrushdieonreligioushatred, accessed 18 July 2006.

especially among young professionals, who would sympathise with the following contribution to a web-based discussion:

> I still defend the right of the play to be staged – but I think people should be honest about what it is and not try to paint it as some kind of gospel come to light up our lives – this premise might cause white liberal chests to swell with pride at their ability to "civilise the natives" [but the] bottom line is, don't think because liberal Sikhs disagree with the Sikh establishment that they saw this play as some kind of truth telling exercise – the truth is we all got smacked in the mouth in the aftermath – and for that reason we say – a plague on you both.[6]

Others, too, reflecting such misgivings, were uncertain as to the rights and wrongs, seeing strengths and weaknesses in the arguments on both sides (Grillo 2007). Moreover, the positions which people took, the values they emphasized when defending or criticising the play, were not always what they seemed. For example, the play's principal critics, the elders, stressed the offence caused by locating the action in a holy context, but since the play was, *inter alia*, a fierce indictment of patriarchy, *Behzti*'s offence may have had as much to do with what it said about gender as about religion. On the other hand, while the defenders of *Behzti* rested their case on freedom of speech and artistic licence, their views sometimes entered other territory seeing the affair as an attack on Western values and an illustration of where multiculturalism leads (e.g. Minette Marin, *Sunday Times*, 26 December 2004). Such critiques slid all too readily into Orientalism, if not racism.

5.3 *Behzti* in Context

In understanding *Behzti* and other affairs it is important to contextualize them locally, nationally, and internationally. The value of focusing on the local context of the Rushdie affair was illustrated by Yunas Samad (1991), discussing the social background of Muslim youths in Bradford, and their experience of school, work and racism in the 1980s. The local context of the *Behzti* affair includes gurdwara factional politics, factional politics within the Birmingham City Labour Party, and on a wider canvas, the politics of caste, generation and gender as they affect relations between Sikhs. Locally and internationally, the struggle for the Sikh homeland (Khalistan) is also highly relevant. This chapter, however, situates *Behzti* within the British *national* context, and considers how the affair may be understood in relation to developments in British multiculturalism, and indeed what it says about the latter.

6 Jay Singh, 26 January 2006 in http://www.pickledpolitics.com/archives/258, accessed 18 July 2006.

The phrase 'clash of civilizations', associated with the American political scientist Samuel Huntington (1993) stresses the incompatibility of values held by different global blocs (notably of course the Islamic world and the West). This idea has been taken up to refer to the clash of cultures *within* contemporary multiethnic societies. The eminent Italian political scientist, Giovanni Sartori, for example, argues that immigration leads to what he calls a "superabundance of diversity, an excess of alterity" (2002: 93). Too great a cultural distance, Sartori contends, is an obstacle to integration, and the difficulty increases when immigrants belong to a theocratic, faith-based culture which equates citizenship with religious faith. Sartori, with his worries that Italy has become a "dismembered society", reflects a viewpoint increasingly widespread in Europe and elsewhere (e.g. North America, Australia) which has been characterized as a 'backlash' against difference or diversity or multiculturalism (Grillo 2005). In the UK, for example, a much-cited article by David Goodhart in *Prospect Magazine* (2004), addressing what he called the "progressive dilemma", asked: "Is Britain becoming too diverse to sustain the mutual obligations behind a good society and the welfare state?" In answering that question Goodhart, like Sartori, distanced himself from multiculturalism, and this has now become commonplace, with critics including, among many others, Trevor Phillips, the Chairman of the UK's Commission for Racial Equality (interview, *The Times*, April 3, 2004).

"Although I use the term myself occasionally", confessed the British Prime Minister, Tony Blair, in his August 2005 press conference,[7] "I never know quite what people mean when they talk about multiculturalism". Indeed, multiculturalism is a contested notion in two senses. Most people are unsure what it signifies, but are either for it or against it. Multiculturalism is in fact best thought of as a political project (strategies, institutions, discourses, practices), which consciously seeks to address multicultural reality, but multicultural initiatives fall along a spectrum from 'weak' to 'strong', with 'strong' multiculturalism entailing a widespread and thorough recognition of difference, encompassing both private and public spheres, with groups having their own institutions and being in large part responsible for their own affairs. While many of multiculturalism's critics treat it as if it were always at its 'strongest', British policy has since the 1960s been guided by what the then Home Secretary defined as 'integration': "equal opportunity coupled with cultural diversity, in an atmosphere of mutual tolerance" (Jenkins 1967: 267). There is now, however, a growing belief that Jenkins-style integration has failed, indeed undermined social cohesion, with minority ethnic groups ceasing to be part of an integrated, cohesive society. The contemporary term for this, popularized by the Cantle

7 http://www.number10.gov.uk/output/Page8041.asp, accessed 18 July 2006.

Report (2001) into disturbances in the northern cities of Britain, is 'parallel lives', and hostility to multiculturalism reflects how it has been identified as intensifying minority and majority ethnic group separatism. Yet seemingly in contradiction, the government has also stressed the virtues of so-called 'faith communities'.

Faith communities based on shared religious beliefs and practices were incorporated into the governance of the Ottoman Empire, and were the basis of the legal pluralism operated in some British, French and Dutch colonies. In the Ottoman *millet* system faith leaders represented their communities to the authorities, and often had a considerable degree of autonomy in how they ran their affairs. There is nothing comparable in contemporary Europe, though some voices in Britain extol the virtues of the *millet* system or the system in India in which there were and are distinct systems of personal law operating for each religious community (Menski 2001). What we have, however, is an increasing use of faiths as channels for representation, consultation and dialogue in the major conurbations.

Faith communities and associated Inter-Faith Councils and Networks, Inter-Faith Weeks and so forth, have been on the scene for many years (the Birmingham Council of Faiths, for example, one of the earliest of such bodies in the UK, was established in 1974). They have attracted little academic attention (e.g. Beckford 1998, 1999, Farnell et al 2003). Furbey and Macey (2005), who discuss the relationship between religion, community, urban neighbourhood and social cohesion in government policy, argue that this association began to be important in the early 1990s with the formation in 1992 of the Inner Cities Religious Council. It was boosted by a New Labour government drawing on 'communitarian' ideas favoured by the Prime Minister. Furbey and Macey cite a speech of his from 2001 extolling the virtues of religion:

> Our major faith traditions – all of them more historic and deeply rooted than any political party or ideology – play a fundamental role in supporting and propagating values which bind us together as a nation (in Furbey and Macey 2005: 97).

The policy emphasis on faith communities has been reinforced through the increasing numbers of faith schools, private and public, which now exist, and the way in which the voluntary aided sector has, for good reasons of equity, been expanded beyond the Christian and Jewish faiths to include growing numbers of Muslim and Sikh schools. Furbey and Macey note that in the light of the disturbances in the northern cities the government saw faith communities as "having the potential to enhance community involvement in urban regeneration" (2005: 99). They observe, however, that this reflects a simplistic view of such communities as homogeneous and endowed with legitimate and broadly accepted representatives available for consultation. As they themselves comment these representatives tend to be male, and "highly traditional and unrepresentative of the views or needs of women and young people" (p. 113). They also point out that far from being potential vehicles of cohesion, faith communities are all too often the very institutions around which parallel lives are constructed and legitimized (p. 110).

Faith communities are also associated with 'interfaith' activities, as in Birmingham's Council of Faiths which brings together ten faiths in the city. Nationally, there is the Inter Faith Network for the UK linking 100 organizations including some 30 'Faith Community Representative Bodies'. Birmingham's interfaith network played an important role in alerting various parties to the problems posed by the play *Behzti* and then offering the Sikhs fraternal support, including the support of the Catholic Church and the Church of England (see Baumann 1996: 173-78, on faith networks in Ealing, a London borough with a substantial Asian-origin population). These faith and interfaith groups and their representatives have been incorporated into governmental processes through consultation.[8] *Inter alia* faith communities were formally consulted about the entry requirements for religious ministers coming from abroad (Hansard, 2 March 2005, col. 1213W), and about religious hatred legislation.

As Beckford (1999: 52) puts it, "agencies of the British state are sometimes frustrated by the lack of formality and the lack of clearly representative organizations among other faith communities". The search for representatives to speak for minority faiths, reminiscent of colonial systems of indirect rule, is not confined to Britain: France (like Italy) has long sought to establish a 'legitimate' voice of Islam to inform and regulate relations with government (Bowen 2004). It was no surprise to find in the Autumn of 2005 Imams recruited into the effort to contain and control riots in the French *banlieues*. Initiatives to create faith communities and develop faith networks in Britain do not, however, come solely from the top. There is a growing tendency especially but not exclusively among minority ethnic groups to stress religious faith as a key element of public and private identity. In the aftermath of 9/11, when Hindus and Sikhs sought to differentiate themselves from Muslims, there was a shift from the use of 'Asian' as an all-embracing ethnic category to ones which specified religion (Sarfraz Manzoor, *Dawn*, 12 January 2005; Hindu Forum of Britain 2006). Indeed, observers already noted in the 1990s an increasing tendency to defend the faith, for example, among Sikhs (Nesbitt 2000: 257), and this in turn fitted with the way multiculturalism was becoming organized on a religious basis.

8 See, for example, http://www.leicestercounciloffaiths.org.uk/LCoFNewsArchive.htm, accessed 18 July 2006.

In a comment on the *Behzti* affair, Gurharpal Singh has argued that this has

> not only legitimised rotten multiculturalism – where culture has long given way to religion, particularly if it is capable of delivering ethnic minority votes. It has also created space in institutional forums that has been exploited by communities such as the Sikhs. While the sentiments of inter-religious dialogues are noble, the result is often to stifle dissent within religions and essentialise particular traditions as representing the Sikh, Muslim, Christian or Hindu way. In a highly plural and secular society, nothing could be further from the truth (*Guardian*, 24 December 2004).

Both locally and nationally, then, government policy and practice, e.g. in the matter of schools or of consultations, respond to, but through recognition thereby heighten, the public profile of faith leaders, who may be encouraged to pursue their own agendas.

5.4 Racial and Religious Hatred Act 2006

The emergence of faith-based multiculturalism is an integral part of the background to the *Behzti* affair and to the succession of proposals to make religious hatred a crime which culminated in the 2006 Act. Lester (2005) gives an excellent account of the history of the debates leading to this legislation, including, *inter alia*, the criticism, in the 1980s, and subsequently in the wake of the Rushdie affair, of the failure of the existing blasphemy law to deal with insults to Islam. This issue was taken up by the Runnymede Trust's report on *Islamophobia* (1997: 40) which recommended amending the 1986 Public Order Act "to make incitement to religious hatred unlawful". The government made a failed attempt to do so in post-2001 anti-terrorist legislation (a clause concerning incitement to religious hatred, originally in the Anti-Terrorism, Crime and Security Bill, 2001, was dropped), and a private member's bill, proposed by the Liberal Democrat peer, Lord Avebury, which sought to create an offence of religious hatred, and *inter alia* abolish the law on blasphemy, was equally unsuccessful. In May 2002, however, the House of Lords established a Select Committee to consider the need to protect followers of religious faiths. After hearing much evidence, the Committee concluded:

> There is no consensus as to whether such protections should exist and, if so, the precise forms they should take, but we do agree that the civil and criminal law should afford the same protection to people of all faiths, and of none (House of Lords 2003: Section 137).

The latter point was central to the debates about blasphemy and the Race Relations Act 1976. This Act covers Judaism and Sikhism, but not Islam or Hinduism, because it is accepted that Jews and Sikhs constitute ethnic or racial groups. A key figure in the *Behzti* affair was instrumental in the case (*Mandla v. Dowell Lee* [1983] 2 AC 548 (HL)) which established Sikh rights under that legislation.

In 2004-5 the government sought to tackle what was widely described as 'racism by [religious] proxy' by including a Schedule in the Serious Organised Crime and Police Bill making it an offence to incite hatred against persons on religious as well as racial grounds. This was welcomed by, among others, the Churches' Commission on Inter Faith Relations in a joint statement (January 18, 2005) signed by various faith community representatives, including the Director of the Network of Sikh Organisations (UK), on the grounds that "stirring up hatred on grounds of religion is as damaging as stirring up racial hatred", and that

> in the context of combating hate crimes at least, there is a significant overlap between racial and religious identity, with communities sometimes targeted on the basis of their religious, as much as any racial, identity.

They were well aware of counter-arguments concerning freedom of speech, but contended, as did the Home Secretary, that the amendments would not

> limit the freedom to criticise religious beliefs and practices or to engage in robust argument about these or to tell jokes. The legislation seeks only to proscribe the use of threatening, abusive or insulting words and behaviour with the intention of, or likely effect of, stirring up hatred against groups defined by their religious identity.[9]

The measure was opposed by many liberals, including members of the acting profession.[10] The *Behzti* affair coincided with the passage through Parliament of the Bill, and from the beginning the affair was seen as a test

9 In http://www.ekklesia.co.uk/content/news_syndication/article_050118hatred.shtml, accessed 18 July 2006.

10 See the largely hostile comments by Philip Hensher, *Independent*, 9 February 2005, Timothy Garton Ash, *Guardian*, 17 February 2005, and Kenan Malik, *Prospect Magazine*, February 2005. The Minister responsible, Fiona Mactaggart MP, defended herself in the *Guardian*, 14 March 2005. Appignanesi 2005 contains many thoughtful contributions to the debate, and Appignanesi's own introduction gives details of PEN's campaign against the legislation.

case for the proposed legislation. Would the author and/or the theatre be liable for prosecution under its terms? Would the legislation encourage protesters to try to bring to court anything with which they disagreed? *Behzti* was mentioned by several MPs in the Standing Committee debate on the Bill, in January 2005, and was discussed in a Home Office 'FAQ' on the legislation:

> Although it is clear that the opera [*Jerry Springer*] and the play [*Behzti*] have caused offence, there is no evidence that they have stirred up hatred against any religious group and they would not be caught by the proposed incitement to religious offence. It is already an offence to stir up hatred against Sikhs, under the current incitement to racial hatred offences, whether because of their race or religion. The police have decided that there are no grounds for action against the play *Behzti*, which some Sikhs felt targeted their community. The proposed offence of stirring up religious hatred, which will extend the same legal protection to other faith communities, is not a blasphemy law and will not penalise criticising articles or symbols of faith or causing offence. It will not therefore interfere with freedom of expression any more than the existing offence on inciting racial hatred has done.[11]

In the event, the controversial Schedule was withdrawn to hasten the passage of the remainder of the Serious Organised Crime and Police Bill through Parliament before the 2005 general election.

Following the 2005 election the government introduced a new Bill to extend the existing offence of racial hatred to cover religion. This Bill was heavily amended in its passage through the House of Lords, consequently, according to the Home Office,[12] "limiting its scope to only the most serious and easily proven cases of incitement to religious hatred". The amendments confined the legislation to 'threatening' rather than 'insulting and abusive' language, and obliged the prosecution to establish intention to stir up religious hatred. When the amended Bill came to the Commons (January 31, 2006) a government proposal to reject it in favour of the original wording was defeated by one vote. This was widely welcomed, not least by PEN who issued the following statement:

> With last night's amendments in place, the Bill now balances the interests of religious groups against those of free expression. The legal loophole which Muslims and others felt did not afford them the same protection

11 http://www.homeoffice.gov.uk/comrace/faith/crime/faq.html, now archived.

12 http://communities.homeoffice.gov.uk/raceandfaith/faith/Religious-hate-crime, now archived.

> as Christians, Sikhs and Jews has now been closed … The intention to incite hatred on religious grounds by using threatening words or images will remain a criminal act. However, the new law confirms the freedom of writers, comedians, artists and dramatists to create imaginative works or use language which may criticize or ridicule, cause offence and insult, or robustly debate any aspect of religion or religious practice (PEN Press Release, February 1, 2006).

On the other hand, Sir Iqbal Sacranie, of the Muslim Council of Britain, said:

> The Bill had been intended to close a loophole in the law which meant that while some faith groups, such as Jews and Sikhs were rightfully protected against incitement under our existing racial hatred laws, others were not. Far right groups have availed themselves of this loophole and have been increasingly and explicitly targeting British Muslims in recent years. Unfortunately, the misinformation and mischief making from popular comedians and some influential sections of the media, supported by certain political groups, has led Parliament to continue to sanction a wholly unjustifiable hierarchy of rights among British citizens (MCB Press Release, 1 February 2006).

The debate created strange bedfellows. Opponents included, among many others, PEN, the Evangelical Alliance of the UK, Ian Paisley's DUP, the Southall Black Sisters, the Muslim Parliament, the Old Catholic Church of Great Britain, and the actor Rowan Atkinson. On the other side, the government found itself lining up with the Socialist Worker's Party, the Muslim Council of Britain, the Catholic Association for Racial Justice, the Commission for Racial Equality, and the Churches' Commission for Inter Faith Relations. Undoubtedly many, though not all, Muslim organizations were in favour of the legislation, and opponents argued that the government was courting their vote and mending its fences with the Muslim community. In the event, the Racial and Religious Hatred Act 2006 actually dealt with a number of crucial points, extending to Muslims the protection which the law already accords to other faiths, while protecting the freedom to criticize, or indeed satirise them. In typical British fashion legislators muddled through to a reasonable compromise, though the significance of the law will only become apparent when it is tested in the courts.

Prakash Shah (personal communication) has pointed out that other legislation, including the Equality Act 2006 now closes the gap for religious groups under anti-discrimination law. Moreover, the Crime and Disorder Act 1998 which had "created new offences, with increased maximum penalties, where a basic offence [e.g. against the person] is committed in circumstances which are racially aggravated" (Edge 2003: 10), had been extended by the Anti-terrorism, Crime and Security Act 2001 to cover offences which were both "racially or religiously aggravated" (Edge 2003: 18).

This is further evidence of the way in which multiculturalism in Britain now emphasizes religious as much as cultural or ethnic identity, and in turn relates to the 'space' that minority groups find within the law to justify their claims. Thus, in 1983, British Sikhs were obliged to argue that they constituted an ethnic or racial group under the Race Relations Act 1976 in order to support their claim that children should be allowed to wear the turban in school (*Mandla v. Dowell Lee* [1983] 2 AC 548 (HL)). On the other hand, in France in 2004, when Sikhs were caught by legislation to ban the wearing of religious headgear (e.g. the Muslim *hijab*) in schools, they argued that the turban was a cultural not a religious requirement:[13] the French Ambassador in London rejected the argument on the grounds that culture was optional, reportedly saying that "Religion prescribes. Culture doesn't".[14] In a subsequent petition to the European Union Sikhs emphasized the religious character of the turban, as did Sikh elders in the *Behzti* affair:

> French-Sikh children are placed in a very difficult position as the turban is an integral part of their faith. Consequently, French-Sikh school children are being forced to choose between their education and their religion. Their freedom to practise and manifest their religion is, therefore, being denied.[15]

Pragmatically, Sikhs, like others, must argue according to context and situation.

5.5 *Behzti* and Other Affairs

Although this chapter has sought to locate *Behzti* in its British context, and in current British debates about multiculturalism, faith communities, and religious hatred, there are many similarities and some differences with other episodes.

There is, first, the obvious point that they have an international and transnational character, most noticeable in the Rushdie affair and that of the Danish cartoons, but apparent also, albeit to a lesser degree, in *Behzti*. They demonstrate "the creation of a modern, unified field of world politics" (Fred Halliday, *Open Democracy*, 13 February 2006). Certainly some

13 http://www.sikhtimes.com/news_011204a.html, accessed 18 July 2006.

14 http://www.sikhnet.com/s/USDiplomat, accessed 18 July 2006.

15 http://www.unitedsikhs.org/rtt/doc/Right_to_Wear_Sikh_Turban_MEP_Letter.doc, accessed 18 July 2006.

events barely make national headlines, but others become international *causes célèbres*. The mechanisms through which this happens require investigation. The crucial role of the conventional media (press and TV) in conveying and nourishing these affairs is significant, as is that of the Internet in all its manifestations, along with technologies such as text messaging.

Secondly, if these episodes are globalized or internationalized, they are also caught up in local issues and power struggles in the countries where they originate and those to which they spread (Jonathan Steel, *Guardian*, 11 February 2006, discusses several examples). They may rapidly become political footballs at and between each level. In the Rushdie affair the local social and economic situation in Bradford was important. In *Behzti*, gurdwara and other politics in Birmingham, and disputes within the wider community of Sikhs around such issues as support for the independence of Khalistan played a part. In the cartoons affair, the situation of the (right-wing) Danish newspaper and its position vis à vis Danish multiculturalism was important, as were internal divisions between Danish Muslims, and the groups and individuals claiming to represent them (Tabish Khair, *Guardian*, 7 February 2006), also a significant factor in other episodes. Governments are sometimes caught in this global/local nexus, anxious about their international contacts, but concerned with the effect of these events on public order back home, and on minority populations, especially those living in areas represented by the governing party.

Thirdly, and relatedly, these cases say something about global and local *rapports de force*, and the social capital on which protagonists can draw. In the cartoon affair, Danish Imams could call on the assistance of several Middle Eastern ambassadors to intervene with the Danish Prime Minister but, when that intervention was rebuffed, toured Muslim countries and secured an impressive array of international supporters. It may well have been in the interests of their supporters to exploit the issue (as in the Rushdie affair), though exploitation is often mutual. The Sikh diaspora is much weaker, given the powerful position of India and its importance for Britain both in foreign relations and in relations with Britain's minority ethnic population. On the other hand, and this is something they share with Muslims, British Sikhs are able to draw on the support of local councillors, MPs in constituencies with a significant Sikh electorate, and, through interfaith networks, representatives of other religions.

Fourthly, in all these episodes there is a similarly wide spectrum of opinion including fundamentalists of all hues whose views are frequently Orientalist or Occidentalist (Carrier 1995), at times outrightly xenophobic, as in the Rushdie and *Behzti* affairs. A telling example was the way in which the van Gogh murder on 2 November 2004, was very widely described in the media through the phrase 'ritual slaughter', for example, Theo van

Gogh was "ritually slaughtered on the street in Amsterdam" (*Daily Telegraph*, 22 December 2004).[16]

This is related, fifthly, to a tendency for these episodes to be construed as confrontations between two sides, 'them' and 'us', and it is striking how often what is said and done feeds and in turn feeds upon each parties' fantasies and nightmares of the Other, how rapidly dehumanized and essentialized the imagery becomes, and how these episodes escalate in word and deed, in action and reaction. Thus, the Danish cartoons fed the Western fantasies of Islam, and at the same time Muslims' own fantasies of where the West stands in relation to their religion. They were an "absolute gift to the extremists", as Karen Armstrong put it.[17] Likewise, placards calling for the beheading of traducers of Islam (as displayed in a demonstration in London) fed Western images of Muslims, with the response to this episode in turn feeding Muslim images of the hostile West. Tariq Ramadan commented:

> The crises provoked by these cartoons shows us how, out of "seemingly nothing", two universes of reference can become deaf to each other and be seduced by defining themselves against each other – with the worst possible consequences (*Guardian*, 6 February 2006).

One consequence is, finally, that those in the middle, Muslim and non-Muslim, Sikh and non-Sikh, hesitant, ambivalent, "hav[ing] their cake and eat[ing] it", accused Madhav Sharma, one of the actors in *Behzti* (2005: 36), find themselves squeezed, "struggl[ing] to reconcile … free speech and tolerance" (Madeleine Bunting, *Guardian*, 3 February 2006). Like Jay Singh, cited earlier, Danish Muslim, Tabish Kahir (*Guardian*, 7 February 2006) writing as a 'moderate', records that his silence on the cartoons and the protests against them was not through lack of an opinion, but because there was no room available for him to voice it, neither in Denmark, nor in Muslim countries.

5.6 An Emerging Consensus?

Behzti, like the Rushdie affair, seemed to pit the right to artistic freedom against the right to have religious sensibilities protected from transgression. Yet, in the UK in 2006, in the light of the furore over the Danish cartoons, a consensus appeared to be emerging which said, in effect: "Freedom of speech, but no licence to offend". British newspapers by implication adopted that view when, unlike newspapers elsewhere in Europe, they

16 The problems raised by such representations are discussed further in an appendix (*infra*).

17 http://news.bbc.co.uk/1/hi/world/europe/4676632.stm, accessed 18 July 2006.

refrained from republishing the cartoons. Their restraint was approved by the British Foreign Secretary who was widely reported as saying that the republication had been "unnecessary, insensitive, disrespectful and wrong". In France a Foreign Ministry spokeswoman commented "Free speech is a sacred right on the condition that it neither violates privacies nor incites hatred".[18] This was the position taken by the philosopher Onora O'Neil (*Guardian*, 13 February 2006); Andrew Anthony (*Observer*, February 12, 2006) took the opposite view while Ronald Dworkin argued that although the British press was right not to publish the cartoons, "Even bigots and Holocaust deniers must have their say" (*Guardian*, 14 February 2006).

That there is no licence to offend does not mean the law must intervene. Tariq Modood, for example, specifically called for censuring offensive writing, not censoring it (*Open Democracy*, February 8, 2006), as did Tariq Ramadan.[19] Along with other observers (e.g. Timothy Garton Ash, *Guardian*, 9 February 2006), Ramadan stressed the importance of self-restraint, though what happens if self-restraint fails is unclear. Certainly when a literary or other product threatens or incites violence most agree the law must be involved, and there has long been a battery of instruments for this which the religious hatred legislation simply extends. Nonetheless, there remains a grey area. What about productions which contribute to a climate of hatred and fear without directly threatening violence? The *Christian Science Monitor* (7 February 2006) compared the publication of the Danish cartoons to organising a Nazi rally in a Jewish neighborhood, and others, too, made the connection with the anti-semitic cartoons published in Nazi Germany in the newspaper *Der Stürmer*. The point is that *Der Stürmer*'s cartoons were not just offensive, but inflammatory, and crucially helped to create a climate of opinion in which the unthinkable could happen.

Should such cartoons which are not just offensive, but deeply xenophobic and inflammatory be published at a time of social tension? Context and history are all. The cartoons, "distil the experience of inferiority" (Tariq Modood, *op. cit.*), and "feed into profound feelings of disempowerment, fear and insecurity" (Sarah Joseph, *Guardian*, 3 February 2006). As others have pointed out (e.g. Salman Sayyid, *Open Democracy*, 15 February 2006), episodes such as *Behzti* or the Danish cartoons cannot be viewed in isolation but as one of a series of events, within Europe and beyond, in which Muslims (but not only Muslims) believe themselves increasingly under siege from a hostile 'West'. They are embedded in a long history of relationships between East and West, Muslims and Christians, colonizers

18 http://www.islamonline.net/English/News/2006-02/01/article06.shtml, accessed 18 July 2006.

19 e.g. http://www.tariqramadan.com/article.php3?id_article=572&lang=en/, accessed 18 July 2006.

and colonized, and one of the lessons from *Behzti* and other affairs is that the consequences of that history remain to be addressed.

5.7 Appendix: The van Gogh Affair

The representation of the van Gogh assassination as 'ritual murder', raises many questions (see Eyerman 2005 for one interpretation). How was the murder actually committed and how was that interpreted in the Netherlands by Muslims and non-Muslims? Was van Gogh deliberately killed so as to call to mind a (Muslim) religious practice such as the slaughtering of sheep for the *Aïd*? Was the performance of the act interpreted in that way by Muslims? Or was this a construction by non-Muslims? Alternatively, did the act incorporate ceremonial aspects as happens in the case of some serial killers (Jack the Ripper is an obvious example) who may choreograph their dreadful work using symbols of private and public significance?

Certainly, the murder, which involved both shooting and stabbing, was physically horrible and had an overt and very strong religious motivation. It was undoubtedly a religious assassination whose significance was set out in detail in two long and incoherent letters which the murderer wrote. One he pinned to van Gogh's body; the other, containing his "final words", he had about his person. The language is violent and the text exudes hatred, but reading those letters (in English translation) leaves the impression of a deeply disturbed individual. Nonetheless, whatever his intention or state of mind, to report what he did as 'ritual slaughter', is to re-locate the event in a very disturbing discourse. One might compare the way in which the fiction of the 'blood libel' was a staple of anti-semitism, and elements of that surfaced in the Jack the Ripper case. As a result, the van Gogh murder became linked with, for example, the beheading of kidnap victims in Iraq in a manner which created a general view of Islam and Muslims as savages, leading to the conclusion that such acts signal "the end of Europe's multicultural utopian dream", to quote one commentator (Magdi Allam, *Corriere della Sera*, 6 November 2004). The use of such phrases, especially including 'ritual', also places the act in the context of barbarism, primitive human sacrifice, Satanism etc. The British media used such terminology when reporting on the struggle for Kenyan independence in the 1950s.

It is interesting to trace the development of this usage in the Dutch press. Earliest reports recorded the brutal nature of the murder (e.g. *Volkskrant*, 3 November 2004), but 'ritual murder' or something similar soon became commonplace, along with references to the murderer's appearance (supposedly in a kaftan, *Het Parool*, 2 November 2004, or in "fundamentalist Islamic dress", *Het Parool*, 6 November 2006). A catalyst seems to have been a TV talk show, on the evening of the murder, in which journalist Sylvain Ephimenco, referred to the "beastly manner" in which van Gogh was "ritually slaughtered". Subsequently, a syndicated article by MP

Ayaan Hirsi Ali (e.g. in *Het Parool*, 4 November 2004) employed the phrase without explanation. The use of a knife, as well as the manner in which the murder was committed (*Trouw*, 6 November 2004) also suggested a link between van Gogh's murder and the work of the 12th century 'assassins'. Thus although a ritual character was sometimes hesitantly ascribed to the murder ("almost ritual murder", "with a feeling for ritual"), and some reports in the British press employed cautious language ("ritual style killing", "apparent ritual nature of the murder", and "what the media has described as a 'ritual killing'"), more often it was taken for granted, one writer following another without anyone ever explaining how and why it might justifiably be so described.[20]

20 I thank Sussex MA student, Loes Vaessen, for locating and translating extracts from the Dutch press.

Chapter 6 Planning Law and Mosque Development: The Politics of Religion and Residence in Birmingham

Richard Gale

In the wake of the events of 11 September 2001 and, more recently, the attacks on London in July 2005, relations between British Muslims and various agencies of the state has been a sustained focus of public and academic debates. With the current prominence of wide sweeping anti-terrorism measures, which many regard as a threat to freedoms enshrined in international and domestic human rights legislation (Liberty 2005), much of this debate has understandably coalesced around the role of the criminal justice system. However, attention is also now beginning to turn to the long-established role played by other public bodies and institutions, at local as well as national levels, in compounding British Muslim experiences of social and political marginalisation. One arena of governmental administration that has become a source of focus, both in Britain and across other European states, is urban planning (see the November 2005 special issue of the *Journal of Ethnic and Migration Studies*, on 'Mosque conflicts in Europe').

Whilst the effects of planning may be less immediate and its operations less overtly politicised (and politicising) than those of the police and wider criminal justice system, the interactions between British Muslims and the planning system nevertheless constitute an important dimension of the wider pattern of inequality to which Muslim groups are exposed. At the most general level, as Huw Thomas (2000) has rightly observed, the planning system does not operate in a social and cultural vacuum, but in a context where group relations, socially and spatially, are characterised by significant patterns of racialisation. Viewed in this light, planning has a considerable stake in contributing to – as well as an important potential role in overcoming – the reproduction of inequalities experienced by Muslims and other minority groups. Secondly, at the more specific level,

Prakash Shah (ed.), Law and Ethnic Plurality: Socio-Legal Perspectives. *pp. 127-144.*
 ISBN 978 90 04 16245 7.

through exerting control over the use and development of (urban) space, the planning system is a crucial institutional nexus for deciding the fate of Muslim and attempts by other religious groups to establish viable places of worship, with bureaucratic input into not only the location, but also the design and use of religious premises. The present chapter presents the results of qualitative research to explore how some of these issues have played out in the experiences of a number of Muslim groups, taking the West Midlands city of Birmingham as a case study.

Pioneering research undertaken in Birmingham in the early 1980s revealed some of the effects of planning procedure on Muslims attempting to establish mosques and education centres (*madrasas*) in the city. This research was highly critical of the local planning authority. Following a review of contentious planning cases, the research concluded that there had been "a shameful record of planning refusals and enforcement notices" in Birmingham throughout the 1970s (Hodgins 1981: 24). Furthermore, it was argued that there had been "a *prima facie* case of racial [sic] discrimination" in the city, in terms of the City Council's treatment of Muslims who had applied for permission to establish religious facilities (Hodgins 1981: 24; see also Grudzinska 1982). Somewhat later, in a survey of British local authority responses to Muslims needs, Jørgen Nielsen (1988) found the situation to have improved in the city, with Birmingham being one of a handful of planning authorities in Britain to have adopted detailed planning policies specifying how the authority would respond to applications to develop Muslim and other religious premises. Specifically, Nielsen found that the City Council had adopted a new policy in 1981 that allowed "a much more flexible approach" than had previously been the case, easing some of the earlier restrictions, particularly upon the use of houses for religious purposes (Nielsen 1988: 60). Nielsen found that many of the cases in which premises had been used without planning permission had been resolved, thus providing "evidence of the improvement brought about by the new policy" (Nielsen 1988: 60).

However, there has been little recent research to bring these earlier findings up to date.[1] The purpose of the present chapter is to resume the focus of this earlier research and assess how the situation in Birmingham has developed in the intervening years.[2] The paper is divided into two sec-

1 Although see Nye (2001) for an important discussion of the experiences of the International Society of Krishna Consciousness (ISKCON) in a planning case against Hertsmere Borough Council near London; see also Gale (1999) for Leicester.

2 The research on which this chapter is based was made possible with the use of awards from a number of funding bodies to whom the author would like to express thanks: firstly, the Economic and Social Research Council (ESRC)

tions. The first examines a debate that emerged over an application from the Birmingham Central Mosque to broadcast the call to prayer (*azan*) in the 1980s. The topic of applications to broadcast calls to prayer on the outside of mosques in Britain has already received some academic attention, most notably in the work of John Eade (1993, 1996). The Birmingham case was also mentioned, but not comprehensively examined, in works by Nielsen (1988) and Joly (1995). The contribution of the present discussion is its examination of the specific role of urban planning procedure in providing an institutional setting for the social and aesthetic contestation that took place over the *azan*. The positions of the mosque committee, local non-Muslim residents and the City Council are considered in turn. Particular attention is paid to the way in which urban planning established the parameters for this contestation, and to how the language of planning discourse became infused in its articulation.

The second section of the chapter provides an overview of contemporary patterns in Birmingham, with regard to the effects of urban planning upon Muslims. Drawing upon interviews with members of various mosque committees, as well as quantitative data on planning decisions, it is argued that, whilst advances have been made by the City Council in the light of experience gained in the 1970s and 1980s, there remain areas of tension that merit further consideration.

6.1 The Birmingham Central Mosque and the Call to Prayer

According to the 2001 Census, Birmingham's population of slightly less than 1 million includes 140,033 Muslims, i.e. about 14 per cent of the population (Office for National Statistics 2003). Correspondingly, mosques and *madrasas* are now an established feature of the built environment of the city, having been developed progressively by different local Muslim groups to service their religious and social needs. The number of officially registered mosques in the city has increased steadily since the early 1970s, from only 2 in 1970 to 13 in 1980, 47 in 1990 and 73 in 1998.[3]

The 2001 Census also shows that the majority of Muslims in Birmingham are of South Asian heritage, with Pakistanis accounting for 70 per

from whom the author received a doctoral award between 2000-2003; the Leverhulme Trust who funded the 'Ethnicity and Cultural Landscapes' project (grant no. F/773) based in the School of Geography and the Environment at Oxford University and lead by Professor Ceri Peach between 1998 and 2001; and the Nuffield Foundation, who provided an award to the author and Professor Ceri Peach under the 'Small Grants Scheme' in 2004. This paper is a revised version of Gale (2005).

3 Source: Office for National Statistics, Register of officially certified places of worship in England and Wales.

cent, Bangladeshis 14 per cent and Indians 4 per cent of the total Muslim population. Most reside in the inner city, with 72 per cent living in seven electoral wards located to the north, south and south-east of the city's central district.[4]

Approximately half of the mosques in Birmingham are converted residential premises[5], located in areas where they serve the needs of highly localised communities (see Geaves 1996). However, for historical reasons discussed below, the Birmingham Central Mosque now stands in an area in which Muslims constitute only a small sector of the local population, a factor that was of some significance to the way in which public discussion over the *azan* developed.

Birmingham Central Mosque is not the oldest mosque in Birmingham, but was the first to be purposely constructed, and to consciously draw upon Islamic architectural antecedents (Gale 2004).[6] The building is situated in Highgate, a mixed residential and commercial area lying a short distance from the central city. The area was extensively redeveloped during the 1950s and 1960s, and the land on which the mosque now stands was allocated as part of the initial redevelopment plans.

Immediately contiguous to Highgate is Balsall Heath, one of the initial areas of settlement in Birmingham for Muslims of mainly South Asian, but also of Yemeni, origin in the 1950s and 1960s (Dahya 1974). Accordingly, the Central Mosque was designed to serve Muslims living both locally and throughout the city.[7] However, as the President of the mosque commented, a further consequence of the redevelopment scheme was that it displaced many of the Muslims who had lived in the area at the time when the plans for the mosque were conceived:

---

4 For a detailed discussion of the residential patterns of different South Asian groups in Birmingham see Slater (1996).

5 This refers to the proportion of officially registered mosques in the city that were formed through house conversions.

6 It is uncertain which was the first mosque to be established in Birmingham. The oldest existing mosque is that at 294 Edward Road, a converted semi-detached house in Balsall Heath, which is affiliated to the Islamia Allaouia Religious Society, principally a Yemeni organisation with establishments in several former ports, including Cardiff, Swansea, Hull, Liverpool and South Shields.

7 A 1956 report provides further evidence of the dual function of the mosque, with the statement: 'Provision has also been made for a mosque to be located on a site adjacent to the intermediate ring road to serve *not merely this area but the city as a whole.*' (Public Works Committee, 'Gooch Street Redevelopment Area—zoning layout', 2 February 1956; emphasis added).

> When the idea was originally conceived, this whole area was mainly populated by Muslims. By the time the construction was complete, the population had changed completely. The Muslims had moved out, and it was a mixture, a sprinkling of the Muslim population here around the mosque, so all the people that you see coming to the mosque are coming from all over Birmingham. It has got no central catchment area.

Partial confirmation of this statement is provided by data from the 2001 Census, which shows that Muslims constituted approximately 27 per cent of the Highgate population, in contrast with Christians, who constituted approximately 45 per cent. There were much smaller numbers of Sikhs and Hindus, who constituted three per cent and one per cent of the Highgate population respectively. Those who identified themselves as having no religion, and those who declined to state their religion, each accounted for a further 11 per cent. It is of course necessary to guard against the assumption that the composition of the local population was an inevitable precondition for the dispute over the *azan*. Nevertheless, the relative sizes of different religious communities in the area was an important issue insofar as it was articulated by those who took part in the planning dispute, and lay at the core of several claims and counter-claims concerning the legitimacy of broadcasting the *azan* in the local public space.

As a result of financial constraints, the mosque committee was not able to erect the minaret planned for the building until some time after the completion of the main prayer-hall in 1975. Due to the amount of time that had elapsed since the approval of the original design, the construction of a minaret in the early 1980s required additional planning permission.

A planning application for the minaret was submitted to the City Council in October 1980, and was approved without opposition. Indeed, the planning report[8] concerning the proposal applauded the design of the minaret, concluding that it would make an important aesthetic contribution to the urban landscape:

> [The] design is elegant and well proportioned. [It] will form a good foil/contrast with the main domed building. Visible over wide area along Belgrave road/Lee Bank Middleway and across Balsall Heath. No objections to this interesting addition to the sky-line.

Whilst the application was thus approved, it was, however, subject to the condition that "no sound reproduction or amplification equipment shall be installed or used on any part of the said minaret at any time". The condi-

8 Birmingham City Council, Planning Application number PA E/C/23328/1–8. Further quotes below are drawn from this 1980 report.

tion thus imposed a separation between the form of the minaret, which was accepted into a controlled landscape aesthetic, and the customary practice of using the minaret to call the *azan*, which was explicitly disallowed.

In November 1982, the mosque committee contested this restriction on the minaret and applied for the condition to be relaxed. They did so with reference to two principal arguments, both of which challenged the City Council on the basis of the inequality that was perceived to ensue from its restriction on the use of the minaret for the *azan.* The first argument drew upon a representation of the local environment, with the claim that "as neighbouring churches are allowed to ring peals of bells on any day of the week", the request of the mosque committee to install amplification equipment for the call to prayer "was not unreasonable". The local origins of this argument were recalled during an interview with a founding member of the now-defunct organisation, the Council of Birmingham Mosques, which had supported the application:

> We gave an example: there is the Central Mosque, there. On the top of it [sic] is an Anglican church, on the top. And we used this [argument], 'if you allow the bell there, and it's alright, what about our prayers?' That was the example we used. And they were shocked…

Comparisons between church bells and the *azan* also formed part of public debates over the transmission of the *azan* at the East London Mosque in Whitechapel Road (Eade 1996: 224–25). However, the difference in the Birmingham context was that this comparison formed the basis of an attempt to generate political sway within the planning process itself.

The second argument used by the mosque committee challenged Birmingham City Council on the grounds that another planning authority, Calderdale Borough Council, had previously allowed the *azan* from a mosque in Halifax, thus setting a national 'precedent'. The use of this argument ultimately had little impact upon the planning process surrounding the *azan*, but was sufficient to impel Birmingham City Council to correspond with Calderdale Borough Council to establish the veracity of the mosque committee's claim. It thus signifies the readiness of the mosque committee to mobilise in opposition to the limits imposed on the mosque by the planning authority.[9]

9 The reply from Calderdale was ambiguous: whilst they referred to correspondence between the local planning authority and the Central Mosque in Halifax dating to 1977, which indicated that the call to prayer would be allowed, they were uncertain whether amplification equipment was presently being used. More conclusive evidence of Calderdale Borough Council's position on the *azan* was provided by Nielsen's survey. In response to the question in the

These forms of interaction between the mosque committee and the City Council articulated what the Muslim group saw as their legitimate claim to manifest their religious practices in public space, through means of negotiation and compromise. Referring to tensions that have often arisen over the call to prayer in Britain, the representative of the Council of Birmingham Mosques cited earlier commented upon the fact that it has often been perceived by non-Muslims as 'point-making':

> The call to prayer has always been the sticking point of people saying it is 'point-making', and we have to be patient, like we have been patient with the planning permission. Time will come when people will accept. But when you are calling the prayers, you should call the prayers in a way that you do not upset the majority of the people.

It was for this reason, the respondent added, taking into consideration the diversity of the surrounding population, that the application sought permission to call only the midday (*salāt al-zuhr*) and afternoon (*salāt al-'asr*) prayers, and the Friday congregational prayer (*jum'a*), rather than all five daily prayers. Moreover, this attitude of compromise with regard to the *azan* was interpreted by the respondent as a matter of religious obligation:

> The word compulsion of religion, it is not practiced in my vocabulary in the Middle East, because it is *harām*, even to *think* to force you against your will is *harām*, is forbidden. It's forbidden, it's forbidden.... It is their country, they could tell me to get lost, what could I do? Well this is the truth, at the end of the day.

However, this in turn raises the issue of how the application was viewed by local non-Muslim residents. Between 1982, when the original application was made, and 1986, when the application was finally approved, many letters were submitted to the City Council in relation to the call to prayer, the large majority of which were expressions of opposition. The issues raised in these letters showed a considerable degree of consistency, and revealed several recurrent themes, including: that Muslims don't live in the area; that to approve the call to prayer would be taking 'race relations' too far; that England is still a Christian country, whilst Islam is a 'false' religion; that the call would devalue properties and contribute to the degeneration

survey on local authorities' planning policy guidelines, Calderdale answered that 'a condition would normally be included with any permission [for a mosque] restricting any amplification except for the midday call to prayer' (Nielsen 1988: 58). In the light of the controversy in Birmingham, this was, as Nielsen notes, 'quite permissive despite the wording' (Nielsen 1988: 58).

of the area; that the sound of the call is unpleasant and 'alien' to English heritage; that this application is the 'thin end of the wedge' and will lead to other similar applications elsewhere; and that the sound of the call will be a distraction to motorists, leading to road accidents. Here, I concentrate on comments that involve constructions of the symbolism of the mosque in relation to its local environment.

The overt message of letters stating that to allow the *azan* would be 'taking equality too far' was that the *azan* would make Muslims too prominent, with the result that they could be the victims of heightened 'racial tension'. However, these comments were themselves characterised by strongly racialised overtones. The following are fairly typical examples:

> As a rates payer and loyal citizen of Birmingham I feel that this would be a mistake as it would make racial problems (which we have in this city) much worse by irritating the indigenous, native population. There is room for all races in this great city of ours but care must be taken in the equal distribution of rights and privileges.
>
> As a householder and hence a rates payer within the vicinity of the mosque, I wish to outline the basis of my objections to what is proposed.... I feel that the proposal seeks to exploit the unique tolerance of racial and religious minorities in this country.... In any event, the proposal is not in keeping with the character of the area. This is, after all, England!

Each of these statements involves a more or less explicit opposition between the notion of 'authentic' citizenship and 'minority' presence. The notion of 'citizen' as employed here is qualified with such terms as 'native', 'indigenous' and 'loyal', and makes reference to more concrete attributes that purport to legitimise the claim to citizenship, such as 'householder' and 'rates-payer'. In contrast, the Muslims are characterised as 'intrusive' and 'exploitative', and found to be 'pushing their luck'.

In other letters, this opposition between 'citizens' and 'minorities' underpinned commentary upon the aesthetics of the *azan* itself. Some of these, such as the following two quotations, actively refuted the comparison made by the mosque committee between the call to prayer and the ringing of church bells:

> The argument that if the Church of England can have bells why should not a mosque have loudspeakers, avoids the point that bells are rather musical, beautiful and natural instruments, whereas the idea of a voice calling the faithful to prayer is anything but aesthetic. What is being proposed is quite alien to our way of life and, if approved, would be a

> constant source of annoyance to the vast majority of people living in the area – who are certainly not Muslim.
>
> [I] sincerely trust that permission will not be given for the sounding of the minaret. The noise can best be described as a cow in pain and is quite alien to our British culture. At the moment it would be in Birmingham twice daily – soon, it would be nationwide five times a day. Minarets are going up at great speed (planning permission would never be given to any other building so foreign to British architecture). The only purpose for them being built is to be used.

In these remarks, representations of the residential area around the mosque, the city and the nation have become linked together in an *imagined community* that is opposed to the presence of the Muslim 'Other' (Anderson 1991). A concomitant of this construction of identity is a comparable projection of the 'threat' that the immediate case seems to prefigure; "…soon it would be nationwide five times a day', etc. Moreover, this construction encompasses a racialised representation of the built environment, whereby the minaret, the *azan* and the mosque itself are identified as 'foreign', in contradistinction to '*British* architecture'.

Turning now to the position of the planning authority, it is worth considering how these arguments, both in support of and in opposition to the *azan*, were mediated by the deliberative processes that constitute urban planning procedure. In terms of the history of the case, there were two occasions on which applications for the call to prayer were considered by the authority, once in 1983, when it recommended refusal, and again in 1985/6, when, following a trial period of one month, it granted approval. These two occasions are considered briefly in turn.

The first report prepared by the planning authority in July 1983 responded to the comparison previously made by the mosque committee between the call to prayer and church bells, and stated that:

> Although church bells are part of this country's heritage, they produce a high noise level and have given rise to complaints.

Thus, the planners were able to avoid denouncing the comparison in the way that some local residents had, and to obviate the implication that they had treated the Muslims unfairly by setting their decision on a 'material' footing that disregarded religious differences.[10] By developing this argument, the authority was able to re-inscribe the comparison between church

10 See Cooper (1998) for a similar argument in relation to an application to establish a Jewish Eruv in north London.

bells and the *azan* in a way that emphasised the greater intensity of use proposed in relation to the call to prayer:

> The equipment proposed would be used on a far more regular basis than church bells and, together with the high noise level predicted, would be likely to constitute a nuisance to local residents.

Nevertheless, the opposition of local residents was accorded considerable importance as a factor in the planning authority's initial decision to recommend refusal of the application, as the conclusion to the report makes clear:

> Although the applicants have agreed to a trial period, I feel that in view of the strength of local opinion and the high noise level involved, I see no alternative but to recommend refusal to vary the condition.

However, immediately prior to the meeting of the City Council planning committee at which the application was to be considered, the mosque committee withdrew the application, in all likelihood to prevent it from being formally refused. There was then a two-year period in which the question of the call to prayer lapsed into silence. The mosque committee resubmitted their application in 1985, and on this occasion, the planning authority agreed to a trial period, after which there was a public consultation exercise. In the light of this, the authority recommended approval of the application for the calling of the midday and afternoon prayers, commenting that:

> [the test of the sound equipment] resulted in a range of comment, from just acceptable to highly intrusive. However, bearing in mind the number of objections received is small, and [that] it could be reasonably assumed that as the noise level, although high, lasted only two minutes in each case, it was generally acceptable to residents.

As this quotation illustrates, the decision continued to be couched in the instrumental terminology concerning what constitutes the 'public interest'. Accordingly, it is difficult to assert that the decision to approve the *azan* correlated with a shift away from the entrenchment of the interests of neighbours that seemed to mark the initial stages of the debate. Nevertheless, the fact that the City Council agreed to a trial period when the application was considered on the second occasion, having refused to allow such a trial on the first occasion, suffices to show that a shift in the limits of tolerance imposed by the Council had occurred in practice. Moreover, this procedural shift has been maintained in the form of a (local) 'precedent'. Thus, a mosque that was completed in the Small Heath area of Birmingham in 1997 was granted permission to broadcast calls to prayer for the same prayers and according to the same constraints of time and volume that were established in the Central Mosque case.[11]

On account of the strength of feeling engendered by the application to broadcast the *azan*, as well as the extent of the deliberations that led up to its approval, the case remains unrivalled in magnitude by any other planning issues that have been raised by the development or use of mosques in the city. However, in another sense, it is the more frequently repeated forms of interaction between religious organisations and the local planning authorities that hold the key for assessing whether there are more systematic imbalances woven into planning policy and procedure. Thus, the following section moves on to examine planning issues that have recently been of concern to Muslim groups in Birmingham, as reflected, firstly, in statistics on planning decisions, and secondly, in the views of representatives of a number of mosques in the city.

6.2 Recurrent Themes and Tensions

Between January 1990 and October 2002, Birmingham City Council processed approximately 300 planning applications relating to Muslim religious buildings (including mosques and *madrasas*), compared with 248 relating to Christian buildings (including churches and church halls), 55 relating to Sikh *gurudwaras*, and 12 relating to Hindu *mandirs*. The data in Table 1 show that, *prima facie,* there are some notable disparities in planning decision patterns pertaining to the places of worship of different faith groups in Birmingham. Thus, only 56 per cent of applications relating to mosques and *madrasas* gained approval. In fairly marked contrast, 82 per cent of applications relating to Christian buildings and 70 per cent of applications relating to *gurudwaras* were approved. The rates at which applications were refused also make for some important comparisons. Thus, nearly a quarter of all applications for mosques and *madrasas* (24 per cent) were refused. This compares with 9 per cent of applications relating to Christian buildings and 11 per cent of those relating to Sikh *gurudwaras*. There were only twelve applications identifiable as relating to Hindu *mandirs*, and these are not analysed further here.

11 Birmingham City Council, Planning Application number E/01112/90/FUL.

Table 1. Planning decisions relating to Muslim, Christian and Sikh places of worship in Birmingham, 1990-2002

Decisions	**Numbers**			**Percentages**		
	Muslims	Christians	Sikhs	Muslims	Christians	Sikhs
Approved	144	181	33	49	74	61
Refused	71	22	6	24	9	11
Invalid application	23	7	2	8	3	4
Approved temporarily	22	19	5	7	8	9
Withdrawn	21	15	6	7	6	11
Deferred	6	0	0	2	0	0
Other	7	0	2	2	0	4
Total	**294**	**244**	**54**	**100**	**100**	**100**

Source: Birmingham City Council Planning Department, Register of Planning Applications.

Further research in this area is necessary to provide a full account of these differences. However, the statistics themselves suggest that there is an association between the types of building used by different faith groups and the planning decisions that correspond to them. Thus, the majority of applications pertaining to Christian religious buildings and 35 per cent of applications for Sikh *gurudwaras* were for permission to develop or extend purpose-built premises. Moreover, a further 17 per cent of applications relating to *gurudwaras* corresponded to buildings that were converted Christian churches. In contrast, the majority of applications for mosques and *madrasas* related to buildings that had been converted from other uses, with applications relating to purpose built premises accounting for only 18 per cent of the total for which the building type could be identified.[12]

The decision patterns relating to mosques and *madrasas* were analysed further in terms of building type (Table 2). The right-hand column of the table indicates that the converted house category accounts for the largest proportion of planning applications for mosques and *madrasas*, 45 per cent of the total. This confirms the observation made in the first part of this chapter that nearly half of all registered mosques in Birmingham are established in former residential premises. However, the statistics show that this was not only the largest category, but was also the most problematic within planning procedure, accounting for 60 per cent of all refusals.

12 Out of the 294 applications relating to mosques and *madrasas* in Birmingham between 1990 and 2002, it was possible to identify the building types for 274 of these.

These data indicate that the observed frequency of refusals for mosques and *madrasas* located in converted houses exceeded the expected frequency by a substantial margin. In contrast the actual frequency of refusals for applications relating to purpose-built premises was substantially lower than the 'expected' frequency. A simple chi-square test applied to the statistics in Table 2 supports the hypothesis that planning decisions on mosques etc. do indeed vary significantly by building type. (The chi-square test gave a value of 23.5 with 6 degrees of freedom, which is significant at the $P < 0.001$ level.) Clearly, applications relating to purpose-built premises are much less likely to be refused than applications relating to converted residential premises.

Table 2. Planning decisions on different types of building used as mosques in Birmingham, 1990-2002

Building type	**Refused**	**Approved**	**Other**	**Totals (%)**
Houses	41	61	21	123 (44.6)
Shop/commercial	11	24	12	46 (16.7)
Purpose-built	3	42	4	49 (17.8)
Other	12	33	10	58 (21.0)
Total	**67**	**160**	**47**	**274 (100)**

Source: Birmingham City Council Planning Department, Register of Planning Applications.

These statistical results are reflected in some of the themes that were raised during semi-structured interviews with the representatives of various mosques in Birmingham, as well as with a number of Muslim architects/designers who have handled planning applications for mosques and *madrasas* in the city.[13] Indeed, juxtaposing these interview data with the quantitative patterns sketched above enables more detailed exploration of why certain building types have been problematised within planning procedure. In addition, these interviews provide insights into the way in which the planning process in Birmingham is currently perceived by some of its Muslim residents.

A key concern repeated by several respondents was that planning officers lacked understanding of the religious practices of Muslims, which would be necessary for their policies on places of worship to be sufficiently aligned with Muslim needs for religious premises. In this context, planning

13 These interviews were conducted as part of my doctoral fieldwork undertaken in Birmingham between October 2001 and September 2002.

was experienced as a significant constraining factor in the development of religious facilities. In reference to the problems that have frequently surrounded the conversion of houses for Muslim religious use, one Muslim architect commented as follows:

> The problem is, right, I feel they [planners] don't understand the community's need, because if you study the mosques, they need to have specific, small centres in each sort of area, and they've got to be by residential areas.... People living here [Small Heath] they can't go to Balsall Heath, right, on a normal, daily basis, so they need to have them in specific areas, a number of mosques, and smaller mosques, so the people in the immediate streets can walk to that place. So I think, every time you put an application in for a mosque, they start questioning the parking, and the noise and the disturbance to the people in the local area.

This statement conveys the tension perceived between the need for localised religious premises on the one hand, and the tendency of planning procedure to intervene in the process of meeting this need on the other, by raising concerns about issues such as noise disturbance and parking provisions. It also suggests possible reasons why applications relating to converted residential premises tend to be refused more often than for other types of premises. Another Muslim architect, who has worked on several mosque-building projects in Birmingham, also expressed this tension, arguing that, in practice, decisions relating to mosques and *madrasas* do not necessarily coincide with the stipulations of the places of worship policy contained within the Birmingham Unitary Development Plan (Birmingham City Council 2001: 202–3):

> Where people want mosques is in residential areas close to their houses so they can walk to the mosque, and in some respects the planning policy seems to favour that, but in practice it makes it impossible to do, and that's where you get problems.

None of these comments refutes the possibility that the use of premises in residential areas for religious activities can cause disturbance to neighbouring property owners. However, they articulate the view that the concern of planning with the external impact of religious practices may negate religious needs, rather than these concerns being balanced in relation to one another.

A further development of this theme was provided by another architect/designer, also a Muslim, who commented in relation to *madrasas* that, because such facilities are generally located within areas of predominantly

Muslim concentration, the concerns of planners over noise and disturbance tend to be exaggerated:

> You must have policies that look at the need of the community as well, because it is predominantly a Muslim community [in reference to Small Heath]. That noise and disturbance doesn't bother them, because to them, it's a holy thing to do, like in a church for example ... the Muslim community that's there, they are not going to feel bad about say half an hour of people coming and dropping kids off on the streets in cars, they won't feel bad about it.

According to the logic of this argument, the development of Muslim residential enclaves results not only in the spatial expression of Muslim religious practices (in particular, through the establishment of religious facilities), but also in the ways in which such practices are perceived by residents in the locality, on account of their shared religious belonging. This introduces a degree of cultural (and indeed spatial) relativity into questions over how activities are to be construed as intrusive, bringing into doubt – at least for this respondent – the view that notions such as 'noise' and 'disturbance' constitute objective, culturally independent criteria for establishing control over the impact of particular types of land use.

Other comments expressed the view that planning had played a role in either displacing or attempting to displace mosques from residential areas. Thus, one respondent commented:

> I've come across many, many applications where they want them to go into a factory or they want them to go and use commercial premises where, um, you know, they expect them to go to that site, and it's more appropriate if there's a purpose-built [facility] in the community.

One of the architects commented in a similar way upon a specific mosque that he had worked on in Birmingham:

> The one we did in [name of place], that is a conversion of three houses, there was a terrific amount of opposition to that.... They succeeded, they put the mosque at the back of the houses and they want to extend it now, and whether they'll be able to I don't know, but it's in the community and most people walk to it, so it's where they want it to be. They were offered a new site two miles away [by the City Council] and it's of no use to them at all.

Another theme that arose during the interviews concerned the professional attitudes of planning officers. One respondent was especially critical of the way applications from both Muslims and from other 'minority' [sic] groups were processed:

> I feel they [planning officers] look at it from 'how can I refuse the application?', you know? Mostly, when you're a planning officer, you should look at it, 'how can I approve this application?' right? Not 'how can I *refuse* the application'.... Not only that, the other thing is, I feel that 'who is the applicant?'—that shouldn't be the issue. Do you see what I'm saying? And to be honest, a lot of the time, those two elements crept [in].

From the viewpoint of this respondent, therefore, the attitudes of planners towards particular types of planning application and towards the identities of applicants themselves appeared to become infused into decision-making processes, thereby becoming inseparable from the resulting interpretation of planning law and policy.

A related sub-theme was that there were individuals within the planning department who, over time, had developed expertise that gave them insight into the planning requirements of the various religious groups. However, whilst indicating an essentially more positive assessment of the relationships between planning and faith communities than was implied in the previous quotation, such comments tended to be made by way of contrast with what was perceived to be planning officers' otherwise pervasive lack of awareness of the social and cultural needs of Muslim groups. Thus, one respondent referred to a development control officer in the following way:

> They [planners] don't understand, unless they're someone like [name of person], who has been dealing with the area for a long time. So he has got a better appreciation than someone who has just moved here from an area where there isn't [sic] any such community assets for which people need planning consents. So he will understand why do they [Muslim children] need to come to study at 4.30 [in the *madrasa*] after they have spent a whole day at school.

Not all of the remarks made during the interviews were censorious in tone. Thus, one respondent at a purpose-built mosque in Handsworth noted the improvements that had been made with regard to planning and the provision of facilities for Muslim communities in Birmingham:

> Well at the present moment, with the change of officers and with a few more Muslim councillors involved, we're getting co-operation from the city and from planning officers and funeral people, and we're having

> meetings with them to point out what our needs are. And I think once we can get them to understand what our needs are, we can go forward and get them to respond a bit quicker.

Similarly, other respondents referred to the "good relationships" that had been maintained with planners during the time that their planning applications were being processed. Thus, one respondent stated that "from the beginning, the City Council has been very co-operative". Similarly, a representative from another purpose-built mosque stated that "we've got a very good relationship, working with the planners." As such, it would be incorrect to suggest that there is anything approaching uniformity in the way in which Muslims in Birmingham perceive the policies and practices of the local planning authority. Nevertheless, this section of the chapter has highlighted some of the recurrent issues that have arisen through the interaction between Muslim groups and the planning process in the city.

6.3 Conclusion

In the time since Henry Hodgins' (1981) pioneering paper on mosques and the planning process, there have been significant changes in Birmingham in terms of how it constructs symbolically the religious buildings of different faith groups in the city. In the early 1980s, Hodgins noted that applications to develop purpose-built mosques were "submitted to pressure for them not to look like mosques", and that some were refused because their designs were considered "too Eastern" (Hodgins 1981: 19). However, since then, the discourse surrounding the architecture of purpose-built mosques has shifted, placing increasing emphasis both upon the role such buildings play in promoting the 'image' of the city, and upon the importance of the social functions they fulfil (Gale 2004). It is important to note in this context that many of the changes that have taken place have emerged through the sustained engagement of Muslim and other religious groups with planning bureaucracy. As the debate over the *azan* from the Central Mosque indicated, this engagement has often been productive in challenging the limits that have been imposed upon religious practices through planning constraints.

Nevertheless, some of the findings discussed in this chapter suggest that the planning process continues to present Muslims in Birmingham with a series of constraints that unduly restrict their religious observances. In areas where Muslims are highly concentrated, there is often a need for small, localised facilities that are accessible for daily use, both for prayers and for the after-school tuition of Muslim children. Whilst converted houses are often ideally suited to fulfilling these needs, in proportional terms, they also constitute the category that is most contested within planning procedure. It would be difficult to sustain the view, on the basis of these findings alone, that these tensions amount to what could be labelled as religious discrimination. However, at the very least, they suggest that there is a need to assess and continually monitor planning policies, in Birmingham and elsewhere, in terms of their impacts upon different religious groups.

Chapter 7 Alternative Dispute Resolution in a Diasporic Muslim Community in Britain

Mohamed Keshavjee

This chapter,[1] highlights the preliminary findings of a study still in progress which addresses the questions: in what ways do Muslims in the United Kingdom resolve their family disputes, and more specifically, what are the reasons for, and nature and significance of, a continuing preference on their part for reliance on the informal, primary decision-making processes in such disputes. The study examines the processes in a given UK-based community and explores how they are similar to, or different from, the processes followed by alternative dispute resolution (ADR) practitioners in the Anglo-American common law world – in particular, assessing their general efficacy and practicality. It shows how the principal players get engaged in the resolution of disputes, the understanding and role of the sharia – religious law of the Muslims – in this process, and how the laws of the land come to be invoked and why. The chapter outlines the various fora and the interactions that take place within them, explaining their choice, as well as the implications of the study on inter alia, ADR practice in the UK, ADR research direction, policy planning and legal education in Britain.[2]

---

1 The author has retained the copyright of this chapter and has given permission to the Publishers to publish it. Any further reference to the chapter or a republishing of it or any part of it will require specific permission from the author.

2 For the purposes of this study, 'mediation' has been defined "as a form of intervention involving a process by which a third party – the mediator – assists the parties to a dispute to negotiate over the issues that divide them". The mediator has no stake in the dispute and is not identified with any of the competing parties. The mediator has no power to impose a settlement on the parties, who retain authority for making their own decisions. The mediator is

Prakash Shah (ed.), Law and Ethnic Plurality: Socio-Legal Perspectives. *pp. 145-175.*
 ISBN 978 90 04 16245 7.

Given the dispersal of Muslims in the United Kingdom today, this study could well have been conducted in any part of the country. However, there were compelling reasons for conducting it in the Hounslow area of London. First, a study of this kind required a fairly organised group of immigrant Muslims, preferably homogenous in culture and linguistic background and constituting a critical mass. The Hounslow Muslim community of some 19,000 people, predominantly from the Indian subcontinent, provided this dimension. Secondly, it was felt that the research would gain a great deal if the bulk of the population under study was from the same jurisprudential school of Islam. The Hounslow Muslim community largely belongs to the Hanafi school of Islam.[3] The area, however, also has a smaller group of recently arrived immigrants from Somalia, most of whom belong to the Shafi school. This school is a sister Sunni school but its adherents are not included in the study.[4] Thirdly, the Muslim community in the Hounslow area reflects the main difficulties faced by any Muslim immigrant community going through the process of acculturation in Britain. While most other areas of Muslim settlement in the United Kingdom would have also provided this dimension, Hounslow, given its other advantages (e.g. proximity to various national institutions dealing with ADR), made for an appropriate context for this study. Fourthly, and most importantly, a study of this nature required the ability to gain sufficient access to people and issues – something that was not easy to obtain. The author, while studying for his LLM at London University, had conducted a small ethnographic study in the area and had established a good relationship with some of the people there. The present study was able to build on

therefore responsible for the conduct of the process – while the parties control the outcome. 'Arbitration', on the other hand, for the purposes of this study, involves an important independent third party hearing both sides on a matter and issuing a binding decision to resolve the dispute. 'Conciliation' refers to a process in which an impartial third party helps the parties to resolve their dispute by hearing both sides and offering an opinion on settlement. It has many overlaps with mediation.

3 This school emerged in Kufa, in present-day Iraq, under the eponym of Abu Hanifa (d. 767) but was developed by his students Abu Yusuf (d. 798) and al-Shaybani (d. 805). For further elaboration see Rippon (1990: ch. 6).

4 Al-Shafi'i (d. 822) was the eponymous founder of this school. He demanded the use of systematic reasoning without arbitrary or personalised deduction in formulating the law and thus created a system that was far more cohesive on a theoretical level than had previously been the case. Somali Muslims, although Sunni, come from a different racial, ethnic, linguistic and cultural background, hailing predominantly from Africa and, although they share the same mosque for prayers, they have their own specific issues and their own social welfare institutions to deal with them.

that relationship on a subject that is very delicate and sensitive because it involves religious law, religious sentiments, customary norms and practices, community institutions and above all, interpersonal relationships.[5] Finally, the Hounslow Muslims refer their jurisprudential matters to the Muslim Law (Sharia) Council (UK) at Ealing (hereinafter called the Muslim Law (Sharia) Council) with which its mosque has a privileged relationship. This study became possible largely through the trust relationship developed by the author with the Muslim Law (Sharia) Council and, more particularly, with its head, the late Dr Zaki Badawi, a former imam of the Regent's Street Mosque.[6] However, it must be stated that while this study was conducted in the Hounslow area of London, the context by no means constitutes a discrete hermetically-sealed geographical entity. Hounslow does 'spill over'. For example, some of the key respondents in this study live in Southall but attend the mosque in Hounslow for their services and other communal interactions. Others, such as Relate, the mediation agency which covers the area, is based in Harrow, while the Muslim Law (Sharia) Council, the point of reference for the imam of the Hounslow Mosque, is based in Ealing Common. Generally, the area merges seamlessly with other, contiguous boroughs and for this study to have taken an artificially–drawn, arbitrary boundary line, would not only have been inappropriate but would have deprived the study of the rich interactions that take place between people and institutions spontaneously across various borough lines in the field of dispute resolution.

7.1 Historical Connections between Muslims and Britain

Muslim presence in Britain goes back at least three hundred years to the time of the East India Company which recruited *lascars* – seamen from Yemen, Gujarat, Sind, Assam and Bengal who settled in different parts of the country (Runnymede Trust 1997: 13).[7] Many of these seamen settled

5 The author did his LLM at School of Oriental and African Studies (SOAS), University of London, in 1998-2000. As part of his ADR course, he undertook a short ethnographic study of the Hounslow Muslims titled: *The Mosque, Family Disputes and ADR in the UK: A Case Study*. This small (unpublished) study largely drew on the insights of a young imam from that area, Muhammad Yazdani Khan, who was a fellow student in the Islamic Law class at SOAS.

6 Dr Badawi assigned his senior-most scholar, Mawlana Shahid Raza Naimi, to assist the author in this work. Many issues with regard to the *sharia*, as they relate to the area and to the particular school of jurisprudence to which most of the Muslims of Hounslow belong, would not have been possible, without his assistance.

7 For a detailed account of the long Muslim settlement in Britain see Ansari (2004).

in port towns and cities in Britain and set up *zawiyahs* (places of prayer, generally associated with Sufi Islam[8]) which, in addition to being places of congregation, became arenas for celebration of rites of passage such as birth, marriage, circumcision and funerals. This connection with Muslim countries and Muslim peoples continued throughout the eighteenth and nineteenth centuries. In the 1920s and 1930s, a large proportion of Muslims were in the merchant navy and many of them stayed on in Britain after the Second World War. These pioneers acted as points of contact and sources of assistance for the substantial chain migration from East and West Pakistan that took place in the 1950s. Groups of Muslim intellectuals also emerged in Britain in the late nineteenth century (Lewis 1994: 13). Both in the last quarter of the nineteenth century and most of the twentieth century, Britain witnessed a steady flow of Muslim students from various colonial territories, and following their independence, from the member states of the British Commonwealth of Nations.

While the connection of the Muslims with Britain goes back some three centuries, migration to Britain on a large scale began only in the 1950s. According to Peach (1990: 13), the probable Muslim population of Britain in 1951 was about 23,000. Ten years later, it was 82,000 and by 1971, it was about 369,000. Migration was spurred on as a result of major labour shortages in Britain, particularly in the steel and textile industries of Yorkshire and Lancashire. Workers who first came to the United Kingdom were needed by the economy with "wages for labouring jobs in Britain in the early 1960s … over 30 times those in Pakistan" (Shaw 1988: 9). These workers came mainly from the Mirpur district of Azad Kashmir or from the North West Frontier region of Pakistan, or from the Sylhet area of Northeastern Bangladesh, known then as East Pakistan. Immigration to Britain was thus from a rural setting to an urban one, as well as to a different country and culture and involved an increase in wealth and income, as well as a change in occupation (Runnymede Trust 1997: 14). According to Modood (1990: 143-60), this group constitutes a "semi industrialised, newly urbanised working class community that is only one generation away from rural peasantry". Migrant workers also came from India – largely from three districts in Gujarat – Baroda, Surat and Bharuch – areas having a long tradition of migration and trading, especially with East Africa (Lewis 1994: 16).

About 15 per cent of the 150,000 Asians who came from the East African countries in the late 1960s and early 1970s were Muslims, with their family roots in Pakistan or Gujarat. In the 1970s also, substantial communities from Turkey and the Middle Eastern and North African countries

8 Term used for those who have chosen the path of mystical understanding and devotion to God. Sufism is the dimension of Islamic spirituality.

began to be established. Of late, Somali, Iranian, Arab and Bosnian communities have been established in many cities of Britain and more recently, following the breakdown of Communism in the former Soviet Union, followed by the civil wars in Yugoslavia, a number of Central Asian and Eastern European Muslims, respectively, have settled in Britain. It must be noted that Muslims from Yemen, though in smaller numbers, have had a very long connection with Britain, as have the Somalis – some of whom have been in the country for three to four generations. The 2001 Census data in Britain showed that Muslims make up 3.1 per cent of the population of Britain at around 1.6 million, projected to rise to 2 million by 2010. The largest group originates from Pakistan, followed by Bangladesh, India, Cyprus, Malaysia, Turkey, the Arab countries and parts of Africa.

In the early days, most Pakistani migrants to Britain saw themselves as temporary visitors who would one day return to their country of origin (Anwar 1979). By the 1960s, however, they began to see themselves as settlers, rather than as temporary residents. They established families whose future, it was increasingly clear, was going to be in Britain. A major impetus to this was the Commonwealth Immigrants Act 1962, for it was as a direct result of this legislation that families had to choose between being together in Britain or being divided for lengthy periods of time between Britain and Pakistan. In the five years, between 1961 and 1966, the Pakistani population grew by over 400 per cent, from about 25,000 to 120,000. Between 1973 and 1981, a further 82,000 people came as settlers, almost all of them being the dependents of men already in Britain (Runnymede Trust 1997: 15).

As a reflection of the transition from mere transients to settlers, British Muslims established a wide range of community organisations in the 1960s. They began to become more self consciously Muslim in their sense of identity than had previously been the case and more observant in the practice of their faith. Factors leading to this strengthening of their religious belief and practice included the desire to build a sense of corporate identity in a situation of material disadvantage in an alien culture; the desire, now that communities contained children on the one hand, and elders, on the other, to keep generations together and to transmit traditional values; and the desire for inner spiritual resources to withstand various pressures, for example racism, Islamophobia and the threat posed to their own customs and cultures by Western materialism and permissiveness (ibid.). Hence, for Muslims, a major preoccupation was to create "a space for Islam" in Britain. This took many shapes. The most visible was the establishment of mosques. Before 1964, only seven new mosques had been registered in Britain. In 1964, itself, a further seven were registered and over the next decade, there were about eight new registrations each year. From 1974 onwards, new registrations were running at 25-30 a year. The creation of mosques was both a cause and a consequence of increased self-definition and, in the autumn of 1996, it was estimated that there were 613 mosques in Britain, of which 96 were purpose-built (ibid.: 16).

7.2 Muslim Settlement in the Hounslow Area

The majority of the Muslims in the Greater Hounslow area come from the Indo-Pakistan subcontinent and the area reflects the same diversity and pluralism of Islam in Britain as is found elsewhere in the country. Ethnically, most of them are from Pakistan and comprise mainly two groups – the Kashmiris[9] and the Mirpuris.[10] There are, however, some people from other areas, as well, such as Gujarat in India, Central Africa, East Africa and most recently, Somalia.[11]

Asian settlement in the Hounslow area goes back to sometime in the 1950s, and in some cases, even earlier, with students from various parts of the British Empire coming to London to study and finding places to live in the area.[12] The major influx, however, started in the 1960s as part of the larger Muslim influx to Britain. This was mainly due to the labour shortage in the area and, more particularly, to the labour requirements of Heathrow airport and its allied services. It is not coincidental that among the early Muslim pioneers in the area who played such an important role in the establishment of the community, the majority were in the employ of the British Airport Authorities.[13]

Like Muslims elsewhere in the country the first immigrants to Hounslow came to Britain with a view to returning to their lands of origin (Anwar 1979). The Commonwealth Immigrants Act 1962 however imposed

9 Those people from the Pakistani side of the disputed territory of Kashmir.

10 People from the Mirpur district of Pakistan Punjab, many of whom got displaced in the 1960s when the Mangla Dam was constructed. Many of them got compensation and used this to immigrate into Britain in the 1960s.

11 One of the main respondents of this study, Soli Osman, a solicitor to the Trustees of the Hounslow Mosque, is from Malawi in Central Africa. His mother was born in Mozambique. According to him, Suleiman Chachia, one of the pioneers in the area and a leading social worker in the community, is also from Malawi and is a Memon Muslim. Two of the younger respondents, Samir and Shehbana Malik, are from Kenya. They are Punjabi Muslims. The author has often attended afternoon prayers at the Mosque and the congregation each day, largely made up of Pakistani Muslims, also includes some Arabs, Somalis and Eastern Europeans. The average daily congregation is around 60 people.

12 Although the census of 1921 showed the total number of Asians living in the whole county of Middlesex to be 84, it would not have been unusual to see Asians in the Isleworth area during the 1920s. See Chippendale (1993: 7).

13 These were Raja Yakub, the late Assen Shah and Haji Gondal. The latter two have been respondents in this study.

on immigrants in Britain an obligation to make a choice as to where they wished to make their definitive home. From that time Britain has been quite desperately seeking to control secondary immigration, that is, the settlement of spouses and other family members after primary immigration or labour migration was officially stopped since the 1962 Act. Immigration law has thus played a major role, both in Muslim settlement patterns in the UK, as well as on the nature and resolution of their inter-personal conflicts.

By 1970-71, the greater Hounslow area already had a small, but burgeoning, Asian population of which Muslims constituted a majority – some 2,500 to 3,500, scattered across the Great West Road. 1972 saw another major influx of Asians to the area, as a result of the Uganda Asian expulsion (Mamdani 1973, Listowel 1973, Melady and Melady 1976). Many of these new immigrants were Muslim. While the earlier influx was largely of semi-skilled workers, with some from the middle professional level who found work easily with the British Airport Authority, the later influx was largely of professional people and small businessmen – those who were known as *dukawallahs* in East Africa (Bhatia 1973) whose entrepreneurial vigour and settlement in Britain helped to revitalise the retail trade for the next three decades.

The nascent community faced many of the same problems as Muslims faced elsewhere in Britain. As in most cases, the first task of the community was to lay down the "infrastructure of continuity and belonging" (Sardar 2004: 22). This entailed ensuring that people were able to get together, at least once a week (on Fridays), in order to offer congregational prayers. Among the early pioneers who provided their residence for this purpose was Raja Yakub, a devout individual who espoused the vision that the community would one day have a purpose-built mosque in the area where everyone – regardless of denomination – would be able to come and pray. He instituted a system whereby each individual could give £1 a month to a fund from which communal expenses could be defrayed. From such a fund, he felt, one day a mosque could become a reality.[14]

Other concerns of the community at the time included a search for more 'Islamic' ways of doing things. These ranged from finding or establishing shops selling *halal* food and placing their children in schools with norms compatible with their 'Islamic' principles, to getting their marriage ceremonies recognised and ensuring that their customs and practices, particularly those having legal implications, conformed to the laws of the United Kingdom (Ashan 1995). The nascent Muslim community faced many other basic settlement problems. It had very few professional people. Those that had professional qualifications from back home found that

14 Soli Osman – interview, 21 August 2004.

these were not easily recognised and some had to go through protracted retraining at enormous cost, in order to follow their original professions.[15] Some were able to do so, while others just did not have the wherewithal to even consider the option.[16] The immediate preoccupation for the majority of the immigrants was to ensure that they got a job as soon as possible in order to be able to put food onto the table. In many cases, remittances had to be sent to India and Pakistan to support extended family members in the home countries – something that led to conflict between spouses in those initial days.[17]

To keep expenses at a minimum, men shared accommodation, even sharing a bed by using it according to the shifts they would be working. This was at a time when 'Pakibashing' was on the increase, with graffiti sprawled on walls asking for immigrants to "go back home". While the older generation had no choice but to accept such undignified behaviour, the younger generation, brought up in Britain, refused to accept the situation (Anwar 1991: 32). The riots in Southall in 1982, according to Soli Osman, were the turning point. Until then, Asians were seen as a docile and guileless group.[18]

For the early community, in addition to a number of socio-economic and racial problems, there were also emotional problems. For those who came with their families, there was some sort of support mechanism. Others faced serious problems of loneliness and, in some cases, depression. The major problems were lack of education, lack of linguistic proficiency, racism and the inability to find a suitable job compatible with the training they had received in the countries of their origin. To tide over some of these early settlement problems, community members came forth and offered their services. One Dr. Khan, President of the Pakistan Welfare Society – founded in the 1960s to help members of the Pakistani Muslim community settle down – ministered to people's problems. Often, he helped negotiate settlements when interpersonal problems cropped up – meeting people in his surgery. Problems generally revolved around husband and wife issues or issues engendered by forced marriages whereby a girl brought up in England would be forcibly married to a boy from Pakistan or India, who may not be of her educational level. In such cases, the first resort was usually to internal clan members.[19] The clan members always tried to effect a reconciliation. Generally, the divorce rate in the community was low

15 Taher Aslam – interview, 20 November 1998.

16 Hussein Qureishi – interview, 13 September 2004.

17 Assen Shah (late) – interview, April 1999.

18 Soli Osman – interview, 21 August 2004.

19 Assen Shah (late) – interview, April 1999.

– about 2 per cent. Since divorce would raise concerns about loss of *izzat* (family honour), the nascent community wanted to contain the matter and for many of them, "marriage becomes a value and if you value it, you hold on to it".

Another bulwark was to establish a permanent structure for congregational worship. It is often around a place of worship that a Muslim community normally organises its identity. It is also around such a place that their children learn the rudiments of the faith and where their rites of passage, such as those attendant on birth, marriage and death are performed. While the nascent community tried to contain its conflicts and challenges, it also laid down the principles of a community organisation and spent much of its time trying to establish more permanent structures. Among these, the construction of a purpose-built mosque became a priority and some of the same elders got involved in this endeavour.

The Hounslow Muslims spent many years in the early 1980s trying to get their own purpose-built mosque constructed, but this exercise proved to be a challenge. They set up the Hounslow Jamia Masjid Trust for this purpose and in the early 1980s, the Trust campaigned to build the mosque on a piece of land adjacent to the Heathland School in Hounslow. Over a protracted period of time objections were raised by the Heathland School, coupled with complaints from the neighbours that the mosque would upset the peace and tranquillity of the area. Following a series of applications and appeals, permission was finally granted. No sooner was this sorted out, the Trust ran out of funds and was unable to commence construction within the time allowed under the terms of the planning permission. The Trust was then obliged to start all over again. One of the elders, Suleiman Chachia, a Trustee, went to Pakistan and managed to raise some money, although this was nowhere near enough to build the mosque.

In 1991, the Trust launched another application, and this time, the objections from the neighbourhood were even more virulent. A series of hearings took place in 1991 and in August 1992, the Government decided to finally back the Hounslow Muslim community and gave the Trust the go ahead to begin construction. The Environment Secretary's seal of approval brought to an end a bitter 11-year battle between the mosque Trustees and the neighbours along the road where the mosque was to be built.

The Jamia Mosque, as it is called, has also given the first generation immigrant Muslims in the area a greater sense of belonging and rootedness. It has become an important focal point of their religious formation and identity. Completed in 1998, with its beautiful 46 feet high dome and 65 feet high minaret, directly below the flight path of the aircraft landing at Heathrow airport at the rate of one every minute, the mosque stands as a silent but eloquent witness to the long struggle on the part of the Muslims of Hounslow to be recognised in their own right as part of the multiethnic mosaic of Britain. The sense of pride and belonging it has engendered in them is quite palpable on the faces of the many worshippers who use its services every day.[20]

7.3 The Interface of Religious Law and Customs with British Laws

Religious law governs many aspects of the lives of Muslims today and constitutes a critical element in any discussion about the application of the principles of their faith to their contemporary needs. Despite modifications to the *sharia* in countries of the Muslim world, according to Coulson (1964: 147), Muslims still regard its family law aspects as an integral part of the scheme of religious duties. Consequently, for them, the classical doctrine of the Arab authorities remains inviolate as expressing the only standards of conduct valid in the eyes of God and any "such deviations from this norm", condoned as legal practice in certain areas is "never recognised as legitimate expressions of Islamic law" (ibid.). This issue still lies at the heart of the challenge facing Muslim societies today, that is, how to reconcile their religious law with their obligations as citizens of a secular, non-Islamic nation state (Ansari 2002: 22). This matter also came up for discussion at a conference on Islam in Britain in 2004 where it was stated that Muslims in Britain want greater recognition of their faith with the introduction of Islamic law for civil cases.[21] It is in the realm of the family and all the interactions that take place within it that this challenge is most strongly felt.

The family is a central institution in Muslim society. In Britain, most families today have to cope with problems of rapid urbanisation and the pressures of living in cramped conditions in cities. This has had an impact on Muslim family relationships. Although there has been an alarming increase in divorce rates among Muslims, Muslim marriages tend to be more stable than Western ones, because they are based on a different set of assumptions. According to Ahmed (Ahmed 2002: 150), these assumptions

20 On a weekday, between 50 and 75 male worshippers attend the afternoon prayer session (*zuhr*) which is often followed by a sermon by the imam in English. On one occasion, in May 2004, the sermon touched on conflict resolution where the imam cited the example of Prophet Muhammad (PBUH) saying that Hazrat Abu Bakr, the first Caliph, was once talking to an individual in the presence of the Prophet and during this discussion, an argument ensued and Abu Bakr lost his temper, at which point the Prophet walked away. When asked by Abu Bakr why he did this, the Prophet's response was that when Abu Bakr kept his composure even the angels were with him but when he lost his temper they abandoned him and therefore he (the Prophet), as well, followed suit.

21 *Guardian*, 30 November 2004, *"British Muslims want Islamic Law and Prayers at Work"*, <http://www.guardian.co.uk/uknews/story/o,,1362533,00.htlm>.

are founded in the Muslim notion of the cosmos. As there is order and balance in the universe, there is a similar natural pattern in society, which is reflected in the Muslim household. In a conceptual sense, one mirrors the other, with each individual member playing an equally significant role in his or her own capacity which is related to the other members of the family. The family in Islam is a divinely inspired institution that came into existence with the creation of man. "The human race is a product of this institution and not the other way round" (Ahmed 1974: 13). Not surprisingly, the most intricate rules and regulations guide family life. Almost a third of the legal injunctions in the Quran deal with family matters (Ahmed 2002: 150).

The areas in which a Muslim family normally faces difficulties in living in Britain include marriage, *iddat* (the waiting period after termination of marriage), *mahr* (the contractual sum due to a woman in the event of a divorce), custody of children, mixed marriages, plural marriages, change of faith and inheritance.

Marriage in Islam is an essential part of the Islamic way of life. It is the only way in which a man and a woman may lawfully have sexual contact and establish a stable relationship based on mutual love, affection and psychological, emotional and spiritual support. Marriage is essential to keep the relationship between the two individuals and families prosperous and happy, as it is to preserve the human race, Islamic values and Islamic traditions (Ahsan 1995: 22). An important misgiving which many people in the West have about a Muslim marriage is the role of the parents in arranging a marriage for their children and the right of the girl to accept or reject such an arrangement. In Islam, both sons and daughters have an absolute right to select their partner and fashion their future life within the framework of Islam. However, while in theory, this right exists, in practice, parents tend to arrange the marriage of their children although arranged marriages do not appear to be very prevalent in the Hounslow area. For some reason, this study has not been able to locate many examples but that does not mean that the problem does not exist. It bears mentioning that many debates take place today over the rights of a *wali* to give a woman in marriage, a particularly problematic issue for Hanafi South Asian Muslims, both in Pakistan as well as in the United Kingdom.

Dissolution of marriage is another area where the interface between the *Sharia* and the laws of the United Kingdom can be problematic. Although marriage is described in the Quran as a strong and binding contract (*mithaqan ghaliza*), it is not a sacrament or indissoluble. Islam permits divorce, but only as a last resort and refers to this option as "the most abominable of permissible acts" (*abghaz al mubahat*). Islam, contrary to popular belief, also allows women the right to divorce in certain circumstances. A woman can repudiate her marriage under a form of divorce, known as *Khula*.[22] Since the Muslim law of divorce is not recognised by the laws of the United Kingdom, Muslims cannot simply follow the laws as given by Islam. Should a Muslim couple decide to divorce, the matter must go through an English Court. Muslim women in the United Kingdom face an added difficulty: even the granting of a divorce by an English Court does not entitle a Muslim woman to marry someone else under Islamic law. The divorce has to be 'Islamised' so that she can marry again.[23]

Mahr or dower is another such situation where British laws do not recognise the right inherent in a Muslim marriage. The Quran commands men "to give women their dower". This is a contractual sum stipulated in the marriage contract and payable to the wife by the husband. The effect of this is simple. The Quranic rule, then, is to transfer the wife from the position of a sale-object to that of a contracting party, thus giving her a legal competence she did not possess before (Coulson 1964: 14).

Another area where Islamic law differs considerably from British laws is with regard to custody. Young children (the boy up to the age of 9 and the girl, up to puberty or marriage, depending upon the specific school of Muslim law) remain in the custody of their divorced mother. As long as she nurses the young children and looks after the others, it is the father's responsibility to bear the full cost of their care. In addition, he alone, is responsible for their housing, clothing and food, even though they are in the mother's custody or home. This is one area where a great deal of conflict takes place, particularly in the case of mixed marriages.[24] The problem becomes more complicated when a Muslim parent abducts an infant and takes it back to a Muslim country. With the majority of Muslim countries not being parties to the Hague Convention dealing with the abduction of children, this gives rise to great hardship to the other spouse (usually a woman) even if she has converted to Islam.

A Muslim is not allowed to marry a non-Muslim whether such a person is a Hindu, Sikh or follower of any other religion. The only exception is given in respect of the People of the Book – *Ahl al Kitab* – that is, for Christians and Jews and applies to women only. Thus, under Islamic law, a Muslim man can marry a Christian or Jewish woman, but a Muslim woman cannot marry a man of a Christian or Jewish faith without his having to convert to Islam. This whole subject of mixed marriages has implications on the issue of dower rights and the rights of a non-Muslim wife to have

22 Divorce obtained by a wife when she gives or agrees to give consideration to the husband for her release and the husband accepts the offer.

23 Zaki Badawi interview, 27 July 2002.

24 Mixed marriages, for the purposes of this study, is where one party is a Muslim and the other is a non-Muslim. In most cases, it involves a marriage where one party is 'white' British, and married to a Muslim born within the faith.

control of her property. It also has some implications on the issue of custody and access as well as on the right to inheritance (Ahsan 1995: 26).

Polygamy is another area where British laws clash with Islamic law. Under Islamic law, a Muslim man is allowed to marry up to four wives, but this permission is hedged around some strict conventions. British laws do not allow Muslim men to take a second wife. As Islam forbids extramarital relations, Muslims are not permitted to have extramarital relationships or live together outside wedlock. The concepts of cohabiting through unmarried partners, the unmarried mother or bachelor father, are foreign to Islam and regarded as abhorrent aberrations (ibid.).

In the field of inheritance law, Muslims in Britain also face difficulties. Islamic law of inheritance is very comprehensive in nature and is based on doing justice to all the members of the extended family, according to their rights and responsibilities. Western laws of inheritance are completely different from the *Sharia* and if a Muslim wishes to divest of his property according to the principles of Islamic law, he would have to do this by will. Although this practice is not yet widespread, some Muslims authorise well-qualified and knowledgeable individuals to distribute their inheritance according to Islamic principles in their wills (ibid.).[25]

Before embarking on a discussion of the various agencies and institutions to which disputants resort in the event of a conflict, it would be important to review some general or common perceptions about the *sharia* in order to appreciate the fact that for a Muslim in the United Kingdom, the choice of resorting to 'the law' or resorting to 'ADR' is not a simple matter. Muslim family disputes have many complex legal dimensions and in most cases, law and ADR have to work in very close collaboration in order to resolve an issue. It is not a simple either/or situation but more one of finding the 'forum to meet the fuss'.

7.4 Stereotypes and Knowledge Gaps

The *sharia* is a complex phenomenon and its interface with various laws and conventions gives rise to a host of potential conflicts and tensions (Coulson 1969), many of which Muslim institutions as well as ADR organisations find difficult to come to grips with. This issue features prominently in this study.

Before the establishment of the Muslim Law (Sharia) Council at Ealing, religious law issues were handled by the Hounslow community itself, largely through their elders, or by the imams of the mosque. Often, cases would get referred for a *fatwa* to a jurisconsult and matters would get resolved in the normal course of things. The issue of the 'Islamising' of a divorce granted to a Muslim wife by a UK Court did not really arise and

25 Also Zaki Badawi – interview, 10 May 2005.

for those women who wanted to remarry Islamically, there was unfortunately no recourse because there was no competent '*sharia*' court available in the UK to do so (Shah-Kazemi 2001). Generally, while the process of acculturation was still in its initial stages, people accepted what was told to them and this was a period when a fair amount of forced marriages took place across the country, under the garb of the practice being part of Islamic law. With the effluxion of time, as children grew up in Britain, they began to question this notion and asked whether this was really something 'Islamic' or whether it was a customary practice from back home masquerading as 'the law'. A distinction had to be made between principles of the faith which were immutable and transcendent and practices that were time-specific and contingent and therefore, depending on the particular context, subject to change under the principles of *darura* (necessity) and *maslaha* (public interest) – principles of classical Islamic law. Important changes have taken place in Islamic personal law in many Muslim countries since the early twentieth century. Unfortunately, these changes do not get reported in the media. The media, often, emphasises the more sensational cases which range from the call for stoning for adultery of a woman in Nigeria and the call for the excommunication of an author in Egypt to the clamour for the execution of an aid worker in Afghanistan for apostasy and the whipping of a female victim of rape in Pakistan for not being able to produce the four witnesses hitherto required under the Hudood Ordinance.

Very little is really known about the transformation of "jurisprudential thought, from its traditional attitude of detached idealism to a functional approach to the question of law in society", (Coulson 1969: 107) which have made the "courts applying Sharia law to deal with the problems of society [in such a manner] so that they now assume, to a much greater extent than hitherto, the responsibility of organs of real social purpose" (p. 108). The effect today is that the external perception of the religious law is still very negative while those who adhere to the faith tend, at times, to have a reified impression of it, either essentialising it or anchoring it in time. To a large extent, however, people today tend more to follow the ethics behind the law and let these guide them in their general relationships unless specific rulings are warranted for any specific purpose.

The imams are generally well versed in the normative dimensions of the law but do not seem to have a clear understanding of how these interface with the laws of the country. For this, they defer to the Muslim Law (Sharia) Council in Ealing. It bears mentioning that while the imams may not be knowledgeable about the interface with official British laws, they are very conscious of their existence and gladly defer to the Muslim Law (Sharia) Council for help and guidance on matters in which they do not feel they have the legal competence. This realisation of the need for a better understanding of the *sharia* and a recognition of the limitations of various agencies and institutions to deal effectively with *sharia* issues and their interface with the laws of the land have been an important determinant in the choice of the forum to which disputants resort in the case of their disputes.

7.5 Main Fora to which Disputants Resort

Disputants generally go to the forum they feel is best able to help them. Sometimes, the help required is immediate, as in the case of domestic violence while at other times, the issue may involve a complex *sharia* dimension in which case, through proper referrals, a disputant will end up with an agency that is able to help. Sometimes two or even three agencies may be simultaneously involved. Sometimes the involvement is sequential. The agencies do not rank in hierarchy. Most often, people's choices will depend on a number of variables including the cultural, socio-economic and educational. The main agencies to which the Hounslow Muslims resort are: the imams of the mosque, the *biradaris*, the Pakistan Welfare Association, the elders, the Muslim Women's Helpline, the police, the solicitors, the ADR agencies and the Muslim Law (Sharia) Council in Ealing.

7.5.1 The Imams

These are the male religious functionaries who are attached to the mosque and are responsible for leading the prayers. In addition, they attend to many other functions such as officiating at marriages and funerals, delivering the daily *khutba* and rendering pastoral care. The study shows that the imams do play an important, although not an extensive or even exclusive, role in dispute resolution in the community.

Contrary to popular perception, the imams are sensitive to the changing times and as many female informants who intuitively felt that they were not clued in with the times, were matched by an equal number who actually felt that they were and had proved this. The general impression seems to have gained currency because of two factors: first that some women tend to feel that the application of the *sharia* is patriarchal in its bias and the imam, by virtue of being a custodian of this tradition, will take a male-dominated approach and secondly, women do not usually attend the mosque for daily prayers. The imam thus gets automatically implicated in a stereotypical image. In reality, this study shows that not only does the imam get consulted but often also participates actively in resolving disputes.[26]

26 Two incidents that the author has personally witnessed attest to this. While the author was a student at London University doing his LLM, he studied with a young imam, Mohamed Yaazdani Khan who was attached to the Hounslow mosque at the time. On various occasions, the imam would receive a call on his mobile from a woman congregant who wanted to know of her rights under

The imam's scope in dispute resolution is constrained by various factors. First, not all the Muslims in the area are regular mosque-going Muslims with the result that not everyone would bring their dispute to the imam. Secondly, the imam is always pressed for time – he has to attend to many other daily activities to service the needs of the community. Thirdly, he is in the employ of the Trustees of the mosque and this calls for great diplomacy as intra-trustee disputes can become problematic and the imam has to ensure that he does not upset any sensibilities. Fourthly, and most importantly, while he knows the *sharia* principles, he would not be competent to deal with their interface with the laws of the land, particularly in issues such as custody, divorce and inheritance matters. Lastly, he has no enforcement powers.

The imams use traditional methods of dispute resolution and although they may not utilise key mediator skills as these are known in contemporary ADR terminology, there is a great deal of resonance between what they do and what exists in the ADR toolbox such as engaging the parties, active listening and trying to understand the viewpoints of both the parties. The imam does not 'mediate' in the technical sense of the term. Parties come to him voluntarily and he facilitates the discussion but the primary role he plays is in enunciating the *sharia* and leaving it to their individual conscience to decide what they wish to do. He deals with issues such as anger management and here he draws from the example of Prophet Muhammad (PBUH), extolling his virtues when similar situations arose. The imam often quotes Ayats from the Quran with regard to dispute resolution and in specific cases refers to principles of Hanafi jurisprudence by citing from texts and commentaries on Hanafi law such as the *Hidaya* and *al Fatawa al Alimgirriya*.[27] The imam has no enforcement authority. By and large, his force is moral and for those who wish to remain within the community and abide by its norms, the imam's advice would have persuasive authority.

the *Sharia* as her husband would want her to leave the matrimonial home and the children. In the second incident, when this study commenced, Shahid Raza Naimi of the Muslim College (Sharia) Council personally escorted the author and introduced him to Imam Sulaymani of the Hounslow Mosque. While the author was in the office, an irate man barged in and asked the imam to intervene with his in-laws who had gone to the lawyers to get an injunction preventing him from talking to his wife or to themselves except through the lawyer.

27 These are texts and commentaries based on the principles of Hanafi law which imams and muftis refer to. See Masud, Messick and Powers (1996: 14).

7.5.2 The Biradaris

Although the great majority of South Asian Muslim households are physically nuclear and comprise of a man, his wife and their children, most such households have other close relatives living nearby: this may include as many as ten further households. Extended kinship networks of this kind are normally identified as a *biradari*. The *biradari* is best understood as a context-dependent idea, rather than a rigid and concrete entity. Thus, besides its local manifestation as a network of co-resident kin, it may also include relatives elsewhere in Britain, and in its widest extent may span different countries. Indeed, when only few members live locally, a family may well consider this trans-national network of relatives as constituting a *biradari* (Alavi 1972: 2).

The *biradaris*' approach to dealing with disputes would be broadly patriarchal but largely benign – using their influence and their largely pre-immigration cultural norms and values as guiding principles.[28] Given the general predilection on their part not to speak about family disputes to people outside their close-knit clan, not many people would get to know about a dispute – not even the imam of the mosque. By and large, on the altar of clan harmony and group cohesiveness, disputants are encouraged to settle their disputes amicably within the principles of customary practices and, where it helps, general Islamic principles are cited to effect a reconciliation between the parties. The *biradaris* still operate within a very close-knit circle. In the Hounslow area, they are estimated to constitute some 20-30 per cent of the population, mainly made up of the *Mirpuris*. Their intervention in dispute resolution can only be invoked by their own clan members.

7.5.3 The Pakistan Welfare Association (PWA)

This organisation, a charity registered with the Charity Commission was established in the London Borough of Hounslow in 1966 with the aim "to relieve the inhabitants of the London Borough of Hounslow and its adjacent towns, particularly those of Pakistani origin or descent who are in condition of need, hardship or distress". The Association today provides advice and counselling and represents some 6.5 per cent of the population of the Borough. The PWA's main remit when it was established in 1966, was to help newly-arrived immigrants from Pakistan to settle down in the area. This included a host of services ranging from identifying suitable places for

28 For this study it was not possible to meet with the *biradaris* but whatever has been gleaned is through a third party who belongs to a *biradari* whose members helped his mother when she was having a divorce with his father. The respondent was too young at the time to understand all the processes but feels that they were very supportive and fair to his mother.

worship and negotiating for Muslim burial facilities to imparting cultural education in Urdu and Arabic to children in the weekends and helping people find jobs and suitable housing. As the population increased, many of their original activities got hived off and allocated to specific committees more suitable to do certain tasks.

Many of the elders who got involved in solving inter-personal disputes were initially associated with the PWA. Hussain Qureishi, its General Secretary at the time of this study, originally got involved with some of the founding members in the 1960s. The PWA today deals with peoples' interpersonal problems and has a trained social worker, Anila Chaudary, who is a community development officer with the organisation. She has trained with the Federation of Independent Advice Centres and normally handles issues of domestic abuse. People come to the organisation through referrals or reading about the service in the Muslim Directory. They come for advice on housing matters and financial issues. Domestic violence, most often, is linked to the request for housing. The service does not provide mediation in the sense that it is known today in ADR terminology. Women tend to feel more comfortable coming to the PWA and discussing their issues because such facilities are not readily available to them in the mosques. The service generally comprises listening to people and helping them apply to the appropriate social services – assistance which is more akin to counselling than mediation.

With regard to *sharia* issues, according to a co-worker with the organisation, people today prefer going direct to the Muslim Law (Sharia) Council, because they find it more professional and affording greater confidentiality. Also, in the earlier days of settlement, people were more amenable to utilising the support afforded by the extended family. This is reducing in significance at a time when people arguably need it most. Another phenomenon they noticed was the plight of the estranged husband, often it is a sponsored immigrant who, in the event of a personal dispute, found himself totally helpless and at the mercy of the in-laws who sponsored his immigration into the UK. Power imbalances in mediatory contexts normally tend to be associated with female victims (Grillo 1991: 1545-1610), but despite a so-called patriarchal cultural background, this study found that male spouses are often also victims of a power imbalance. Often, the PWA is unable to assist in such cases beyond basic relief assistance. Whether mediation even works in such situations is a moot point. Individuals generally get referred to a solicitor for specialised assistance.

7.5.4 The Elders

The Hounslow area has a cluster of adults who constitute a discrete although informal group of dispute resolvers. They include two lawyers, an ex-teacher, a chartered accountant and a medical practitioner – all of whom are semi-retired or in civic services. All of them, at one time or the other, were involved with the PWA. Although they do not identify themselves as a group, they do get called upon to negotiate in peoples' disputes. Their position as respectable elders was earned during their hard work for the construction of the Jamia Mosque as well as in the PWA.

In dealing with inter-personal disputes, they largely give advice to disputing parties, exhorting them to appreciate the value of compromise by reminding them of the harm that would befall their families and their children if they divorced. Given the early nature of the settlement, coupled with the basic type of issues the nascent community then faced, there was a general degree of receptivity on their part to this type of advice. The elders had no special knowledge of the *sharia*, as such, but understood the general ethics of the faith which teaches compassion, tolerance, equity and fairness. The elders fully recognised that their advice carried no legal weight and that anything that was agreed upon could be easily reneged upon. In dealing with issues they are seen as acting with integrity, impartiality and fairness. One of them, Mo. Chaudary, has become a Town Counsellor for the area. In this capacity, he is able to refer people to the proper social services departments. Another, Ashraf Gondal, has since become a member of the Mosque Funeral Committee. A medical practitioner, Bhabi Khatija continues to do a great deal of social work. The techniques that this group uses are neither mediation nor arbitration, but a combination of various approaches which encompass counselling, exhorting and cajoling – all closer to the directive end of the mediation spectrum.

In keeping with Islam's general injunction, they always emphasise reconciliation as a virtue to be followed by stressing on the Prophet's hadith which says that of all things abhorrent, divorce is the most abhorrent of acts. Hence, their major focus has always been on reconciling disputing parties. The elders still play some role in this field, but given the complex nature of issues today and the availability of a greater number of services such as Muslim solicitors and *sharia* specialists, the role of the elder dispute resolver is slowly beginning to wane – something that the elders regret and attribute (somewhat mistakenly) to the blind acceptance of the values of the host culture by the new generation brought up in Britain.

7.5.5 The Muslim Women's Helpline (MWH)

This agency, a telephone-based emotional support service for Muslim women, was started in 1989 by a small group of volunteer Muslim women. The organisation does not get involved directly in mediation and reconciliation but provides support by referring callers to organisations that provide such services. The MWH is self funding and operates on a very small budget – always finding itself strapped for resources. Sara Shariff, one of the founding members of the organisation felt that many of the type of disputes that come to the MWH would clearly be amenable to arbitration or mediation but, very often, Muslim women do not want any external interventions in their inter-personal problems, as they feel that such intervention would exacerbate the situation. So, often the agency is sworn to secrecy, as women do not wish their husbands or their fathers to know that they have spoken to someone outside the immediate family. Women generally get to know of the agency through friends or even statutory organisations – many of whose websites have MWH's contact address on them. MWH's work indicates that conflict is still a very private matter among Muslims in a diasporic context and people are often not able to get the appropriate services because they cannot even speak of this to anyone else. Despite this constraint, people still tend to have very high expectations about what the agency can do for them at a time when they are "distressed, confused and not knowing what to do".

Generally, women feel very comforted when they know that someone has listened to them and acknowledged that they have a grievance. They feel a greater sense of comfort when this is done anonymously, given the fear that some of them live under. According to Shariff, just listening to them gives them a sense of empowerment and they do not wish to go to anyone else. They begin to look at their issues themselves.[29]

The service which receives between 1800 and 2000 callers a year provides advice to people on matters ranging from inter-generational clashes and matrimonial matters to domestic violence and requests for housing. The agency shies away from immigration and financial problems as it does not have the wherewithal to deal with follow ups. Matrimonial matters top their list of issues. The agency generally refers people to specific social service agencies which people are afraid to contact directly. On *sharia*-related issues, the agency refers to specific muftis (jurisconsults) as well as to the Muslim Law (Sharia) Council. In this way, the mufti makes his opinion confidentially known to an anonymous caller thus adding to the level of comfort and trust.

Mediation is not really known by the callers and often, when it is suggested, the response is: "my husband would never agree to that". According to Najma Ibrahim, one of the officers, Muslims in Britain come from countries where they have never had to mediate in a structured manner. People come from villages and towns where there was a head of the family or an uncle to whom people would go. They would talk to such people and the problem would get sorted out. Today, those people have disappeared.[30]

29 Sara Shariff – interview, 1 September 2004.

30 Najma Ibrahim – interview, 1 September 2004.

7.5.6 *The Police*

The imams have no enforcing powers and many issues associated with a dispute require urgent attention – issues such as emergency help in the case of domestic violence. It is here that the police come in and play an important role. Although they do not 'mediate' as such, in the true sense of the word, their intervention is very much mediatory and critical. Their understanding of cultural issues and religious sensibilities could help, and in the past has helped, solve many problems at the earlier stages of a dispute. Disputants often resort to the Hounslow Police for help in their inter-personal issues.

In the case of the Hounslow area, one police officer, Peter Jordan, spent 15 years of his 35 year tenure with the Metropolitan Police Force in the Hounslow area. Having been a Community Beat Officer for 9 of these 15 years, he found himself in the midst of all the problems that arose as a result of the construction of the mosque. He noticed the racism the community was facing and became a part of the committee involved in the mosque development with a view to getting a 'hands-on' understanding of the issues. Through this involvement he got to know many of the children who were then growing up in the area and a strong trust relationship developed between them. Jordan saw the community undergoing a process of acculturation and trained other officers within the police force to understand different cultural mores. Understanding the need to help without causing any destabilisation in the community, he developed the concept of 'third party reporting', making Hounslow the first Borough in the country to introduce a system whereby a woman could go to a mosque or a *gurudwara*, and report a crime and a third party could go to the police station and report this on her behalf. Over a period of time, the police got socialised to the cultural specificities of the Muslim community in the area. The police force also became sensitive to the extended family networks which helped them to gain a deeper insight on how to manage domestic abuse in the general Asian community. The trust that developed over a three-decade period made the police force an even more important agency for disputants to resort to in the event of their inter-personal disputes. [31]

7.5.7 *The Solicitors*

The Hounslow area has a small number of Muslim lawyers but the mosque seems to have a very close rapport mainly with one of them, Soli Osman, who was brought up in the area and today renders voluntary service to the trustees and many of the congregants. Disputants resort to him not only when there is an impasse on an issue but also in the normal course of a dispute such as a divorce. Since divorces have to go through the official courts Osman helps by referring people to appropriate solicitors who deal

31 Peter Jordan, interview, 1 December 2005.

with divorce matters. Generally, the imam of the mosque refers matters to him which have an immigration dimension or a public law element, or where matters of custody or abduction are involved. In general, regardless of the fora to which disputants otherwise resort, solicitors will invariably be involved. As a Muslim solicitor, Osman tries to help effect a reconciliation wherever this is possible. Although law in many areas is premised on an adversarial process, he still favours mediation and whenever parties can be encouraged to indulge in a negotiated settlement, he promotes the process.

Osman's remit as a lawyer also includes advising both the mosque functionaries as well as individual congregants about the interface of various cultural practices and the principles of English law. He cites the example of a phone call he received once in the middle of the night from a family in Cardiff that wanted to abduct their daughter and send her out to another country to forcibly marry a relative because she had fallen in love with someone the family did not approve of. He immediately admonished caution and asked everyone to calm down reminding them that such actions would amount to the violation of the criminal law since the family wanted to sedate the girl and put her on an outward bound plane. The processes the solicitor utilises are a combination of adversarial ones and mediation, but tempered by community and faith considerations, where applicable, without infringing the laws of the country.[32]

7.5.8 The ADR Agencies

Various ADR agencies service the area. For this study, four of the main ones were interviewed. These are: Relate, Mediation in Divorce (MID), the National Children's Home (NCH) and Hillingdon Mediation Services. Muslim disputants in the area go to any of these depending on their needs and whether they get referred to them by the Social Services.

Relate is a charity which gets its referrals from the Legal Services Commission. They do homeless mediation which, at times, has a domestic violence and immigration dimension to it. The agency has no contact with the Hounslow Mosque or the Muslim Law (Sharia) Council. One area where it has great resonance with the mosque and the Sharia Council is its emphasis on reconciliation where this is possible. The agency always leaves it to the parties themselves to come to that decision and offers a counselling service to facilitate that. People come to the service primarily because of homelessness. Disputants may be inclined to go to the mosque first but often they have been advised to try and keep the marriage alive and, in situations when that is not possible, there is no real alternative. The approach

32 Since this study started some 5 years ago, Soli Osman has himself taken up a course in mediation and has introduced mediation in his practice.

the agency uses is mediation as it is understood in the contemporary ADR terminology.

Mediation in Divorce (MID), based in East Twickenham, also does mediation. It is a non-governmental agency whose clients get referred by solicitors, general medical practitioners, health visitors, self referrals as well as the Legal Services Commission. Despite its name, MID's main remit is to assist young people as a result of the British Government, in April 2002, placing upon the Local Authorities the responsibility for assisting young people up to the age of eighteen. This is the age when young people leave home and there is a great deal of homelessness. The agency tries to help a young person and the parents repair and preserve their relationship. This is consistent with Fuller's idea of the central quality of mediation, as lying "in its capacity to reorientate the parties towards each other… by helping them achieve a new and shared perception of their relationship" (Fuller 1971: 305-39). The agency deals with issues affecting the Muslim community in the Hounslow area when children leave their homes as a result of inter-generational tensions.

The agency attempts to be culturally sensitive but has no real contact with the Muslim community as such. The approach that is followed is mediation according to the way it is understood in contemporary ADR terminology. MID also provides counselling services and often asks people from different cultural backgrounds whether they would like a counsellor from their own community. Responses to such a question vary. Some would like someone from their own background whereas others will say that the confidentiality aspect will be compromised. The agency also provides All-Issues mediation.

The National Children's Home (NCH), started by a Methodist minister some 150 years ago with its head office today located in Highbury, offers residential accommodation to children with disabilities. It offers family group conferencing in cases of family conflict where the family recognises that the child needs to stay within the family. Space is given to family members and friends who are close enough to the family to come together and to work out a plan for the young person. 'Family' includes the extended family, i.e. grandparents, uncles, aunts and friends. The family itself works out the plan and the child has a say in what the family thinks is best. The service operates under the Children Act 1989 and the Children Act 2000. The spirit behind the whole approach is that families themselves are experts on what works best for them – therefore it leaves it to them to work out their arrangements. The system is voluntary and any party can leave the process at any stage. The NCH does not deal with issues affecting children at the time of a divorce. These are issues that would go to mediation rather than the social services.

The Asian community today seems to be using the social services more than they did in the past. This possibly is due to greater socialisation and confidence. In the past, there was a stigma attached to getting help for a family that may have become dysfunctional but today the understanding is changing. The NCH works with various communities although it does not have any contact with the mosque. NCH's main focus is social work but the techniques it employs are very close to mediation such as voluntariness, allowing each person to put his viewpoints forward, listening to each party, showing neutrality and impartiality, and exercising complete confidentiality, unless a child is in physical danger. NCH also has ground rules akin to mediation such as "not interrupting, listening to what they had to say and then responding after they had finished".[33]

Hillingdon Mediation Services, established in April 2000, provide mediation in neighbourhood disputes. Family disputes are seen to be a more specialised area related to the courts and the service therefore does not involve itself in them. This is left to Relate which covers Hillingdon, Ealing, Brent, Harrow and Uxbridge.

Although family disputes are not within the remit of the agency, it can mediate over them – on a remunerated basis. People do approach the agency but they do not really come back. The agency is not keen on taking on matters for which they are not funded as they already have more cases than they can handle with regard to neighbourhood disputes.

7.6 Situations where ADR may not Work or Work Partially

There is an axiom that mediation works best when parties go to it voluntarily. Equally, it must be recognised that where one party refuses to go to mediation, it cannot take place at all. In such a case, the official law is the only recourse. Also, certain types of issues are only amenable to a legally-determinable treatment because of their very nature. Family dispute situations in the UK where the official law has had to intervene include custody cases, child abduction cases, issues of forced marriage, disputes with an immigration element and divorce. In all these cases, negotiation, wherever it has been possible, always has to take place "within the shadow of the law" (Mnookin and Kornhauser 1979). In some cases, lack of enforceability of an agreement may lead to the invocation of the official law. The payment of a dower right (*mahr*) is a case in point.

In the case of *Shahnaz v Rizwan* ([1965] 1. QBD 390), the parties had married in accordance with Muslim law in India. The fact that the marriage had been concluded in accordance with Islamic Law presented the court with jurisdictional problems. The court resolved this problem by treating the claim of the wife as a contractual, rather than a matrimonial matter.

33 Angie Moore, interview, 11 May 2005.

Winn. J. held that the right to dower is "a right ex-contractu which, while it can, in the nature of things, only arise in connection with a marriage by Mohamedan law (which is ex-hypothesi polygamous), is not a matrimonial right. It is not a right derived from the marriage but is a right in personam, enforceable by the wife or widow against the husband or his heirs". The English courts have since followed a similar line of thinking in other cases involving *mahr*.

Re J ([1999] 2 FLR 678) is a case where ADR on its own would not have been effective or time sensitive. Here, the Muslim father sought two specific orders in relation to his 5 year old son, one requiring the non-Muslim mother to raise the child as a Muslim and another requiring her to have the boy circumcised. The father acknowledged that he was not a devout Muslim, that he rarely attended the mosque and ignored many of the tenets of the faith, but gave evidence that he was anxious for the son, who was a Muslim under Islamic law, to follow certain basic practices including circumcision. The mother opposed both applications, as did the Official Solicitor acting as guardian *ad litem*.

Rejecting both the father's applications and prohibiting the child's circumcision in any jurisdiction, Wall J held first that only in unusual circumstances would the Court require that a child be brought up in a religion that was not that of the parent with whom the child was residing. In a case such as this, where the child was unlikely to have much contact with the Muslim world even when staying with his father, it would not be appropriate to require the mother to follow Muslim practices. Secondly, while it was lawful for two parents jointly exercising parental responsibility for a male child to arrange for the child to be ritually circumcised in accordance with religious beliefs, where the parents or other persons having parental responsibility for the child, including a local authority, were in dispute over whether or not to circumcise a child, that dispute should be referred to the court for resolution, if need be as a matter of urgency. The court would then decide the question by applying section 1 of the Children Act 1989 to the facts of the case.[34] In this case, circumcision was not held to be in the child's interests as, although circumcision would firmly identify the child with his father and confirm him as a Muslim in the eyes of Islam, it was a painful operation, which was opposed by the mother and which would make him an exception among his peers.

Court decisions such as the above are an important consideration when it comes to deciding which fora a matter is to be referred to. For the Muslim Law (Sharia) Council, it is important to ensure that its decisions do not violate the principles of official United Kingdom laws. It is for this

34 Section 1 of the Children Act 1989 provides that the child's welfare is to be the paramount consideration.

reason that the Muslim Law (Sharia) Council has three UK-trained lawyers on its panel.[35]

7.7 The Muslim Law (Sharia) Council at Ealing (MLSC)

The Muslim Law (Sharia) Council, by no means the only Sharia Council in the UK, was the first that was set up, largely through fortuitous circumstances. Its founder, the late Dr. Zaki Badawi, a knowledgeable mufti and a charismatic individual, responded to the entreaties of a desperate Muslim woman who had attained her divorce in an English court but was unable to remarry Islamically, as her divorce was not recognised under Islamic law and consequently she was undergoing great hardship. Calling upon two imams Dr. Badawi pondered her predicament and, drawing upon the philosophy and principles of the eponymous founder of the school of jurisprudence, Abu Hanifa, to which both parties belonged, he called upon the husband to come forth and explain why he was refusing to grant his wife the divorce (Shah-Kazemi 2001). Dr. Badawi invoked the principles of classical Islamic jurisprudence *darura* (necessity) and *maslaha* (public interest) and followed Abu Hanifa's advice that in a non-Muslim country, it would be absolutely in keeping with the principles of Islamic law for the wise among the community to constitute themselves as a *qadi* court and mete out the necessary justice where public interest so warranted.

This endeavour and the work done by the MLSC over the past 25 years can be viewed as an interesting example of restoring to the *sharia*, Islam's original message of justice, freedom and equity (Abdalla 2001) – something which Muslim ADR processes would need to address today. Reinforced with this philosophy and coupled with the practical ability to mete out justice, the MLSC, while following basic *sharia* textual principles, went beyond them to their original purpose (the *maqasid al-sharia*) which is to protect the higher values of: life, intellect, property, genealogy and faith. The MLSC is an institution which in Lederach's (1995) words is "wet up to its ears standing midstream in the river of conflict". While its original remit was to help 'Islamise' divorces granted by the British courts to Muslim women, it is also the main point of reference on *sharia* issues for the Hounslow Muslims. In addition to its declaratory function, through acting as an appellate court, it also undertakes dispute resolution and counselling services at the earlier stages of a conflict. It acts as an appeal court because the English court becomes *functus officio* once the English divorce is granted yet a female Muslim has no recourse to get her divorce Islamised. She has to appeal to some court. The MLSC becomes that court.

The processes it follows are more directive than facilitative – leaning closer to the arbitration end of the ADR spectrum than to the mediation

35 Raficq Abdulla – interview, 24 February 2005.

one. This is understandable when one takes into consideration that the *sharia* is the dominant framework. However, it must be emphasised that by going back to the founding principles of the *sharia* and utilising Islamic law principles of *takhayur* – resorting to other schools of law (including the Shia schools), it has, through neo-*ijtihad*, been able to reinterpret the *sharia* in a contemporary context. From an ADR point of view, this study shows that its thinking on the *sharia* is constantly juxtaposed with the principles of United Kingdom laws although its analytical clarity with regard to the various ADR processual tools it uses remains unclear. This apparent shortcoming needs to be reviewed in the context of whether there is a pristine ADR corpus existing globally and what the primary purpose of ADR really is. If a greater focus is placed on the intrinsic value of mediation as a transformative experience then the emphasis can arguably be shifted from means to ends, that is, from processes to outcomes which is what the MLSC actually aspires to in any dispute.

This study shows that most of the extra-judicial entities, at one stage or another, have to resort to the MLSC. MLSC's own refurbishment to bring it up to speed with regard to developments in the ADR world, is something that emerges fairly clearly in this study. From its grassroots contacts with many of the imams of the mosques of the UK, to its understanding of classical Islamic jurisprudence and a readiness to calibrate its principles with the laws of the land, the MLSC is an ideal candidate for 'indigenous empowerment', 'conscientisation' and 'recycling', basic concepts for the development of a culturally-sensitive ADR system in a diasporic context (Lederach 1995: 111-14).

7.8 Significance and Implications of the Preliminary Findings

7.8.1 Findings

This study shows that first, there is no structured ADR system in place among the Hounslow Muslim community, although ADR, based on Quranic principles, Islamic law and customary practices, does take place. Very few people have really heard of mediation as a processual tool, let alone ever having used it. Whatever mediation does take place in the family arena (though minimal) is through housing services and this is done by non-Muslim agencies.

Secondly, ADR is done largely through referrals, with each agency doing its own little bit, depending at what stage in the dispute trajectory it gets called in to intervene and on its own capacity to help by way of resources, enforceability, etc. There is relatively little inter-agency contact. This partly may be due to client predilection for anonymity. In some cases, agencies feel that they have to refer for example, the imams may refer a case to the Muslim Law (Sharia) Council in cases involving complex *sharia* issues, or solicitors may do the same in cases of 'Islamising' a civil divorce decree.

Thirdly, the average person's understanding of the *sharia* varies from what it may have been when he or she left his/her country of origin to what the imam of the mosque says it is today. This may be at variance with what the Muslim Law (Sharia) Council may decide, for their remit is to match a *sharia* principle with the laws of the land. Furthermore, the Council's decision may be different from what is happening in the Muslim world itself, because of the different socio-economic and political conditions obtaining in some 57 different Muslim countries. Menski[36] refers to this phenomenon as *angrezi shariat* and concedes that there is no one monolithic conception of it. Each Muslim group, however, will develop its own approach within the principles of its own jurisprudential school, its history, its traditions, its interpretation and, in fact, its own particular circumstances.

Whether this development can be termed 'law' or 'ADR' is not clear. It is more akin to the concept of 'unofficial law' postulated by the legal pluralist, Masaji Chiba (Chiba 1986). An interesting question arises as to the extent to which the notion of *angrezi shariat* is informed by local positive laws or whether it is the development of 'Islamic law' in the stratosphere which will look homogenous, regardless of wherever the evolution is taking place. This issue will need further research. For the moment, based on the present study, it would be fair to assume that *angrezi shariat* is the outcome of the interface between United Kingdom official laws and the principles of Islamic law and custom as they are developing within the local context, and also within a very specific jurisprudential context.

Fourthly and most importantly, there is no clear-cut understanding of the fundamental difference between mediation and arbitration. Various agencies refer to their intervention as 'mediation' but do not follow its basic principles. While espousing a more directive approach that is akin to arbitration, they may not even be following the basic principles of arbitration. This is one area where greater training is called for and where MEDARB could be developed and used more self-consciously as well as more self-confidently.

Fifthly, there is an overarching need for culturally-sensitive counselling skills in the community. Until now, there has been an aversion on the part of Muslim boys and girls to go into this profession. Equally, the study shows that there is a commensurate reluctance on the part of Muslim families to resort to counselling services. It is seen as an admission of 'family failure' which would bring shame on a family. However, this situation is now beginning to change with the second generation of Muslims brought up in the country. This study also shows that the imams of the mosque are

36 Werner Menski – interview, 2 November 2005.

themselves keen to go for counselling training. For this to happen, they would need to be given the necessary encouragement and financial assistance by the Trustees of the mosque, coupled with extra time so that they can get some relief from their existing duties. The imams could play a very important role in the whole process of social engineering in the community. As Zaman (2002) has shown in his influential work that the role of the *ulama* in contemporary Islamic issues often gets overlooked despite the fact that they are very important stakeholders in the whole process of change.

Sixthly, conciliation plays a very important role in the whole dispute resolution trajectory among Muslims. This study shows the importance attached to it, largely because of the injunction in the Quran but also the *sunnah* (practice) of the Prophet. Contemporary mediation practice does not give enough primacy to conciliation. Also, very little training is given to practitioners on how to detect possibilities for engendering a genuine reconciliation where one is still possible.[37]

Finally, the whole aspect of domestic violence screening has a different dimension in a faith-based community where people do not speak about the subject. The study shows the need for a more culturally-sensitive understanding of discernment where domestic abuse is extant. A mere perfunctory session with the disputants which present ADR practice seems to imply will not yield the necessary insights in a diasporic Muslim setting.

7.8.2 Significance of the Findings

The findings reflect the travails and aspirations of a relatively new community – largely transported from a rural, Third World setting and regrafted on a highly urbanised, First World one, crossing major divides. It shows a community that is undergoing rapid acculturation and is only now beginning to come to grips with some major issues through multiple transitions. Its predilection to choose its own rudimentary processes of dispute resolution are compatible with a number of hypotheses, all consistent with how a newly-arrived community goes through different evolutionary phases and finally finds its niche in a multi-cultural landscape (Doo Leigh-wai 1973: 652-54) – albeit, for the Muslim community in Britain, this has not been an easy task given today's highly conflictual world.

37 The author is a Director of Training Programmes for the National Conciliation and Arbitration Boards (NCABs) of the Shia Imami Ismaili Community worldwide. Since 2000, training programmes have been conducted in Asia, Africa, Western Europe and North America. This issue has arisen in each training programme the author has conducted. To address this need, the NCAB training module has been adapted to incorporate reconciliation. Mediators are trained to be particularly discerning of the possibility of reconciliation and, where this is possible, to explore how it can be furthered.

According to Auerbach (1983: 4), "how to resolve conflict, inversely stated, is how (or whether) to preserve community". Some Muslims who came to the area developed a community based on their faith affinity and utilised their own, home-grown dispute resolution processes that worked. According to Roberts and Palmer (2005: 10), a model of informal justice that would be seen as superior to orthodox formal justice should have a number of core elements. These include: being non-bureaucratic in structure, local in nature, accessible to ordinary people, reliant on lay people as third party interveners, outside the immediate scope of official law, based on substantive and procedural 'rules' that are vague, unwritten, flexible and intent on promoting harmony between the parties and within local communities. For them, the history of the search for alternatives should be seen in a broad historical context and should "encompass the experiences of dispute resolution mechanisms of more than Northern Europe and North America" (ibid.: 11). This dimension is apparent in this study but how long this religious impulse to mediation will last is a moot point. Auerbach (1983), referring to the Protestant Sectarian tradition in North America, where the colonial settlers were hostile to any external interference that challenged the religious and social values of the local communities, argues that "the counter tradition to legalism particularly mediation, was impossible to sustain in the face of ever growing pressures of greater economic and social integration, immigration and secularisation". Secondly, and importantly, the preference for resorting, where possible, to internal structures may be due to present-day identity politics. The first generation of Muslims wanted to build a community but they were not inimical to non-Muslim institutions or processes. The second generation, somehow, feel a sense of alienation although in some ways they are more integrated (Alam 2006). For them, resorting to indigenous structures is resorting to one's own traditions. They see this as an important bulwark against the unrelenting forces of rapid globalisation. Thirdly, for the first generation, having had to struggle to effect a smooth transition to resettlement in an alien country, cost considerations were important. For the newer generation, this may no longer be the case. Fourthly, for the first generation, shame and honour (*izzat*) had a greater value, given the close-knit nature of the earlier community. For the younger generation, more integrated as it were into the British way of life, this may not be that important. Finally, and most importantly, Islam still seems to hold centre stage. In a post-modern world struggling against a relentless surge of globalisation, religion may still constitute the strongest anchor in order to maintain a particular religious and cultural identity, as a sort of counter-globalisation.

7.8.3 Implications

This study has potential implications for various entities. These include policy planners, researchers, legal training institutions, ADR specialists and different Muslim communities. For policy planners, if mediation is going to be taken seriously as a genuine alternative to adjudication, much greater resources will need to be allocated to it for training than has been the case hitherto. Mediation should be upgraded as a profession and continuing education should be made into a life-long pursuit with adequate resources allocated for training purposes. Faith communities should be made partners in this endeavour and they could be encouraged to come up with the resources themselves to train their people. With regard to research, academic agendas could be made far more purposive – drawing upon the lived experience of different communities in transition and focusing on specific issues impacting upon Muslim and possibly other communities in Britain. With regard to legal education, much greater focus could be given to ADR courses at the under-graduate level in Universities thus helping to balance a culture that emphasises litigation at the cost of all other dispute resolution processes (Bok 1983: 582-83). For ADR theoreticians and practitioners, ADR itself needs to undergo a change by reviewing its founding principles and renewing its initial promise (Bush and Folger 1994). Universities could invite Muslim lawyers and ADR practitioners who have worked among Muslim communities to speak on their ADR courses.[38] Understandings from different cultural contexts could be played back into the ADR learning chain,[39] thus making cross-cultural ADR a genuine reality rather than an under-resourced wish. This study was undertaken with a view to building on the wisdom of the past without forsaking the future in the spirit of giving the past a vote – and not necessarily a veto, something that cross-cultural mediation theory and practice so desperately needs in today's fast changing world.

38 In April 2006, the London School of Economics invited the author and a member on the panel of the MSLC, both Barristers-at-Law, to present the module on ADR and Muslim communities as part of the LLM ADR course.

39 A great deal of the cross-cultural learnings from the Ismaili NCAB training programmes have been judiciously incorporated in the ADR practice in the UK today. For this, see Keshavjee, M. and Whatling, W., *"Reflective Learnings from the Training Programmes of the Ismaili Muslim Conciliation and Arbitration Boards, globally"*, paper presented at the 5th International conference of the World Mediation Forum in Crans Montana, Switzerland, on 8th September 2005. http://www.iis.ac.uk/view_article.asp?ContentID=106246.

Chapter 8 Rituals of Recognition: Ethnic Minority Marriages in British Legal Systems

Prakash Shah

Given unprecedented levels of ethnic plurality today, Britain can no longer be seen simply as a conglomerate of different national units within a 'United Kingdom', but rather one that can more properly be described as a 'community of communities'. At one level, this plurality challenges dominant legal assumptions and necessitates a re-examination of the modernist separation between 'law' and 'culture' (Cotterrell 2006).[1] Judges and other officials in Britain are now faced with much more complex forms of legal pluralism, which Griffiths (1986: 2) defined as "that state of affairs, in any social field, in which behaviour pursuant to more than one legal order occurs". Thus it is possible to speak about "Asian laws in Britain" (Menski 1993) existing alongside a variety of continually reconstructed Afro-Asian norm systems as hybrid laws in Britain. Similarly, we can also talk about Asian legal transplants in Europe (Shah 2005a).

Seen in this light, it is not very surprising but nevertheless remarkable that in recent decades case law involving members of Afro-Asian diaspora communities has prominently featured in many areas of family law within official British legal systems. This is as true of case law concerning marriage solemnisation, which is the focus of this chapter. The prominence of such cases shows how official Western legal orders, with their claims to dominance, have come under pressure to adjust their legal regimes in the area of family law as a result of the increasing presence of diaspora Afro-Asian

1 Britain is, of course, far from unique in experiencing legal issues in a much more pluralized environment, and other writers have as a consequence also been moved to reconsider the modernist assumptions of law. For Germany see Bierbrauer (1998) and for Australia see Davies (2005). For Europe in general see Shah (2005a) and Menski (2006).

Prakash Shah (ed.), Law and Ethnic Plurality: Socio-Legal Perspectives. *pp. 177-202.*
 ISBN 978 90 04 16245 7.

communities. This is clearly evident from the way in which cultural, religious or ethnic diversity is now flagged up in leading family law textbooks (Hale et al 2002: ch. 1; Probert 2003: 9) although, once an acknowledgement is made of the ever more diverse forms of social organisation, kinship patterns and ritual observances now visible, those texts do not pursue the consequences of this plurality far enough.[2]

Besides the more general questions of the link between culture and law, and new types of legal pluralism, this chapter also explores the ways in which judges struggle when dealing with ethnic minority marriage solemnisation. Trouble most often arises when the registration procedures expected by British laws have not been followed. In this context, a more general point of interest is how judges arrive at their decisions. Do they reject the validity of ethnic minority forms of solemnisation? Or do they recognise them in their own right, in the process having to overlook the demands made by legislation or binding case law? Or do they approach their work by first looking to see whether they can adapt concepts which already exist within British legal systems to confer recognition?[3] In choosing any of these techniques do they favour some of Britain's cultural communities over others?

In discussing ethnic minority family arrangements we must also tune in to the fact that many such arrangements exhibit complex forms of transnationalism. Following some recent writing (Guarnizo and Smith 1998, Ballard 2001), this might even more properly be termed 'translocalism' since we are seeing communal arrangements linking a specific locality to another locality elsewhere. Using the concept of translocalism also helps to avoid casting such arrangements in terms of a nation-oriented analysis which may be methodologically unsound. Indeed, continuing links between people in geographically distant locations brings into question the validity of a nation-oriented prism through which official legal matters tend to be viewed.

Questions involving translocal marriage may also occur in any of a number of contingent social contexts including the phase of initial migration, spousal reunification, or marriage formation across localities. Further, translocalisms exist in a continuum alongside arrangements that concern members of families who are relatively more settled in Britain.

2 Of course some writers have devoted much time to discussing the problems raised by the increasing ethnic pluralisation of Britain, although regrettably these have tended not to be in turn reabsorbed by the textbook writers as much as they could be. See Poulter (1986), Pearl (1986), Bradney (1993), Hamilton (1995), Pearl and Menski (1998), Jones and Welhengama (2000) and Murphy (2005).

3 This line of inquiry draws upon that followed in a more systematic project conducted in Holland by Hoekema and van Rossum (2007).

Whether translocal or settled, marriage solemnisation may involve navigation among different legal orders of one or more states, as well as the laws internal to that community. Thus the choices made by such people may be motivated by any combination of expediency, convenience, necessity and even ignorance as they navigate through multiple laws. More broadly, therefore, instances of navigation by members of diaspora groups at the socio-legal level challenge assumptions of modern law, with its fixation on territoriality and uniformity.

Nor should we lose sight of the fact that questions of marriage solemnisation may be incidentally thrown up when, in fact, the cases in question are part of a wider entanglement of individuals within multiple rule systems. In a sense, this is a natural corollary of legal pluralism. The question of capacity to marry, as in the case of polygamous marriages (Shah 2005b: 89-121), may also bear upon issues of validity of marriage. In addition to formal rules on marriage solemnisation, immigration laws of states often impose additional sets of rules that parties have to work through (Sachdeva 1993, Menski 1999, Wray 2006). At the official level, questions of private international law (or conflicts of law) also feature prominently, where the problem is whether to recognise legally relevant facts which took place in another country. The cases we discuss initially appear in the official sphere as matters of immigration, social security, nullity, divorce, or inheritance. These official contexts may co-exist with a number of unofficial laws whose assumptions and demands, grounded as they are in alternative legal cultures, may not 'fit' together well with official norms. For the present analysis I have selected only those official cases which, while involving linked matters, have specifically focussed their attention on the question of marriage solemnisation.

8.1 The Official Framework

In his study on *English Law and Ethnic Minority Customs* Sebastian Poulter (1986: 8) outlined the framework that forms the basis for according official legal recognition to Afro-Asian forms of marriage solemnisation:

> the formal validity of the marriage is determined by the law of the place of celebration (*lex loci celebrationis*) … In the vast majority of cases these rules [of private international law] can be applied mechanically in order to determine whether a foreign marriage is entitled to be recognised as valid for the purposes of English law. However, certain foreign marriage customs *may be so markedly different from those followed in England as to give rise to doubts as to whether the normal approach should apply*. In addition problems may arise where a foreign marriage custom is practised in this country and is felt to be in danger of conflicting with English norms or laws. It should be borne in mind that since in England

> (as elsewhere) marriage gives rise to a distinct legal status, *English law may only be prepared to accord that status to a foreign union if it displays a clear resemblance to the English conception of marriage.* [Italics added]

Poulter thus sets out the two main methods by which non-English marriages may be accorded or refused recognition. The one is through the framework of private international law which official legal systems invariably use as a way of dealing with legally relevant acts ocurring outside the territorial jurisdiction of the state where a matter arises for decision. With the reversal of dominant migratory patterns, particularly in the post-colonial period, British legal systems (primarily England and Scotland) were increasingly facing the need to recognise legal relationships entered into among Afro-Asian migrants abroad. The colonial inheritance helped here to a certain extent since British regimes overseas frequently recognised, albeit in somewhat distorted forms, the traditional laws of colonised people in Africa and Asia. There was therefore some knowledge of the ways in which relationships were being formalised and some means by which they could be recognised. Yet, in the early decades of large scale immigration there remained difficulties and considerable confusion or uncertainty in deciding whether to recognise legal relationships. These problems account for Poulter's qualification that, when faced with a claim to recognition of legal acts occuring abroad, the basis of those legal acts may differ so markedly from the 'English' model that the presumption of recognition might be seen as needing to be dispensed with.

As some immigration cases from the 1970s demonstrate, British judicial officers, if not immigration control personnel, continued to show an awareness that marriages performed, say in South Asia, may not have an element of official registration, but would still be valid marriages under the local official systems (Sachdeva 1993: 110-11). By the 1980s, however, there seems to have been a definite hardening of attitudes. British law began to erect considerable barriers to the immigration of spouses, particularly men, who were getting married to British-resident South Asian women (Sachdeva 1993). Britain was practically the only country in Europe to refuse to recognise such translocal marriages for the purposes of immigration law. By the time Poulter wrote *English Law and Ethnic Minority Customs* official decision makers were already beginning to exhibit some amnesia about the operation of English law in previous decades when it may well have favoured recognition of 'foreign' marriages.

The ever-growing time distance from the colonial period may have been one consideration in this change of attitude;[4] the more obvious concern

4 Gordon Woodman, Professor of Comparative law at Birmingham University, while endorsing the 'distance-from-the-colonial-period' thesis, has also

of keeping immigration under a firm grip, with consequences for translocal families and on family life, also provides an explanation (Mole 1987: 39-41; Juss 1997, particularly on documentary problems in South Asian marriages). Similarly, Menski (2001: 11) points out that while, Indian law and South Asian laws continue to rely on unofficial methods of marriage solemnisation, this: "... has not stopped British law enforcement agencies, especially the Home Office and its personnel, from insisting that absence of registration of an otherwise valid marriage casts doubt on the validity of the marriage in question." In addition, as Murphy (2005) notes, the failure to link important developments in private international law with family law is ironic given that transnational or translocal family arrangements are increasing in importance. The glaring omission of private international law in law school curricula leaves lawyers unable to handle conflicts of law questions and, in my experience, lawyers are finding it necessary to refer such cases to experts when they could more easily be resolved if the necessary knowledge was built into the corpus of legal training. We will return to the issue of how such pressures have led to adjustments among translocal communities when making marriage arrangements and how these can, in turn, lead to legal problems.

We noted above that Poulter distinguished between the conflicts of law regime applicable to marriages solemnised abroad and those solemnised in England, to which we now turn. What we might call informal or customary marriages, meaning those which did not involve Church-based formality, were recognised officially for a long time in England, while Church doctrine demanded only consent and consummation as preconditions of validity, thus also allowing recognition. This situation changed as a result of the concern among propertied classes that marriages by rich heiresses would allow their wealth to vest in men who were not of the type desired, and because of the potential for polygamy. The purpose of the ensuing Lord Hardwicke's Act of 1753 was to ensure that marriages ought from then be conducted in public. However, by demanding that they be performed in Anglican Churches, that legislation endowed the Anglican religious authorities with a substantial and unprecedented power over the celebration of marriage. Jews and Quakers, but not Protestant dissenters, nor Catholics were exempted from this requirement, although a reform of 1836 allowed solemnisation at non-Anglican places of worship and introduced state registration as alternatives.[5] Thus, notwithstanding the exceptions for

suggested to me that the British Foreign Office and the Home Office have often acted on divergent assumptions, although the amnesia mentioned above seems to operate in the same direction for both offices of state.

5 For accounts of the background to the 1753 Act, see Stone (1979: 29-34) and Hamilton (1995: 42-43). Stone shows that the situation prior to 1754, when

the above-mentioned minorities, by the middle of the 19th century we find more or less a situation of Church-state duopoly, a stealthily modernising orthopraxy over the solemnisation of marriage aiming to secure greater control over the socio-legal sphere. It should, however, be noted that in Scotland the pre-1753 English situation prevailed until 1940, and Scottish law continued to recognise the principle of marriage "by cohabitation and repute" (Cretney et al 2002: 10). The Family Law (Scotland) Act 2006, section 3, however, removes recourse to this ancient principle, except for those cohabiting with repute prior to commencement.[6]

Interest in the study of marriage has more recently concentrated on the frequency with which people *avoid* the institution as it is officially understood, and it seems strongly suggested by Diduck and Kaganas (1999: 59-69) that this is a sign that the socio-legal sphere is reasserting itself against the above-mentioned realignment of Church and state since the 18th century. The rise of cohabitation has been met by an intense academic critique of the official law of marriage. In so doing, however, the mainstream family law writers have been in danger of conflating the trend among members of the white population, who might wish to avoid the state altogether in their conjugal arrangements, and the preferences of ethnic minority groups among whom marriage remains a critical *rite de passage* or, in Hindu terms, a *samskar*. Thus the issues of recognition of cohabitation and that of ethnic minority marriages are actually poles apart in the questions they raise for the official sphere. The former may imply a modernising anti-ritual social movement, perhaps building on Protestant foundations, while the latter demonstrates the increasing presence of Afro-Asian ritual traditions at socio-legal level which remain unrecognised and therefore largely unofficial. The mainstream writers, while sometimes arguing that the official sphere ought to align itself to the new, 'white' socio-legal reality by reformulating the law on the basis of relations of cohabitation (which, incidentally, the official law has made substantial strides towards) have thus failed to take into account ethnic minority concerns.[7]

---

the Act came into force, was characterised by considerable plurality. This history remains of interest to textbook writers: see Cretney et al (2002: 9-12) and Diduck and Kaganas (1999: 59-69).

6 The commencement date is 4 May 2006.

7 Katherine O'Donovan (1993) has argued, however, that it does not follow that the reducing desire for marriage among the majority 'white' population eliminates the strong 'religious', 'sacramental', 'mystical', 'metaphysical', 'sacrificial', 'mythical', 'symbolic', 'sacred', 'totemic', 'ritual' and 'magical' elements from the socio-legal realm. Thus she observes (ibid.: 89) that: 'the question of what is masked by the magical and sacred status of marriage is broader than law and impinges on the very foundations of modern political society'. What

There have been some recent relaxations at state level in the requirements applicable to the places in which marriage can be formalised – by the Marriage (Registration of Buildings) Act 1990 and Marriage Act 1994. While these appear to be generally applicable pieces of legislation, some concern about the effects of the previously rather restrictive rules on ethnic minorities (see Menski 1987: 190-93 for earlier problems) have motivated them in part (Bradney 1993: 39-42). Yet insistence on at least some form of official solemnisation in the form of registration remains. Again, Poulter (1986: 33) is helpful is summing up the arguments for retention of some state control:

> In a modern industrial society it is vitally important for a state to have accurate information about which of its members are married and which are not. Such knowledge is often required to determine status for purposes of nationality and allegiance, to assess liability to tax and social security entitlements, to collect statistics and so on. The normal method of acquiring the necessary details for these bureaucratic purposes is through a compulsory system of registration. However, the state may also take the view that it wishes to exercise some supervision over the actual process of getting married, claiming that there is a public interest in providing adequate publicity, checking that the basic requirements for a valid marriage are complied with in terms of capacity and consent, and preventing fraud and abuse. If this approach is adopted *some limits need to be placed on the freedom of religious sects and other groups to organise their own marriage ceremonies and some minimum requirements about solemnisation must be laid down*. [Italics added]

We see here a transformation from the 18th century justification for having a restricted, state-mandated access to marriage to prevent women's property getting into the wrong hands or to avoid the risk of polygamy and then, in the 19th century, to accommodate excluded minorities such as Catholics, to a late modern concern for the state to know about persons getting married for wider reasons of public interest. Yet more liberalisation as to the place of registration has been advocated in recently mooted reforms, but it seems

---

she seems to be arguing here is that the official law, as well as its (mainly feminist) critics, have failed to take account of the myriad adjectives that persist in popular notions of marriage, which are not necessarily captured by official law, but which retain significance at the socio-legal level. She also frankly admits with respect to arranged marriages among South Asians that 'it may be doubted whether we have the conceptual language necessary to analyse such cases' (ibid.: 84). See, however, Ballard (1982) who supplies some of the conceptual language.

that some opinion still favours the retention of at least a minimal state role (Probert 2004).

Some recent official legal changes have again focused on the link between immigration and marriage. The Immigration and Asylum Act 1999, section 24, placed a duty on marriage registrars to notify the Home Office where they suspect that a marriage, at least one of the parties to which is not a national of a European Economic Area (EEA) state, is a 'sham'. This legislation raises obvious issues of discrimination as between those who are required to register their marriages under current law and those who are not, and as between the nationality of the parties to a marriage. This has been taken a significant step further by the Asylum and Immigration (Treatment of Claimants, etc.) Act 2004, sections 19-25, and the Immigration (Procedure for Marriage) Regulations 2005, which require that for any non-EEA national who is not settled in the UK, permission to marry must be obtained from the Home Office on submission of relevant documents and payment of a fee. Only when permission is obtained may such a person have his or her marriage registered.[8] These requirements do not apply to persons who do not need to register their marriages because, for example, they might marry in an Anglican Church. These provisions were challenged in the case of *R v (Baiai, Bigoku and Tilki) v Secretary of State for the Home Department* ([2006] EWHC 823 (Admin)) in which it was held that the interference with the right to marry is disproportionate and discriminatory. This decision was upheld by the Court of Appeal ([2007] EWCA Civ 478)

8.2 Marrying Abroad

We can now move from the general picture of what is demanded at official level to examining the ways in which cases have been appearing and have been dealt with in official fora. Here diaspora communities will be faced with the prospect of a legal marriage relationship being called into question at some point in their contact with official authorities. We saw above that British authorities have over time reduced their acceptance of non-formal methods of marriage solemnisation although they are extremely common in African and Asian countries. English and Scottish private international law appears to facilitate the recognition of a marriage solemnised abroad as long as that marriage would be recognised officially where it was solemnised. This simple formulation does not appear that simple to follow in practice. Indeed, as we saw above, British authorities have more frequently been insisting, at the point of immigration control, that marriages ought to be registered officially before they are accepted as valid. In a sense this

8 The legislation prevents persons on less than six months leave to remain from registering their marriage altogether.

appears to be a manifestation of Poulter's suggestion that where foreign marriage customs may differ from those in England, they may be refused recognition.

A recent development in this context appears to be the requirement that marriages by Hindus, Sikhs and Jains in Kenya need to be registered before entry clearance to Britain is sought, although this has not tended to be the practice earlier. Indeed, Kenyan law specifically provides for solemnisation without requiring official registration among these groups (as among other ethnic communities) in a manner similar to the Indian model. The recent change in practice by the British immigration officials would therefore appear to be at variance with what the local Kenya official law expects, leading Ramnik Shah (2005) to comment that this is a case where the official British law effectively 'forces' people into a marriage. Such requirements can lead to some strange and unforeseen consequences.

A recent illustration comes in the form of an English Court of Appeal case *Naran v Patel* ([2003] EWCA Civ 259). The facts show that the intended Gujarati 'spouses' went through a register office ceremony in Nairobi, leaving the Hindu ritual solemnisation until after a visa had been granted. At some point, after a discussion between the couple, it was decided not to go ahead with the Hindu marriage ceremony. This case ended up in court, with one party filing for nullity, while the other, contesting the nullity proceedings, filed a parallel divorce petition. On the one hand, the facts indicate that the families concerned were cautious about planning the marriage arrangements pending clearance of immigration formalities. On the other hand, the 'spouses' were also caught between two obligation systems; once it was clear that the arrangements had broken down, they had to negotiate their way out of the 'marriage' entered into at official level, but which probably only existed as a first formality in the longer process of solemnisation within their socio-legal order. The arguments in court did not reflect the Hindu socio-legal sphere here, and the lawyers appear to have proceeded on the assumption that a marriage was already in existence and that it needed either to be nullified or ended through divorce.

Interesting new patterns of solemnisation can be seen to have developed among some diaspora communities, directly in response to the knowledge that the British immigration authorities might refuse to respect the decisions taken among families. Charsley (2006) for example documents, through fieldwork among Pakistani Punjabi spouses, how the real prospect that an immigration application to enter Britain as a spouse could result in a refusal has led to adjustments in the manner in which particular marriage rituals are performed. She shows how particular rituals, especially those that signify the consummation of a marriage, can be left until after admission to Britain has been secured. As discussed further below, this is in keeping with the traditional concern among South Asians about sex prior to marriage. It is quite conceivable that, in turn, such 'partial' performance of Punjabi Muslim ritual celebrations could be used by entry clearance officers stationed in Pakistan to refuse an application on the basis that no lawful marriage exists.[9]

Official reluctance to recognise non-registered marriages taking place in South Asia or elsewhere, even though such marriages would be accorded recognition locally, goes beyond the immigration sphere. Discussing the legal position of South Asian Muslims, Pearl and Menski (1998: 171) state:

> In quite a few cases, absence of witnesses or more generally of documentation of a Muslim marriage entered into in South Asia has been an issue for determination before the British courts and tribunals. While the South Asian courts lean in favour of recognising such marriages as valid, European judges appear to need constant reminders of the existence of a strong presumption in favour of marriage in Muslim law.

Critically, issues about the validity of a marriage may arise in contact with an official authority years after entry may have been granted. A worrying illustration of this sort is provided by the case of *R (Shamsun Nahar) v Social Security Commissioners* ([2001] EWHC Admin 1049) in which a Bangladeshi woman's claim to a widow's pension was disputed on the grounds that a document titled a 'marriage deed', drafted some years after the actual marriage had been celebrated, was offered as evidence that she had been married to the deceased man for many years. In the ensuing social security proceedings it was doubted whether the deed was sufficient to prove the existence of the marriage. Worse, she was then accused of having produced a forgery, with the insinuation that she was attempting to deceive the authorities. Indeed, the procurement of the 'marriage deed' in such a case may show us that the claimant widow may have been responding to what she thought would be expected of her by British officialdom, that is, the production of some piece of paper that looks formal enough, only to be then penalised for following such understandings.

9 An instance of such a refusal is provided by the immigration case of *Basharat Hussain v Visa Officer, Islamabad* [1991] Imm AR 182 where the immigration adjudicator's decision was that the lack of a *rukhsati* ritual led to the conclusion that the parties were not married. In that case David Pearl acted for the appellant and produced evidence to the effect that such a ritual was not a prerequisite for validity in Islamic law. As Charsley's research indicates, however, performance of *rukhsati* remains important among some Pakistanis, as do other rituals.

The decision to refuse the widow a pension was subsequently challenged in judicial review proceedings on the basis that since the immigration authorities, including an immigration adjudicator, had some time ago, and after a long battle, accepted that she had been lawfully married, the social security authorities were bound to adopt that finding. The High Court refused to accept this contention, deciding that it was open for one authority to reject a finding made by another. This case presents a situation all too often encountered in various legal fora, that is, the unnecessary fussiness over minor points by which all concerned appear to have got themselves distracted. In fact, no particular documentation need have been required of the widow given that her marriage was in all probability solemnised according to Muslim law in Bangladesh. A simple expert report would have sufficed to establish that a presumption of marriage applies in Muslim law.[10] Indeed, the lawyers in this case ought to have followed this easier route rather than going into complicated, and ultimately unnecessary, administrative law arguments. Compounding the messy and unhelpful stage at which the proceedings had by now reached, the Court of Appeal ([2002] EWCA Civ 859) threw its lot in and upheld the High Court's decision. This case unfortunately shows how English lawyers in general find it extremely difficult to put forward arguments to the courts that make sense in terms of the parties' own socio-legal understandings, and also demonstrates the courts' resultant lack of awareness of the issues pertinent to Afro-Asian marriage laws.[11]

10 That such a presumption (of marriage and legitimacy of children) exists both in English and Muslim law was accepted by the Immigration Appeal Tribunal in *FI and others (Bangladesh – presumptions – marriage – legitimacy.) Bangladesh* [2005] UKIAT 00016 by reliance on Pearl and Menski (1998), and indeed has been recognised in earlier immigration cases: see Macdonald and Webber (2005: 603). For an example of successful expert intervention in the case of a Ghanaian marriage celebrated by customary Akan rituals see *McCabe v McCabe* [1994] 1 FLR 410.

11 Another decision of some concern, *Azad v ECO, Dhaka* [2000] 1918688 (CA), [2001] INLR 109, involved the status of the child of a third wife of a Bangladeshi man. The Court of Appeal accepted the argument that for the child born in Bangladesh to be considered legitimate, and therefore a British citizen by descent, his mother had to have held a belief that the marriage was valid under English law, even though this was a case of a polygamous marriage lawfully entered into in Bangladesh. Since no such belief could be established on the mother's part the child was considered illegitimate and therefore not a British citizen. This decision must to a large extent have been motivated by the existence of a polygamous marriage combined with its immigration implications. It also illustrates the fact that Bangladeshis, as the most prominent South Asian group in recent years to have undergone large-scale family reuni-

So far we have focused on the kinds of problems that can arise when the question of recognition of a marriage solemnised abroad faces British laws. These issues are normally dealt with under the rubric of private international law, an official classification where European jurisprudence on diasporic laws has also concentrated (Foblets 2003). However, the critical and fast-developing arena in the British case concerns the recognition of marriage solemnised on British territory for which there is no obvious mechanism for the reception of 'foreign' law. We are here firmly, if that is the right term, within the territory of ethnic minority laws and entangled in the problem of the extent to which Western legal orders are prepared to concede some space to facilitate their recognition. While we have already seen that British legal procedures can set up migrants and members of diaspora groups for penalties, there is also much scope for such 'othering' processes to occur within the field of application of British official laws on marriage.

8.3 Fusing of Marriage Practices in Britain

Of primary interest here is the dialectic developing between the state requirement of official registration and that of ethnic minority practices. Plainly, ethnic minorities who have not complied with the requirement of registration would not be considered lawfully married in official terms, which some cases concerning Muslim *nikahs* as far back as the 1940s confirm (*R v Mohamed (Ali)* [1964] 2 QB 350 (a case of 1943!) and *R v Bham* [1966] 1 QB 159), and this remains the dominant position today in English law (Menski: 1987: 189, Cretney et al 2002: 30-31). Writing about Hindus, Menski (1987, 1991) observed that the rigid though relatively simple requirement of registration gave rise to a series of reactions in the communities concerned. Some early unreported cases showed that Hindus had undergone customary forms of solemnisation but had not registered their marriages. When, for example, a daughter was abandoned after the 'first night', shock waves went through the communities forcing them to learn about the need to register. Without registration abandoned women and their families remained without official protection although internal communal pressures could of course be applied where and to the extent possible.

However, while the next stage involved ethnic minority marriages entering into engagement with the state, Menski (1991: 45-46) asks why it was not possible to simply cohabit, following the emerging trend among majority English people, and answers:

---

fication, have encountered the most draconian immigration restrictions. For further discussion of *Shamsun Nahar* and *Azad* see Shah (2005b: 123-40).

> Hindus, however, could not follow this model of avoiding the state law for two reasons. Firstly, they tend to be very concerned about female chastity; extra-marital sex by females would be quite unacceptable socially, a fact which causes many problems to Asian girls growing up in Britain. Secondly, in a modern welfare state so many rights of an individual depend on one's legal status, and many immigrants would have to pay dearly (as some now find) should there be any legal insecurity. As a result we find conscious attempts by Asians to follow the law of the land as closely as possible.[12]

More recent research by Berrington (1994, 1996) also found the overwhelming preference among South Asians for marriage rather than cohabitation, and this observation also holds for the British-born or -raised generations. This pattern is apparently not so prevalent among Afro-Caribbeans, Africans and so-called 'mixed' people, however, and invites further investigation. It is too simple to conclude that these trends are necessarily copies of cohabitation patterns among the 'white' majority.[13] In any case, for many ethnic minority people cohabitation outside marriage is not a solution, but does the recourse to state registration mean abandonment of traditional solemnisation?

This does not seem to have followed. Rather there is much evidence now of hybrid patterns of solemnisation where the state registration procedure forms only one, small part of a much larger ritualised process based on a readaptation of the customs of the parties to the English scene. This is discussed in detail by Menski (1987, 1991) for Hindus. Changes accommodating the registration process are just one element of a constantly developing ritual sphere that adapts according to the constraints and opportunities of the English context, but which has far from withered away by exposure to life in Britain. Ahsan (1995: 22) writes of the position of marrying Muslims:

> According to British law Muslim marriages are not legally recognized unless they are registered at a Registry Office. The marriage certificate issued by a mosque or Muslim organization is not acceptable to the British authorities, unless they are among the few which have been specifically licensed to issue civil marriage certificates. Hence Muslims have effectively to marry twice, once according to their own traditions involving all the rites and rituals, and then at the office of the registrar

12 Similarly for South Asians in general, see Menski (1987: 190, 1993: 259-61).

13 See Poulter (1986: 68-97) for a discussion of cohabitation among West Indians together with some court decisions. See La Font (1996) on kinship and law in Jamaica.

> of marriages, for according to Islamic law, the couple start their life as husband and wife only when the proper Islamic ceremony of marriage takes place.

In some cases it can be observed that the registration procedure is treated as a polluting affair that requires ritual cleansing (Menski 1993: 263)! On the other hand, I have seen evidence that registrars in London will often accommodate people in terms of their wishes to perform certain rituals or their preference for certain music to be played in the otherwise bare registry offices. This may show us that official authorities are gradually showing signs of colonisation by the ethnic minority ritual sphere.

There is also a trend to tie the registration process into the customary process in terms of their timing. This is facilitated by the fact that, given recent official relaxations as to place of registration, all the celebrations can very often take place under one roof and on the same day. This development is driven by the need among ethnic minorities to reduce the period of legal insecurity during which things may well go wrong between the parties, and the marriage arrangements become undone, as seen in the *Naran v Patel* case. Such hybridising patterns can be seen generally among the South Asians in Britain (Menski 1993: 262-63), and preliminary observations also confirm that they are played out in their specific forms among Kurds too. At a wider level these developments can be seen as indications of the gradual emergence of hybrid or plural ethnic minority laws in their various culture-specific and family-specific forms.[14]

A critical question then is to what extent English law responds to the widespread situation whereby ethnic minorities integrate registration as one part of the more elaborately ritualised process of marriage solemnisation. There are indications that some authorities have been asking for evidence as to customary forms of solemnisation besides the marriage certificate (Menski 1987: 193-94). The Court of Appeal declared early on in a Sikh case (*Kaur v Singh* [1972] 1 All ER 292 at 293) that "It is beyond question that in order to fully marry according to Sikh religion and practice, it is necessary to have not only a civil ceremony in a register office but also a Sikh religious ceremony in a Sikh temple." In another briefly reported case (*The Times*, 5 February 1991) the judge had to decide whether a Sikh wedding ritual had taken place on the basis of photographic evidence showing the rose petals on the groom's dress, which were taken as proving that the

14 Anwar (1998: 116) too notes the continuance of South Asian customary solemnisation patterns, without however mentioning the official element, perhaps a hint that this is not regarded as a critical element of solemnisation. He also (ibid.) notes how translocal interest may manifest in the long-distance involvement of relatives.

marriage must have been completed! These cases show that, occasionally, the courts consider it important to have regard to ritual forms of solemnisation. More generally, they might indicate small moves towards legal pluralism acknowledged by judges who may well understand that the parties concerned are bound by more than one rule system. On the other hand, it need not follow that ritual solemnisation is demanded as necessary at the official level which remains focused on registration as the key means by which married status is conferred, although even here, as we will see further below, ethnic minorities appear to be forcing a change in the official position.

8.4 Non-Fusion, or Confusion?

We can see considerable evidence of ethnic minorities responding to the official requirement of registration, and the courts' general unwillingness, at least in the reported cases, to go beyond registration. However, a recent line of cases shows fascinating developments in further cases faced, mainly by the English courts, where they have had to respond to persons who are married in Britain under their ritual forms of solemnisation but who, for one reason or another, have not followed the state-mandated form of registration. These cases show the courts trying to grapple with the issues raised but responding largely by a typical process of muddling through as they grasp for a solution available through British legal principles. British laws in this area are therefore quite confused while still showing deep unease about extending recognition to non-registered ethnic minority marriages.

The first in this line of cases is *Gereis v Yagoub* ([1997] 1 FLR 854) in which a marriage ceremony had taken place in an unlicensed Coptic Orthodox church in London. The parties went through their church ceremony and, as advised by the priest, they also went with witnesses and friends to a registry office to register the marriage, but were turned back because the appropriate notice had not been given and a proper booking had not been made. In evidence both parties said that they were married as members of the Coptic Orthodox church. As Aglionby J found, they cohabited and had sexual intercourse only after the marriage ceremony and the man had claimed married man's tax allowance. After a period of cohabitation, which appears to have lasted at most three months, the relationship broke down. The petitioner woman initially filed a petition for divorce but the respondent man contended that there was no marriage to speak of and those proceedings came to an end. It was then that she filed a petition for nullity. The woman meanwhile also applied for annulment of the marriage to the Council of the Coptic Church in Cairo, which subsequently issued a certificate of annulment. Like for many Muslims in Britain today this case also shows a desire by the parties to secure religious sanction for their decisions to end the marriage.

It is not quite clear that this case fits into the stage outlined earlier, that is, of ignorance of the official requirement of registration among an ethnic minority group. Both parties were made aware by their priest that they ought to register and had simply not organised that as required officially. As indicated in the evidence, it is possible that they had understood the implications of registration differently. In any event, the marriage broke down soon afterwards. The main question for the court was whether, because of non-registration, this was no marriage at all, or whether the marriage could at least be seen as void. Aglionby J reasoned that the ceremony "had the hallmarks of a Christian marriage" to merit recognition as a void marriage. Declaring the marriage void, under English law, made available to the woman the financial provision that would be available to married persons (Cretney et al 2002: 67-68).

How should we interpret this case? Arguably the court's strategy was sensitive enough to respond to the chastity-related concerns of the woman and her family, recognising the marriage just enough to make English law remedies available to her. This was not, however, a full recognition that there was a marriage, and this is seen also in the rejection of the woman's initial application for divorce. The recognition of the marriage as one which was void was motivated by the argument that it was "an ordinary Christian marriage". This line of reasoning unfortunately sets up the problem for English law as to what would happen to those from other minority groups who solemnise marriages which are not as close in form, by virtue of their religious distinctiveness, to the Christian model? We will see this very problem re-emerge in two other reported cases.

In the interim, however, another case, *Chief Adjudication Officer v Kirpal Kaur Bath* ([2000] 1 FCR 419, [2000] 1 FLR 8, [2000] Fam. Law 91), decided by the English Court of Appeal, side-stepped the question, but had recourse to another principle that saved the day. This was a case of a Sikh widow who had many years previously, in 1956, married her husband in a Sikh *gurudwara* "in accordance with Sikh custom and religion", but had not followed any of the English procedures for registration. She now claimed her pension, but the social security authorities contested her right to it on the basis that she had not been married. This case is closer to the kind of situation that many first generation immigrants would have found themselves in back in the 1950s, largely ignorant of Englsh law, and probably working on the assumptions of Indian or East African laws that customary solemnisation was all that was required for validity. In a striking statement (para. 15 of Evans LJ's speech) made for the purposes of the legal proceedings the widow recalled:

> Like most other first wave immigrants, we had no knowledge of the law, were completely illiterate and led to believe, by our elders and peers, that

> we had followed the correct procedures. Both my husband and I have always been religious and we would have been very concerned if our marriage had not been carried out in accordance with the Sikh custom and religion or thought that our marriage was not valid.

It was clear that the couple had lived their lives as if they were married and the pension and tax contributions had been made by the deceased husband as a married man. The judges who gave the main speeches, Evans and Walker LJJ, are said to have gone through "tortuous reasoning" (Probert 2003: 28) about the consequences of the couple not having followed the required registration procedure, and both opted, for slightly different reasons, for the principle of 'presumption of marriage' as a way of conferring recognition.

Since this was not a Christian marriage, the Court of Appeal could not so easily resort to the strategy adopted in *Gereis*, but the judges were obviously concerned not to do injustice to the old lady. The case is therefore of interest since it shows, possibly for the first time, a court using the presumption of marriage principle so as to confer recognition upon a non-registered ethnic minority marriage. In so doing, it used a principle already known mainly through leading Scottish authorities, and transplanted it for use in England. Probably conscious of the possible wider implications of this validation of a non-regisreted marriage, Walker LJ said (para. 7) that the presumption might not be used in the case of a couple who had not had such a long-standing marriage. This leaves the way open for other non-registered marriages to be denied official recognition in future.

And it is still notable that no judge saw fit to recognise the ritual ceremony that the couple had undergone all those years ago. The Sikh ritual sphere is thereby completely disregarded and the status of the ethnic minority law is therefore not given recognition in terms of its own socio-legal context, but in terms converted to English sensibilities (and via Scottish authorities).[15] The case is therefore an interesting illustration of the bending of English law principles to suit ethnic minority facts but does not really merit the conclusion that Engish law now recognises ethnic minority

15 See Cretney et al (2002: 9-12), where those authors think that the principle of presumption through cohabitation and repute is one of Scottish not English law. Hughes J in *A-M v A-M* (at para. 35), discussed further below, specifically mentions that the leading authorities on presumption of marriage were indeed Scottish. Probert (2002: 409-18), on the other hand, criticises the court for using the presumption of marriage principle in a manner quite contrary to previous authority, and argues that it ought to have been restricted to the narrow ground that there was some defect in the registration procedure rather than being applied in a case where there was a wholesale disregard for it.

marriage laws on their own terms. It is possible, however, that this case will be interpreted by some as conferring legal status to unregistered marriages, and create further pressures for British laws.

Two further cases appear to take a more definite position with respect to the solemnisation of ethnic minority marriages. *A-M v A-M* ([2001] 2 FLR 6[16]) is a case of an Arab couple who got married in an Islamic marriage ceremony in London in 1980, and there was no question that it was not properly conducted under Muslim rules. The husband was then advised by his lawyers that the marriage would not be valid under English rules – not only did the husband have another wife, the *nikah* would itself have no validity in English eyes. There followed a series of complicated actions (with some dispute as to what actually happened) in which the husband went through different procedures in different Muslim countries to divorce and then to marry the woman again so as to have the marriage recognised by English law. The marriage then ran into difficulties and the couple separated. When the wife petitioned the Family Division of the High Court for divorce, the husband responded by pronouncing a divorce in a Sharjah court. In the English proceedings he argued that there was no marriage to speak of and the wife should therefore not have recourse to any remedies offered by English law.

It seems clear that the husband attempted to get out of his tricky situation more than once by having recourse to Islamic legal principles and, at the same time, to avoid being penalised by English law for so doing. It may be this situation that led the court again to have recourse to the principle of presumption of marriage. However, Hughes J ruled that the 1980 London ceremony did not lead to a marriage recognised by English law. Rather, he held that there must have been some marriage existing between the parties performed in an Islamic country. In so doing, it appears that Hughes J was using the presumption of marriage as recognised by the Scottish authorities and recently by the English Court of Appeal in *Bath*. It is probable that he did not have in mind the presumption of marriage which Pearl and Menski speak about as being applicable in Islamic law, even though one assumption upon which recognition was being conferred was that a marriage ceremony had taken place in a Muslim country.

Faced with the argument on the part of the wife's counsel that the 1980 marriage ceremony was a marriage within the meaning of the applicable English law (section 11 of the Matrimonial Causes Act 1973), Hughes J (at para. 56) stated:

> If, however, it is, the same would no doubt apply to all manner of self-derived rituals intended to be binding in conscience by those forsaking

16 It is also reported as *Al-Mudaris v Al Mudaris* [2001] All ER (D) 288 (Feb).

> the civil forms of marriage, as well as to 'marriages' according to *foreign religions*, and to other ceremonies which make no attempt to be English marriages within the Marriage Acts. [Italics added.]

Hughes J was clear that the only way that a marriage valid in English law must be carried out was through the methods prescribed in the Marriage Acts, and one which did not purport to do so, as the London ceremony in question, could not be considered a marriage for the purpose of matrimonial relief. Therefore, although the court did not accept the husband's patently evasive actions, holding that the presumption of marriage operated to allow the wife to access remedies as a married woman, it would not go so far as to say that the marriage in question arose from the time of the *nikah* in London.[17] Going one step further than he really had to, Hughes J dismissed Muslim "marriages" (the quotes are notable) as being according to *foreign religions*, a description that must cause some concern at the start of the 21st century. This sort of characterisation does little to enable Muslims to feel assured that they can claim to be part of British society *as Muslims*, and justifies claims that they are treated as 'the other' in Britain. As we see in the next case Hindus are receiving similar treatment by the judiciary.

In *Gandhi v Patel* ([2002] 1 FLR 603), decided some months after *A-M*, the woman got nothing at all. This was another case with a complicated history and also with polygamy in the background. The marriage ceremony was held in 1989 in an Indian restaurant in London according to Hindu rites and "carried out in considerable style" (para. 16). No registration followed; this would not have been possible as the man already had a wife living. The woman in this case, now also a widow, argued that she ought to have had better financial provision made for herself in her deceased husband's will. By several accounts in the evidence presented, she was portrayed as uncaring, particularly when her husband had become ill. However, the main issue of importance here is the manner in which the Hindu ceremony was regarded by the court. The presumption of marriage was not used to uphold the validity of the marriage ritual in official terms, even though the parties had lived together since their marriage in 1989 until the husband was taken ill and died shortly thereafter. There were also two children of this marriage.

Alternatively, as in *Gereis*, the judge could have held that there had been a void marriage which might have allowed the wife a claim to the inheritance. However, Park J in the Chancery Division felt rather that this was a case of a "non-marriage", that is there never had been a valid mar-

17 In this sense, Hughes J went further than any of the judges in *Bath* by specifically ruling out the recognition of marriages which do not follow the stipulated registration procedures.

riage ceremony and therefore no marriage at all. Repeating (at para. 45) Hughes J's dictum in *A-M*, he adopted similar language: "the Hindu ceremony ... purported to be a marriage according to a *foreign religion* and it made no attempt to be an English marriage within the Marriage Acts." [Italics added.] Again, the judge's statement, describing the Hindu context as belonging to a "foreign religion", seems totally inappropriate given the long settlement history of Hindus, as with Muslims, in Britain.

Notwithstanding the issue of validity, the woman might have been able to succeed in her claim had she been able to show that she had entered the marriage "in good faith".[18] However, in that context, it is interesting how Park J seemed to raise the bar, expecting the claimant to have been aware of the necessity of following the English rules on marriage. He stated (at para. 54):

> The ceremony was conducted in a restaurant by Mr Bhatt, who was a devout Brahmin priest but had no official status under the institutions of this country. There was no attendance by any registrar or any other official. There was no record made in any legally recognised register of marriages. Hasmita [the claimant] said that none of that meant anything to her. All that she knew was that she was getting married according to the traditions of her own community. I have to say that I am sceptical about this. Of course Hasmita was a Hindu girl who had been brought up in a Hindu family. Nevertheless, she had grown up in this country and had been educated in English schools. She was, I think, 23 years old in 1989. She is clearly intelligent. I would not have expected her to know what was required if she wanted to be married in this country, but I would have expected her to know, or at least think it likely, that there would be some legal formalities to be observed.

The judge also took into account (para. 56) her knowledge that the deceased husband was already married at the time to conclude that the marriage could not be regarded as void – "Hindu marriages, I believe, are monogamous."[19]

18 Under the Inheritance (Provision for Family and Dependents) Act 1975, section 25.

19 It is clear from the judgment that the judge did not have any expert evidence or other information on Indian Hindu law before him and appears to have guessed what the Indian position would be (see para. 34). While the relevant Indian statute, the Hindu Marriage Act 1955, indicates that Hindu marriages are monogamous, this is far from being the case in socio-legal reality or in judicial findings: see Menski (2001: 143-45; 2003: 389-407). It remains open to question whether such information would have moved the judge to be more

These statements by the judge show the contradictory treatment of the Hindu aspects of the marriage in question. The claimant's legal choice is based on a cultural preference, illustrating what Chiba (1998) might refer to as the subjective situation of an individual in legal pluralism when there is a conflict between two normative orders. On the one hand, the judge was not sympathetic of this position but rather expected conformism to the dominant English standard, particularly in light of the woman's education in the English system, as a result of which a constructive awareness of English norms is imposed upon her. On the other hand, we find the erroneous assumption by the judge that Hindu marriage is monogamous and this 'knowledge' is used against the applicant. In other words, while some aspects of one's Hindu reality are thought fit for suppression before the official bodies, those aspects which are thought to assist conformism to the dominant paradigm (monogamy) can be called into assistance for the imposition of official English norms.

8.5 A Scottish Detour

So far we have seen that, with some important exceptions, the English courts have tended to insist that, without undergoing the process of registration, parties to a marriage in Britain cannot expect to have their marriages recognised officially. We have also seen that ethnic minorities have responded to this expectation by tying in rituals considered important within the socio-legal sphere with registration. A significant case decided in the Scottish Court of Session's Extra Division now calls into question the registration process itself in the case of ethnic minority marriages.

This case, *H v H* ([2005] Fam LR 80, [2005] SLT 1025), was an appeal against a decision of a first instance court which had refused to grant a declarator of nullity to a woman pursuer (appellant) who claimed it on the basis that the civil marriage registration had not been followed by a Muslim *nikah* and *rukhsati* ritual (spelled rushkati in the judgment), and that the defender (respondent) had refused to go through such Muslim and/or customary solemnisation rites. After the civil registration the defender had managed to obtain a one-year visa on the basis of marriage to the pursuer and, somewhat over a year later, had acquired indefinite leave to remain on the same basis.[20] The parties had never cohabited. The defender continually attempted to delay solemnisation of the marriage according to Muslim rites so that the parties could cohabit thereafter; and he had established

sympathetic to the widow's position and her claim as to the official validity of the Hindu marriage.

20 In April 2003 the period between the grant of initial leave to enter or remain and indefinite leave to remain was raised from one to two years: see Macdonald and Webber (2005: 622-24).

a relationship with another woman some time after the civil registration. Lord Penrose gave the main speech in the judgment, stating (at para. 56):

> In my view, however, an agreement that the parties will not become husband and wife in any real sense until some further condition is satisfied in the indefinite future is not a marriage. It might be betrothal. But what is material is that where parties have agreed that, notwithstanding the exchange of words of consent, the relationship that the language used would normally establish will not be established between them, the proceedings are sham, and should not be recognised. I would allow this reclaiming motion and grant decree as concluded for. I would also move your Lordships to report the whole proceedings to the Lord Advocate for consideration whether criminal proceedings should be initiated.

Their Lordships recognised that defining a marriage in a way that is universally applicable is an extremely difficult, if not impossible, job. Lord Penrose based his argument partly on the ground that, from a Muslim viewpoint, there was hardly a marriage here. He stated (at para. 41):

> The parties shared a belief system that explained their position, that marriage could be constituted only by the performance of prescribed religious ceremonies. Whatever they did in performing the civil ceremony, it did not amount to consent to marriage, because they envisaged that the result would exclude all of the irreducible minimal requirements of marriage.

And a little later (at para. 53) he went on to say:

> … religious Muslims do not become man and wife without due observance of the ceremonial requirements prescribed by their religion. They do not live together prior to those ceremonies because they have not entered into the state of marriage.

Despite the importance given to the evidence based on the religious presuppositions of the parties, it was because there was no actual consent by the parties at the time of the registration to assume the status of married persons, with all the obligations that that involved, that a declarator of nullity was said to follow.

To be sure the Court's reliance on the existence or otherwise of real consent is not entirely new. Both the English and particularly the Scottish courts have been willing to grant decrees of nullity in the case of marriages where there is no defect in the solemnisation procedure, but where they find that the consent necessary to a marriage is lacking. In particular, their

Lordships in *H v H* appeared to follow a line of cases in which lack of real consent had been pleaded specifically on the basis that Muslim marriage rituals had not followed registration.[21] Despite these cases, the leading text by Clive (1997) was pleaded and accepted by the Lord Ordinary at first instance. In that text Clive, while recognising the power of the courts to go behind registration and examine the reality of consent, had maintained (at para. 7.047):

> it is not the case that a civil marriage is void merely because the parties to it do not regard it as having any religious significance. Such a rule would render null a great many civil marriages, and would be totally unjustifiable. The religious view which parties have of a marriage ceremony is legally immaterial.

Their Lordships skirted the impact of this statement however, specifically distinguishing Prof. Clive's interpretation of the earlier cases, and held that consent to assume relationship as man and wife as understood in Scottish law was essential for the validity of the civil marriage ceremony. The judgment therefore appears to hold that the statements made during the civil marriage ceremony ought to be regarded as not just a matter of form, but as giving rise to a substantial relationship between the parties.

In so finding, the Extra Division were not so much concerned that the requisite consent was negatived by the defender's actions *after* the registration which showed that he had lost interest in going through the Muslim rites. Rather, the remarks in the judgment appear to be so all-encompassing as to catch within their scope all marriages which might stagger the registration and ritual solemnisation in that order, thereby laying them open to the possibility of annulment. As we have seen, in many such cases, the ritual stage follows closely upon registration. This judgment now allows for the possibility that the longer the gap between the two stages, the greater the likelihood that a marriage will be open to annulment by either party, and the greater the likelihood that official authorities begin to question the validity of a marriage. This judgment could therefore be picked upon to open up complex family arrangements where ethnic communities, within which marriage and its annulment can have important consequences for persons beyond the couple in question. Further, the insistence in the judgment that the parties view the civil ceremony as one which gives rise to their obligations as married persons may not be reflective of socio-legal reality,

21 *Mahmud v Mahmud* 1977 SLT (Notes) 77 and *Akram v Akram* 1979 SLT (Notes) 87. Another case on point, also referred to, was *Orlandi v Castelli* 1961 SC 113.

although it might represent an attempt to reassert the superiority of the Scottish official norm system.

A contradictory position is now developing in the British laws on marriage solemnisation. On the one hand, as we have seen, the immigration authorities appear to be increasingly insistent about the need for those marrying overseas to register, although that may not be a prerequisite for validity in the *lex loci*. This insistence on registration is of course maintained in many court judgments for marriages solemnised within British jurisdictions. On the other hand, *H v H* signals that we might have to get ready for the ever loosening attitude towards registration and its consequences for the status of marriage, with judges likely to come under greater pressure to test whether there was any substantial marriage in a case at issue.

Other issues remain unresolved by this judgment. Given what Lord Penrose said about the status of the registration ceremony, if the requisite intention or consent that he looked for is not present, it may be that it is a betrothal or perhaps something else, but does not constitute the marriage. This then opens up the issue of what precisely the status of the registration ceremony is. If registration is not enough, is it even necessary? If it is not necessary, are we in Britain inevitably moving to a point where we might need to explicitly admit that rituals which result in a recognition among the members of a social or ethnic group that a marriage has been concluded be also recognised for official purposes? So far the English or Scottish courts have not seen fit to recognise this possibility, except in the limited instances of presumption through long cohabitation, the principle behind which has now been overridden by the 2006 Act in Scotland. However, practices in the socio-legal sphere would seem to indicate that, for Muslims at any rate, the practice of non-registration of marriage is becoming quite widespread for a number of reasons. Such practices will in turn place greater pressures on judges to open further gateways to their official recognition. Registration is therefore more likely to lose its appeal on more than one front – by judges increasingly looking behind it and by their more often having to extend recognition to non-registered marriages.

8.6 Concluding Remarks

We have seen that for marriages solemnised abroad, there remains some legal confusion about the extent to which registration needs to be followed upon. While some cases, particularly in immigration law, appear to concede the position that marriages solemnised according to Afro-Asian ritual forms are indeed recognised for the purposes of British legal systems too, this understanding is not necessarily followed either in the administrative context of immigration control, nor in cases which arise in the non-immigration sphere. We also saw evidence that members of translocal communities come under some pressure to either adapt their marriage rituals in anticipation of entry clearance for immigration purposes or, they may simply follow the expected registration procedures only to find that such arrangements then need to be undone even though no *real* marriage actually exists in the socio-legal sphere.

When it comes to marriages solemnised in Britain, the overriding official insistence that they be registered plays a dominant role for official contexts and also results in reactions by members of diaspora or ethnic minority communities as they adapt their ritual performances to include registration. This does not mean that this happens in all cases and the most prominently reported cases are those 'troublesome' ones where ritual performance has not successfully incorporated the official registration stage or has simply bypassed it. These are the main sorts of cases which bring pressure to bear on the official courts to recognise socio-legal reality and to provide remedies. However, there is also a visible tendency to bring to official attention registered marriages which are not solemnised through communal rituals, and these raise the question of the status of registration and force the official courts to acknowledge that without such rituals a marriage may not be one at all in substance.

The main task set for this chapter was to analyse the ways in which judges struggle when dealing with ethnic minority or diasporic marriage solemnisation. Do they reject the validity of ethnic minority forms of solemnisation? From the reported cases analysed so far, it does appear that this is largely the case. While we can see that ritual solemnisation at socio-legal level can be important as evidence which judges will often take into account, this is not the same as judges acknowledging the validity of those same rituals. Indeed, in some cases, notably *A-M* and *Gandhi*, English judges have emphasised the *foreignness* of rituals conducted according to Muslim or Hindu laws, while the case of *Gereis* indicates some willingness to accord partial recognition to a Christian form of marriage not complying with official formalities. As to the question whether there is some sort of hierarchy of importance accorded to various communities, one can therefore answer that there is some evidence that this is so.

Do the courts look to see whether they can adapt concepts which already exist within British legal systems to confer recognition? There is also evidence of this tendency. In both the *Bath* and the *A-M* cases the English courts used the presumption of marriage derived from Scottish law. They did so in order to provide recognition to marriages which were clearly in existence, but in so doing they were not willing to go so far as to say that the rituals themselves have any particular validity. Rather recognition had to follow only on the basis that a pre-existing concept within British legal systems could be adapted to 'fit' the socio-legal reality. It may therefore be valid to say that, at least in some cases, judges will seek conceptual assistance from within official normative understandings which they regard as appropriate to facilitate recognition. The *H v H* case can also be seen as an illustration of the same point, but this time to deny recognition to a marriage which was not in existence in socio-legal reality. In that case the court emphasised the issue of consent, already an important aspect of official norms on marriage, to arrive at the conclusion that there was no marriage at official level. *H v H* goes so far in that direction as to insist that consent must be such as to effect a marriage as understood in Scots law. While this may be seen as an attempt to reinforce the superiority of the Scottish norm system, it has the potential to create mischief for the many legally pluralist marriage arrangements among ethnic minorities.

The cases discussed here therefore illustrate the inherent instability of the British systems of laws on marriage which basically underplay or deny the importance of the socio-legal sphere and, in so doing, judges have to perform gymnastics involving their own principles in order to accord or deny recognition to ethnic minority marriages. If we were to go by the practice of the English and Scottish courts we would learn little about the laws of diasporic or ethnic minorities since their judgments effectively limit our understanding of the socio-legal contexts in which such cases occur. This in turn impacts on legal education if that education is focused on a simple analysis of case law and the rules that arise therefrom. This would encourage students to repeat the patterns of classification accepted officially according to British legal principles and disables attempts at deeper understanding of socio-legal aspects of marriage solemnisation.

Chapter 9 Ethnicity and the Senior Judiciary in England and Wales

Tahir Abbas

The Department for Constitutional Affairs (now, Ministry of Justice) (DCA 2004) have recognised that ethnic minorities are significantly under-represented in the judiciary, and the Commission for Judicial Appointments (CJA 2003) have commented that there is general recognition that the composition of the judiciary is not reflective of society as a whole and that the senior judiciary is overwhelmingly white, male and from a specific social and educational background. This literature review is an attempt to evaluate the extent of ethnic minority disadvantage in relation to appointments to the senior judiciary in England and Wales. Based on an analysis of existing literature and secondary quantitative data, it brings together the crucial strands in academic and policy thinking in this area, and spells out the key issues, suggesting ways forward for research and practice. As stated in the 2004 Department for Constitutional Affairs consultation paper on increasing diversity in the judiciary, "it is a matter of great concern that the judiciary in England and Wales – while held in high regard for its ability, independence and probity – is not representative of the diverse society it serves" (DCA 2004). This chapter mainly relies on secondary published and unpublished appointments statistics held by the DCA, the Bar Council and the Law Society. Given the acute limitations of primary research in this area, a wide range of other sources from which to illuminate the overall findings, including government research, academic study, 'think tank' research, and newspaper reports are also used.

It is important to state clearly at the outset the definitions being used here. The term 'ethnic minority' refers to those groups in society who possess a range of 'ethnic characteristics' in relation to how they see themselves and are defined by others in a society that is different by virtue of culture and class (Fenton 2003). In the UK, the Census categories are used

Prakash Shah (ed.), Law and Ethnic Plurality: Socio-Legal Perspectives. *pp. 203-213.*
 ISBN 978 90 04 16245 7.

as ways in which individual persons, who wish to align themselves to an ethnic category, may self-classify. These categories, however, are also variants of racialised characteristics defining people's imagined or objectified differences. This may help to inform public policy, but there is a danger of over-emphasising differences between groups, leading to a concentration on perceived distinctions. In relation to post-war migrant groups, although it might be relevant to talk of a South Asian and African-Caribbean population dominating the non-white profile, it is also necessary to appreciate that a far greater number of people who arrived and settled in Britain in the 1950s and 1960s (as well as historically) were of Irish origin. Throughout this chapter it has not always been possible to break down the analysis to a level where it might be possible to draw specific conclusions in relation to the experiences of particular groups. Therefore statements made about the experiences of non-white groups in relation to appointment to the senior judiciary are not necessarily group specific – the numbers are small and the classifications used by both the DCA and CJA have been insufficiently detailed until recently.

In order to explore the issues that impact on certain ethnic minorities in successfully gaining senior judicial office, it is important to closely examine the impact of higher education and training. The issues that affect the relative progression of ethnic minorities within the judiciary are closely related to their previous experiences of the social world and the education system, and particularly their early careers as lawyers. It is necessary therefore to develop a fuller understanding of how the legal profession is regarded by ethnic minorities and what impact social class, ethnicity, and gender have on the courses students take, the institutions they attend, and their respective routes to the senior ranks of the judiciary. Although it is plausible that early disadvantage in social life affects the career progression of ethnic minorities, there is a dearth of research to support the claim that there is a direct association. Based on the author's own research on the education of British South Asians it is apparent that social class, gender, and ethnicity do affect educational paths and outcomes (Abbas 2004). South Asians in selective schools are acutely aware of how the higher educational paths they select directly impact upon the likelihood of eventually securing rewarding employment compared with South Asians in comprehensive schools. In the latter, although the wish to read law is strongly demonstrated, they tend to lack knowledge of the importance of certain universities and barristers' chambers in securing more lucrative career trajectories.

9.1 Ethnicity, Education and Outcome

Ethnic minorities disproportionately favour those subjects demanding high A-level scores and at elite institutions (Modood 1993). Ethnic minority university entrants represent 21 per cent of students commencing Law degrees, proportionately greater than in the general population (Cole 2001). The subject is popular among ethnic minority groups, particularly South Asians. However, there tend to be real discrepancies between some ethnic minority groups who are found in the 'elite universities' and others in 'new universities'. These elite universities, which focus on technical and scientific subjects aimed at national and international students, include the 20 that form the Russell Group, as well as other universities with strong law departments.[1] 'New universities' refers to pre-1992 colleges of higher education and polytechnics, where there has generally been a focus on vocationally-driven courses aimed at local students.

Ethnic minorities are strongly represented in law degrees across the different universities but they tend to be concentrated in the new institutions which are favoured less by solicitors' firms and barristers' chambers looking to engage law graduates. This is partly a function of social class differences between groups, but also of access to opportunities. There are no specific quantitative analyses that demonstrate this phenomenon, but it is apparent from a wider analysis of existing research that entering the legal profession is often a precarious procedure. What is identified here is a separate sub-issue relating to access to the bar and/or admittance as a solicitor. Some groups, including a disproportionate number from the elite universities, have direct contact with 'employers'[2] and find it easier to get the postgraduate vocational qualifications necessary to enter the profession. Those from universities less in demand, invariably where some ethnic minorities are more likely to be found, find it much more difficult, which may hinder their postgraduate studies and ultimate employment prospects.

Certain groups are able to capitalise on cultural, economic and social networks and associations, but it is because of access to the elite educational institutions that they can receive preferential treatment in the profession. Groups most likely to be excluded are those with limited incomes and without family connections. Given the lower overall socio-economic profile of ethnic minorities in general, a higher proportion of groups excluded from the legal profession are therefore from this population. Employers disproportionately favour selective–school educated white-English groups graduating from elite universities. Ethnic minorities are less likely to be found among those ultimately selected irrespective of their strong profile

1 The Russell Group consists of the Universities of Birmingham, Bristol, Cambridge, Cardiff, Edinburgh, Glasgow, Imperial College London, King's College London, Leeds, Liverpool, London School of Economics, Manchester, Newcastle, Nottingham, Oxford, Queen's University Belfast, Sheffield, Southampton, Warwick, and University College London.

2 In this chapter I use the term 'employer' to refer to solicitors' firms and barristers' chambers who recruit graduates for a legal career.

among law students – reflecting the differential experience of different ethnic minorities as well as the status of different elite institutions. Without further research it is not possible to determine the full extent of this trend. It is, however, apparent from the evidence on higher education representation and law graduate employment profiles that it is those ethnic minorities possessing the personal and educational characteristics of their white-English selected-school educated counterparts who are most likely to succeed (Vignaendra 2001). Contacts in the profession also increase the graduate's chances of securing a training contract, and ethnic minority graduates are less likely to have such contacts (and the relevant career advice at the right time) than their white-English counterparts (Halpern 1994). This has consequences for the judicial appointments process since it affects the number of ethnic minority practitioners who are likely to be in a position to apply for judicial office, and subsequently the senior judiciary (*Education Guardian*, 21 October 2003).

Not managing to enter the more established universities or take a more favoured degree course frequently results in remaining unselected by solicitors' firms seeking to recruit law graduates from a restricted pool (Rolfe and Anderson 2002). There is, however, no precise or systematic quantitative or qualitative research in relation to the approaches of barristers' chambers. It is important to realise that the extent of bias in the career path of ethnic minority lawyers is differentiated at the very outset, and it appears that this qualitative ethnic penalty can remain with many as they attempt to develop their professional careers as lawyers. In essence, irrespective of the fact that people from ethnic minorities take degree courses and enter the profession at a disproportionately higher rate, lesser proportions of ethnic minorities find themselves in elite institutions favoured by certain employers. This preference is based on what these institutions are thought to generate for the individuals being educated by them – which are based on certain manifestations of cultural, social, and intellectual capital. This sociological effect appears in outcomes in other professions too – particularly in the medical and academic professions.

Therefore, although such patterns of selectivity are not specific to the legal profession, it is necessary to realise the extent of rigidity in certain sectors. Societies maintain economic and social distinctions between individuals and groups based on an education system. Where there are historically strongly-embedded social distinctions, the education system evolves to reflect the needs of different groups in their efforts to maintain the *status quo* or achieve upward social mobility. Post-war social reforms have led to a system where education is increasingly available to all but many of the key distinctions continue to remain however much governments attempt to achieve equality of opportunity and outcome for all. Further research is needed in order to determine the precise nature of the relationship between ethnicity, education, and outcome in the legal profession.

9.2 Policy

A number of organisations have identified reasons why the profile of those who sit in judgement on their fellow citizens should be reflective of society as a whole. For example, 'Operation Black Vote' argues that at a time when South Asians are three times and African-Caribbeans eight times as likely as whites to be stopped and searched by the police the need for the magistracy to reflect the communities they serve has never been more pressing.[3] Similar arguments would support the contention that the composition of the professional judiciary should reflect society as a whole.

Why ethnic minorities are disproportionately under-represented in the legal system is clear from an analysis of ethnic minorities' experiences in higher education, but they are also disproportionately under-represented in the judiciary, especially the senior judiciary. Based on current figures approximately 8 per cent of Deputy District Judges (Magistrates Courts) come from minority ethnic groups, which make up approximately 9 per cent of the population as a whole. These overall figures are encouraging. However, among the 161 judges in England at High Court level, there is only one from an ethnic minority and only ten of the 636 circuit judges are from ethnic minority backgrounds.

Recent research commissioned by the DCA, looking at the experiences of lay magistrates from ethnic minority backgrounds, has highlighted instances where ethnic minorities believe that although their abilities and aspirations to carry out their duties were not necessarily undermined, prejudice, discrimination, and racism still played a part in their working lives (Vennard et al 2004). It is plausible that many of the lessons learned from attempting to make changes to the representation of ethnic minorities in the lay magistracy can be read across to the professional judiciary and that many of the barriers faced by ethnic minority magistrates could affect members of the ethnic minorities looking to establish themselves in the professional judiciary and ultimately to progress to senior judicial office.

Although the experience of senior judicial appointments in the United States is quite different, it is useful to explore it. Here, it is not entirely clear what exactly impacts upon the representation of minorities on a particular bench (Hurwitz and Lanier 2003). Certainly, there is much to suggest that diversity has already been attained, particularly in relation to African-American women (Martin and Pyle 2002). However, there are specific issues that exist in relation to the sentencing of ethnic minorities, who often

3 Operation Black Vote http://www.obv.org.uk/magistrate/ accessed 26 December 2006.

receive harsher treatment (Bushway and Morrison-Piehl 2001, Hood et al 2003). It is not clear how outcomes are affected when the bench is more ethnically diverse. There are, however, some indications to suggest that ethnic minority judges tend to give harsher sentences to *both* ethnic minority and white offenders; "harshness of black judges suggests they may behave as 'tokens' or that they have greater sensitivity to the costs of crime, in particular, within black communities. Although there were small race-of-judge effects, there also was much similarity in sentencing practices—suggesting that the job, not so much the individual, apparently makes the 'judge'" (Steffensmeier and Britt 2001: 763). It is clear that having a bench that reflects the make-up of society can be achieved in some instances, but how that actually impacts on decisions made is also important to consider. These points on sentencing outcomes are relevant to arguments about diversity in the senior judicary.

In Britain, the Queen appoints High Court and Circuit Judges and magistrates on the recommendations of the Lord Chancellor, who is a member of the Government. The most senior judges are recommended by the Prime Minister after consultation with the Lord Chancellor. Almost all High Court Judges are appointed from the ranks of QCs (Queen's Counsel), who are senior barristers. The Lord Chancellor has until recently always decided which barristers are to become QCs. In the past the system appears disproportionately to have favoured 'older white males' (Budge et al 2004). Until 1 November 2004, there were no ethnic minority judges above the level of Circuit judge. Linda Dobbs QC, an African-Caribbean woman, was then appointed to be a High Court Judge.

Analysis of application, interview and selection data appears to show that where ethnic minorities actually make applications for senior judicial posts, their chances of success are increasing relative to those of the majority population. However, when they apply, they are still almost always less likely to be interviewed and subsequently succeed in gaining appointment, although there has been significant improvement in recent years and, the longer-term prospects for ethnic minority candidates applying and succeeding remains optimistic. Because of the few appointments made, a few more or less ethnic minorities impact hugely on percentages and therefore statistics here need to be treated with caution (DCA 2004). From 1992 to 2003, the proportion of ethnic minorities in the judiciary rose from 1 per cent to 2.6 per cent. In particular, there has been a sharp rise in the numbers of Recorders known to be of ethnic minority background and there has been a significant increase at all levels up to Circuit Judge and notably, Recordership, has traditionally been seen as a stepping stone to the High Court. It follows from this that an increase in ethnic minority Recorders may actually result in more ethnic minority High Court judges in the foreseeable future.

9.3 Practice

In the past, appointments tended to remain in the hands of government and politicians, helping to make the process appear "secretive and discriminatory" (Elliot and Quinn 2002). Over the years there has been considerable criticism of the system of appointing judges in England and Wales (*The Times*, 13 July 1986; *The Independent*, 28 June 2004). Traditionally, through questioning leading judges and barristers about an individual's potential, the process of 'secret soundings' has been used to elicit the suitability of a particular candidate. The scope of these soundings varies according to the appointment in question. For example, the DCA's website states that

> ...the Lord Chancellor consults senior members of the judiciary before recommending individuals for appointment to the Court of Appeal or the House of Lords. All Supreme Court Judges and Law Lords are consulted on those who have applied for the High Court Bench, and on other leading practitioners and Circuit Judges. The Lord Chancellor consults the four Heads of Division, together with the Senior Presiding Judge, when considering candidates for appointment to specific posts on the High Court Bench.[4]

Feedback to unsuccessful candidates provides details of individual consultation responses, but only in such a way as to avoid identifying their author. It is argued that if the authorship of opinions is revealed, then judges and barristers would not openly offer their views. Normally, advertisements for jobs are placed in national newspapers or specialist publications, but, until recently, most judicial posts were not advertised at all. Although the process is considerably more open and transparent now, some people will still be invited to become judges without having to apply (particularly when these are promotions rather than invitations to become judges).

Sir Leonard Peach reviewed the appointments system in 1999. At the time it was found that the 'secret sounding' system was *not* inherently weak, but, in fact, delivered professional service and high quality work in general. Sir Leonard recommended a number of changes to the consultation arrangements and the setting up of an independent judicial appointments commission to oversee the judicial appointments process. The Runnymede Trust Commission on the 'Future of Multi-ethnic Britain' (2000), a group of the country's leading race relations experts put to task by the independent race equality 'think tank', published a report at around the same time as the Sir Leonard's report, affirming the need for the creation of a judicial appointments commission in light of the under-representation of ethnic

4 Department for Constitutional Affairs http://www.dca.gov.uk/judicial/appointments/jappinfr.htm accessed 26 December 2006.

minorities: "those who define, administer, enforce and judge in matters of law and criminal justice are still overwhelmingly white".

It needs to be emphasised that the numbers of South Asian and African-Caribbean people are indeed increasing in the magistracy, the probation service, and the practising legal profession but, despite improvements at other levels of the judiciary, they remain especially low in its most senior ranks. Accordingly, because senior judicial appointments tend to be made from the most experienced barristers, the choice of candidate at any one time is likely to be limited, possibly not even extending beyond five or six suitable people. Budge et al (2004) comment that, officially, there ought not to be any regard to 'race', ethnicity, gender, religion, sexual orientation or political affiliation, but the fact that the potential number of candidates is so few results in the vast majority of judges being white, middle-aged or older males. Spending their professional working life as barristers, many senior judges come from privileged backgrounds. Studies tend to show that about eighty per cent of the senior judiciary are products of public schools and of Oxford or Cambridge; that they have an average age of about sixty; that ninety-five per cent are men; and all but one are white. Since the senior judiciary are a restricted group likely to share political, cultural, and social affiliations, the question that remains for social thinking and public policy in general is how far this impacts on the interpretation of the law. Furthermore, as this restricted group perpetuates itself, it continues to limit *all* minorities and the cloning process remains unchecked. However, the appointment of Linda Dobbs QC is a genuine step away from the unchecked cloning processes of the recent past.

In qualitative research commissioned by the DCA, it was found that women and ethnic minority lawyers were affected by a number of factors when applying for Silk (i.e. to become QCs) or judicial office. It appears that the problem is more a case of fewer ethnic minorities feeling confident or being encouraged to apply (Malleson and Banda 2000). A "clear consensus" is found in "support of the need for the appointments processes to be based on openness, objectivity and selection on merit rather than patronage". In general, there was support amongst respondents for the changes introduced by the then Lord Chancellor's Department to deliver these aims through wider advertising, interviews, feedback for unsuccessful candidates, and the encouragement of under-represented groups to apply. The extent to which respondents believed that these changes had made the necessary impact differed between the groups, however. Dissatisfaction with the processes was greater amongst solicitors than barristers, female respondents than male respondents, respondents from ethnic minority backgrounds than white respondents, and amongst those whose applications were unsuccessful compared with those who were successful. Indeed, concerns were raised about the working arrangements of the legal profession as well as the ways in which the appointments process itself worked. In sum, the factors affecting people's decision to apply included:

- The extent to which being in a top-ranking chambers affects barristers' chances of appointment.
- The effects of indirect racial discrimination on the capacity of ethnic minority barristers to build up a successful practice.
- The continuing need to be 'known' in order to be appointed, and the role of social networking in the consultation process.
- The disadvantage faced by solicitors in the consultation process.
- The difficulties faced by solicitors in completing the requirements of part-time sitting.
- The difficulties faced by women lawyers with children in balancing work and domestic responsibilities.

The most commonly proposed changes put forward by respondents included:

- Greater openness and objectivity.
- More active encouragement of qualified lawyers from under-represented groups to apply.
- Reform of thc consultation process.
- The establishment of a judicial appointments commission.
- More flexible working arrangements and a change of culture both in the legal profession and in the judiciary.

The DCA study was a qualitative project exploring experiences and perceptions. As such, it is useful in helping to determine the ways in which different minority groups encounter the appointments process. Wider quantitative and more specific qualitative research is needed before more resolute generalisations can be made. It is true that under-representation of ethnic minorities within the senior judiciary appears particularly acute. However, given the relatively small number of people in the quantitative analysis, it cannot be assumed that the judiciary is systematically discriminative. Ethnic minorities are increasingly beginning to find greater representation in virtually all the other ranks within the judiciary, particularly in relation to tribunals. This suggests that the representation of ethnic minorities within the senior judiciary beyond that of Circuit Judge ought to grow in the near future.

9.4 Discussion

It is apparent that ethnic minorities enter the profession in significant numbers, and this number has been rising for the past three decades. It is also the case that ethnic minorities are beginning to increase their representation within the judiciary. There are no specific statistics that bear out the notion that former barristers achieve high judicial office at disproportionately higher levels, but it is clear that the vast majority of senior judges are recruited from the ranks of barristers, although a few were once solicitors. The perceived wisdom is that Tribunal appointments, Deputy District Judges and District Judges are generally from the ranks of solicitors, Circuit Judges from barristers and Recorders/High Court judges from QCs, but there are no precise statistics to confirm or disprove this observation.

Since 1950 there has been a rising trend in the numbers entering the legal profession as solicitors. Since 2003, the number of solicitors with practising certificates (PCs) has grown by over 50 per cent from 61,329 to 92,752, the number of women solicitors with PCs has increased by 117 per cent from 16,930 to 36,819, the percentage of solicitors with PC working outside of private practice has increased from just over 16.8 per cent to nearly 21.8 per cent, and the percentage of PC holders drawn from minority ethnic groups has increased from 3.1 per cent to 8.9 per cent. In relation to ethnic minority participation, solicitors of minority ethnic origin have entered the profession in larger numbers in recent years. As at 31 July 2003, there were 10,234 ethnic minority solicitors on the Roll, of whom 7,356 (71.9 per cent) held current PCs (*Key Facts* 2003).

Not all solicitors or barristers are eligible to apply for judicial office. Some posts require a certain level of experience and some require potential candidates to have held a certain level of rights of audience (e.g., Recorders require a ten year Crown or County Court right of audience). An increase in the numbers of ethnic minority solicitors therefore only tells part of the story. It would be interesting to see what percentage of solicitors granted a right of audience in the Higher Courts are from an ethnic minority. The aim would be to consider whether the proportions of ethnic minority applicants actually reflect the make-up of people who are eligible to apply (both as barristers and solicitors). It would also be interesting to note the differentials between barristers and solicitors and for different judicial appointments (including Tribunals). However, it is not possible to determine the reasons why ethnic minority solicitors may be less or more likely to apply for such rights than white-British solicitors, although it is likely to be an issue as, again, it may well have indirect discrimination implications.

From a literature review of issues relating to diversity within the judiciary, it has been possible to determine that the proportion of ethnic minorities entering the legal profession continues to rise, both as solicitors and barristers. It is also evident that the disproportionately stronger educational concentration of ethnic minorities in the 'new universities' limits the potential career progression of many and further limits the number who might ultimately be eligible for senior appointment. There are increasing proportions of ethnic minorities appointed to the judiciary (although the base is very small and the overall numbers appointed to circuit bench level and above are still very small), but they are still less likely to apply and subsequently less likely to be interviewed or obtain appointment relative to the majority population. Some of the reasons for this are based on career choices, which are gender or occupation specific. For example, lawyers may prefer to remain in private practice and sit on the bench occasionally as Recorders. Qualitative research is needed in order to examine the *processes* of applications, interview, and appointment to the senior judiciary in order to determine what works and how further to develop the opportunities for ethnic minorities who continue to increase their representation within other parts of the judiciary.

However, specific issues remain. One concerns the ways in which the process of 'cloning' ensures a largely unchanging ethnic and social make-up of the senior judiciary, thereby limiting the range and scope of potential judges to be appointed. The other concerns how this process negatively impacts upon the experiences of ethnic minorities. The case for efforts to support diversity continues in the light of findings that nevertheless suggest an improving position. Although recent developments have suggested a marked shift towards reaching equitable status for ethnic minority groups, the proportions of ethnic minorities who become eligible will continue to rise and every effort ought to be made to ensure that they have the confidence to succeed on their merits in an open and transparent way. In independent qualitative research, the negative perceptions held by ethnic minorities demonstrate that there are concerns, particularly in relation to the question of whether there exists a sufficiently diverse judiciary. The extent to which a 'trickle up effect' can deliver a diverse bench remains unanswered. Advocates of the 'trickle up effect' suggest that the judiciary will naturally become more diverse in time as more ethnic minority (and female) practitioners enter the legal profession and subsequently reach the point where they can be considered for judicial office. In their Second Annual Report CJA commented that they had heard different views on whether time alone would result in a more diverse judiciary and stated that the Commissioners had rejected the notion that 'trickle up' alone could be relied on to redress the gender and ethnic imbalance in the judiciary. Further and more systematic qualitative and quantitative research is therefore needed.

Bibliography

Abbas, T. 2004. *The Education of British South Asians: Ethnicity, Capital, and Class Structure*. London & New York: Palgrave-Macmillan.

Abdalla, A. 2001. Principles of Islamic Interpersonal Conflict Intervention: A Search within Islam and Western Literature. *Journal of Law and Religion* 15, 1/2, 151-84.

Advisory Council on the Misuse of Drugs 1988. *AIDS and Drug Misuse*, Part 1. London: HMSO.

Advisory Council on the Misuse of Drugs 1989. *AIDS and Drug Misuse*, Part 11. London: HMSO.

Advisory Council on the Misuse of Drugs 1994. *Drug Misusers and the Criminal Justice System*. London: HMSO.

Ahmed, A. 2002. *Islam Today*. London: I.B. Tauris, 150.

Ahmed, K. 1974. *Family Life in Islam*. Leicester: The Islamic Foundation, 13.

Ahsan, M. 1995. The Muslim Family in Britain. In *God's Law versus State Law; The Construction of an Islamic Identity in Western Europe* (ed.) M. King. London: Grey Seal Books, 21-30.

Alam, F. 2006. Beyond the Veil. *Newsweek International* Vol. CXLVIII, n° 22, November 27, 2006.

Alavi, H. 1972. Kinship in West Punjabi Villages. *Contributions to Indian Sociology*, New Series 14, 6, 1-27.

Ali, M. 2003. *Brick Lane*. London: Doubleday.

Anderson, B. 1991. *Imagined Communities*. London: Verso.

Ansari, H. 2002. *Muslims in Britain*. Minority Rights Group International Report. London: Minority Rights Group, 22.

Ansari, H. 2004. *The Infidel Within: Muslims in Britain since 1800*. London: C. Hurst & Co.

Anwar, M. 1979. *The Myth of Return: Pakistanis in Britain*. London: Heinemann.

Anwar, M. 1991. Muslims in Britain: Some Recent Developments. *The Islamic Times*, July-September, 32.

Anwar, M. 1998. *Between Cultures: Continuity and Change in the Lives of Young Asians*. London: Routledge.

Appignanesi, L. (ed.) 2005. *Free Expression is No Offence*. London: Penguin.

Appignanesi, L. 2005. Editor's preface. In *Free Expression is No Offence* (ed.) L. Appignanesi. London: Penguin, 1-20.

Auerbach, J. 1983. *Justice without Law? Resolving Disputes without Lawyers*. New York: Oxford University Press, 4.

Aurora, G. S. 1967. *The New Frontiersmen: A Sociological Study of Indian Immigrants in the United Kingdom*. Bombay: Popular Prakashan.

Balibar, É. 2004. *We, the People of Europe? Reflections on Transnational Citizenship*. Princeton & Oxford: Princeton University Press.

Ballard, R. 1982. South Asian Families: Structure and Process. In *Families in Britain* (ed.) British Families Research Committee. London: Routledge & Kegan Paul, 174-204.

Ballard, R. 1990. Migration and Kinship: The Differential Effect of Marriage Rules on the Processes of Punjabi Migration to Britain. In *South Asians Overseas. Migration and Ethnicity* (eds) C. Clarke, C. Peach & S. Vertovec. Cambridge et al: Cambridge University Press, 219-49.

Ballard, R. (ed.) 1994. *Desh Pardesh. The South Asian Presence in Britain*. London: Hurst & Co.

Ballard, R. 1994. Differentiation and Disjunction among the Sikhs. In *Desh Pardesh: The South Asian Presence in Britain*, (ed.) R. Ballard. London & Co: Hurst, 88-116.

Ballard, R. 1996. Panth, Kismet, Dharm te Quaum: Continuity and Change in Four Dimensions of Punjabi Religion. In *Globalisation and the Region: Explorations in Punjabi Identity* (eds.) P. Singh & S. S. Thandi. Coventry: Association for Punjab Studies (UK), 7-38.

Ballard, R. 2001. The Impact of Kinship on the Economic Dynamics of Transnational Networks: Reflections on some South Asian Developments. Paper presented at Workshop on Transnational Migration, Princeton University, 29 June – 1 July 2001. www.casas.org.uk and www.transcomm.ox.ac.uk (accessed January 14, 2007).

Ballard, R. 2006. Ethnic Diversity and the Delivery of Justice: The Challenge of Plurality. In *Migrations, Diasporas and Legal Systems in Europe* (eds) P. A. Shah & W. F. Menski. London: Routledge-Cavendish, 29-56.

Ballard, R. 2007. Living with Difference: A Forgotten Art in Urgent Need of Revival? In *Religious Reconstruction in the South Asian Diasporas: From One Generation to Another* (ed.) J. R. Hinnells. London: Macmillan Palgrave.

Baumann, G. 1996. *Contesting Culture: Ethnicity and Community in West London*. Cambridge: Cambridge University Press.

Beckford, J. A. 1998. Three Paradoxes in the Relations between Religion and Politics in an English City. *Review of Religious Research* 39, 4, 344-59.

Beckford, J. A. 1999. The Management of Religious Diversity in England and Wales with Special Reference to Prison Chaplaincy. *Journal on Multicultural Societies* 1, 2, 56-66.

Benhabib, S. 2004. *The Rights of Others. Aliens, Residents and Citizens*. Cambridge: Cambridge University Press, 136.

Berridge, V. & Edwards, G. 1981. *Opium and the People*. London: Allen Lane.

Berridge, V. 1988. The Origins of the English Drug "Scene" 1890-1930. *Medical History* 32, 51-64.

Berrington, A. 1994. Marriage and Family Formation among the White and Ethnic Minority Populations in Britain. *Ethnic and Racial Studies* 17, 3, 517-46.

Berrington, A. 1996. Marriage Patterns and Inter-Ethnic Unions. In *Ethnicity in the 1991 Census. Vol. 1. Demographic Characteristics of the Ethnic Minority Populations* (eds) D. Coleman & J. Salt. London: HMSO, 178-212.

Bhachu, P. 1985. *Twice Migrants*. London: Tavistock.

Bhatia, P. 1973. *Indian Ordeal in Africa*. Bombay: Vikas Publishing House.

Bhatt, C. 1997. *Liberation and Purity: Race, New Religious Movements and the Ethics of Postmodernity*. London & Bristol, Pennsylvania: UCL Press.

Bhatti, G. K. 2004. *Behzti (Dishonour)*. London: Oberon Modern Plays.

Bierbrauer, G. 1998. Legal Cultures in Ethnicplural Societies. In *Interaction of Legal Cultures* (eds) J. Feest & V. Gessner. Oñati: International Institute for the Sociology of Law (Oñati Pre-Publications, No. 5), 193-205.

Bingham, LCJ 2006. *The Rule of Law*. Lecture to the Law Faculty at the University of Cambridge, November 16, 2006. http://cpl.law.cam.ac.uk/past_activities/the_rule_of_law_text_transcript.php (accessed January 14, 2007).

Birmingham City Council 2001. *The Birmingham Plan (Deposit Draft)*. Birmingham: Birmingham City Council Planning Department.

Birmingham City Council 2002. *A Pathway to Greater Inclusion: Birmingham and its Faith Communities*. Birmingham: Birmingham City Council Equalities Division.

Bok, D. 1983. A Flawed System of Law and Practice Training. *Journal of Legal Education* 33, 570, 582-83.

Borkowski, A. H. 2002. The Presumption of Marriage. *Child and Family Law Quarterly* 14, 3, 251-66.

Bowen, J. R. 2004. Beyond Migration: Islam as a Transnational Public Space. *Journal of Ethnic and Migration Studies* 30, 5, 879-94.

Bradney, A. 1993. *Religions, Rights and Laws*. Leicester: Leicester University Press.

Brubaker, R. 2001. The Return of Assimilation? Changing Perspectives on Immigration and its Sequels in France, Germany and the United States. *Ethnic and Racial Studies* 24, 531-48.

Budge, I., Crewe, I., McKay, D. & Newton, K. 2004. *The New British Politics*. 3rd edition. Harlow: Pearson.

Buruma, I. 2005. Final Cut. In *Free Expression is No Offence* (ed.) L. Appignanesi. London: Penguin, 136-50.

Buruma, I. 2006. *Murder in Amsterdam: The Death of Theo Van Gogh and the Limits of Tolerance*. London: Atlantic Books.

Bush, R. A. B. & Folger, J. 1994. *The Promise of Mediation: Responding to Conflict through Empowerment and Recognition*. San Francisco: Jossey Bass.

Bushway, S. D. & Morrison-Piehl, A. 2001. Judging Judicial Discretion: Legal Factors and Racial Discrimination in Sentencing. *Law and Society Review* 35, 4, 733-64.

Cantle Report 2001. *Community Cohesion: A Report of the Independent Review Team*. London: Home Office.

Carens, J. H. 1997. Liberalism and Culture. *Constellations* 4, 1, 35-47.

Carrera, S. 2006. Integration of Immigrants versus Social Inclusion: A Typology of Integration Programmes in the EU. In *Security versus Freedom? A Challenge for Europe's Future* (eds) Th. Balzacq & S. Carrera. Aldershot et al: Ashgate, 87-114.

Carrier, J. (ed.) 1995. *Occidentalism: Images of the West*. Oxford: Clarendon Press.

Cashmore, E. & McLaughlin, E. 1991. Out of Order. In *Out of Order* (eds) E. Cashmore & E. McLaughlin. London: Routledge, 10-41.

Charsley, K. 2006. Risk and Ritual: The Protection of British Pakistani Women in Transnational Marriage. *Journal of Ethnic and Migration Studies* 32, 7, 1169-87.

Chiba, M. (ed.) 1986. *Asian Indigenous Law in Interaction with Received Law*. London & New York: KPI, 1-9.

Chiba, M. 1998. Other phases of Legal Pluralism in the Contemporary World. *Ratio Juris* 11, 3, 228-45.

Chippendale, N. (ed.) 1993. *Reminiscences from the Asian Community*. London: Hounslow Heritage Publication.

Cholewinski, R. 2005. Migrants as Minorities: Integration and Inclusion in the Enlarged European Union. *Journal of Common Market Studies* 43, 695-716.

Clive, E. M. 1997. *The Law of Husband and Wife in Scotland*. 4th edition. Edinburgh: W. Green.

Cole, B. 2001. *Trends in the Solicitors' Profession: Annual Statistical Report*. London: The Law Society.

Commission for Judicial Appointments 2002. *Annual Report*. London: Commission for Judicial Appointments.

Commission for Judicial Appointments 2003. *Annual Report*. London: Commission for Judicial Appointments.

Commission of the European Communities 2003. *Communication on 'Immigration, Integration and Employment'*, COM (2003) 336 final, Brussels, 3 June 2003.

Commission of the European Communities 2004. *Annual Report on Migration and Integration in Europe*, COM (2004) 508 final, Brussels, 16 July 2004.

Commission of the European Communities 2005. *Communication on 'Terrorist Recruitment: addressing the factors contributing to violent radicalisation'*, COM (2005) 313 final, Brussels, 21 September 2005.

Commission of the European Communities 2005. *Communication on 'A Common Agenda on Integration'*, COM (2005) 389 final, Brussels, 1 September 2005.

Commission of the European Communities 2006. *Annual Report on Migration and Integration in Europe,* SEC (2006) 892, Brussels, 30 June 2006.

Commission on the Future of Multi-Ethnic Britain 2000. *The Future of Multi-ethnic Britain*. London: Profile. [The 'Parekh Report']

Cooper, D. 1998. *Governing Out of Order: Space, Law and the Politics of Belonging*. London: Rivers Oram Press.

Cotterrell, R. 2004. Law in Culture. *Ratio Juris* 17, 1, 1-14.

Cotterrell, R. 2006. Lawyers and the Building of Communities. *Student Bar Review* [National Law School of India], 18, 1, 25-30.

Coulson, N. 1964. *A History of Islamic Law*. Edinburgh: Edinburgh University Press, 147.

Coulson, N. 1969. *Conflicts and Tensions in Islamic Jurisprudence*. Chicago: University of Chicago Press, 108.

Cretney, S. M., Masson, J. M. & Bailey-Harris, R. 2002. *Principles of Family Law*. London: Sweet and Maxwell.

Dahya, B. 1974. The Nature of Pakistani Ethnicity in Industrial Cities in Britain. In *Urban Ethnicity* (ed.) A. Cohen. London: Tavistock, 77–118.

Davies, M. 2005. The Ethos of Pluralism. *Sydney Law Review* 27, 1, 87-112.

de Witte, B. 2004. The Constitutional Resources for an EU Minority Protection Policy. In *Minority Protection and the Enlarged European Union: The Way Forward* (ed.) G. N. Toggenburg. Budapest: EURAC and Open Society Institute, 109-24.

Department for Constitutional Affairs 2004. *Increasing Diversity in the Judiciary, Consultation Paper CP/04*. London: Department for Constitutional Affairs.

Derrett, J. D. M. 1968. *Religion, Law and the State in India*. London: Faber & Faber.

Diduck, A. & Kaganas, F. 1999. *Family Law, Gender and the State*. Oxford: Hart.

Dodd, D. 1978. Police and Thieves in London. *New Society*, 16 March 1978.

Doo, Leigh-Wai 1973. Dispute Settlement in Chinese-American Communities. *American Journal of Comparative Law* 21, 627.

Dorn, N. & South, N. (eds) 1987. *A Land Fit for Heroin?* London: Macmillan.

Dorn, N., Murji, K. & South, N. 1992. *Traffickers*. London: Routledge.

Dworkin, R. 1985. *A Matter of Principle*. London: Harvard University Press.

Eade, J. 1993. The Political Articulation of Community and the Islamisation of Space in London. In *Religion and Ethnicity: Minorities and Social Change in the Metropolis* (ed.) R. Barot. Kampen: Kok Pharos Publishing House, 29–42.

Eade, J. 1996. Nationalism, Community and the Islamization of Space in London. In *Making Muslim Space in North America and Europe* (ed.) B. D. Metcalf. Berkeley: University of California Press, 217–33.

Edge, P. 2003. Extending Hate Crime to Religion. *Journal of Civil Liberties* 8, 1, 5-27.

Edmunds, M., Turnbull, P., Hough, M. & May, T. 1999. *Doing Justice to Treatment*, DPAS Paper 2. London: Home Office.

Elliot, C. & Quinn, F. 2002. *English Legal System*. 4th edition. Harlow: Pearson.

Evans, D. 2002. Drug Crime: What's the Colour of Money? *Fed Express* 2, 4-5.

Eyerman, R. 2005. Art and Assassination as Public Performance. http://research.yale.edu/ccs/research/working-papers/#eyerman (accessed July 18, 2006).

Farnell, R. et al 2003. "*Faith*" *in Urban Regeneration*? *Engaging Faith Communities in Urban Regeneration*. Policy Press: Bristol.

Federation, The 2002. Re-offending by Ex-prisoners Examined by Government Think Tank. *Fed Express* 3, 5.

Fenton, S. 2003. *Ethnicity*. Cambridge: Polity.

Foblets, M.-C. 2003. Muslim Family Laws before the Courts in Europe: a Conditional Recognition. In *Muslims in the Enlarged Europe. Religion and Society* (eds) B. Maréchal, S. Allievi, F. Dassetto & J. Nielsen. Leiden & Boston: Brill, 255-84.

Forst, R. 1997. Foundations of a Theory of Multicultural Justice. *Constellations* 4, 1, 63-71.

Fraser, N. 2003. Social Justice in the Age of Identity Politics: Redistribution, Recognition, and Participation. In *Redistribution or Recognition? A Political-Philosophical Exchange* (eds) N. Fraser & A. Honneth; (Tr.) J. Golb, J. Ingram & C. Wilke. London & New York: Verso, 7-109.

Fryer, P. 1984. *Staying Power. The History of Black People in Britain*. London: Pluto Press.

Fuller, L. 1971. Mediation: its Forms and Functions. *Southern California Law Review* 44, 305-39.

Furbey, R. & Macey, M. 2005. Religion and Urban Regeneration: A Place for Faith? *Policy and Politics* 33, 1, 95-116.

Gale, R. & Naylor, S. 2002. Religion, Planning and the City: The Spatial Politics of Ethnic Minority Expression in British Cities and Towns. *Ethnicities* 2, 3, 387–409.

Gale, R. 1999. *Pride of Place and Places: South Asian Religious Groups and the City Planning Authority in Leicester*. Cardiff: Department of City and Regional Planning, Papers in Planning Research 172.

Gale, R. 2004. The Multicultural City and the Politics of Religious Architecture: Urban Planning, Mosques and Meaning-making in Birmingham, UK. *Built Environment* 30, 1, 30–44.

Gardner, K. 1993. *Desh-bidesh*: Syhleti Images of Home and Away. *Man* 28, 1, 1-15.

Gay, P. 1989. *Getting Together*. London: Policy Studies Institute.

Geaves, R. R. 1996. Cult, Charisma and Community. *Journal of Muslim Minority Affairs* 16, 2, 169–92.

Gilman, M. 2000. A Qualitative View of Drugs Policing: Heroin Markets in Greater Manchester, UK. In *Understanding and Responding to Drug Use: The Role of Qualitative Research* (ed.) European Monitoring Centre for Drugs and Drug Addiction. Luxembourg: Office for Official Publications of the European Communities, 203-09.

Gilroy, P. 1987. *There ain't No Black in the Union Jack*. London: Hutchinson.

Glatt, M. 1974. *A Guide to Addiction and its Treatment*. Lancaster, England: Medical and Technical Publishing Co.

Goodhart, D. 2004. Too Diverse? *Prospect Magazine* 95.

Green, P. 1991. *Drug Couriers*. London: The Howard League for Penal Reform.

Green, P. 1998. *Drugs, Trafficking and Criminal Policy*. Winchester: Waterside Press.

Gregory, J. 1987. *Sex, Race and the Law. Legislating for Equality*. London et al: Sage Publications.

Grewal, S. 2006. Bibliography of work related to Salman Rushdie. http://www.subir.com/rushdie/bib.html (accessed July 18, 2006).

Griffiths, J. 1986. What is Legal Pluralism? *Journal of Legal Pluralism and Unofficial Law* 24, 1-56.

Grillo, R. D. 2005. *Backlash against Diversity? Identity and Cultural Politics in European Cities*. Oxford: COMPAS Working Paper No.14.

Grillo, R. D. 2007. Licence to offend? The Behzti Affair. *Ethnicities* 7, (forthcoming).

Grillo, T. 1991. The Mediation Alternative: Process Dangers for Women. *Yale Law Journal* 100, 1545-610.

Groenendijk, K. 2004. Legal Concepts of Integration in EU Migration Law. *European Journal of Migration and Law* 6, 111-26.

Groenendijk, K. 2006. Family Reunification as a Right under Community Law. *European Journal of Migration and Law* 8, 215-30.

Grudzinska, A. D. 1982. Planning for the Muslim Faith – A Study of the Provision of Mosques in the City of Birmingham. Cardiff: University of Wales, unpublished Dissertation.

Habermas, J. 1993. *Justification and Application: Remarks on Discourse Ethics*. (Tr.) C. Cronin. Cambridge, Mass.; London: The MIT Press.

Habermas, J. 1996. *Between Facts and Norms: Contributions to a Discourse Theory of Law and Democracy*. (Tr.) W. Rehg. Cambridge: Polity Press.

Habermas, J. 1998. *The Inclusion of the Other: Studies in Political Theory*. C. Cronin & P. de Grieff (eds). Cambridge, Mass.: The MIT Press.

Hale, B., Pearl, D., Cooke, E. & Bates, P. 2002. *The Family, Law and Society: Cases and Materials*. 5th edition. London: Butterworths.

Halpern, D. 1994. *Entry into the Legal Professions: The Law Student Cohort Study – Years 1 and 2*. London: The Law Society.

Hamilton, C. 1995. *Family, Law and Religion*. London: Sweet & Maxwell.

Hand, L. 1901. Historical and Practical Considerations regarding Expert Testimony. *Harvard Law Review* 15, 40-58.

Harper, R. & Murphy, R. 1999. *Drug Smuggling: An Analysis of the Traffickers 1991-1997*. Middlesex: Middlesex Probation Service.

Haw, S. 1985. *Drug Problems in Greater Glasgow*. London: Chamelion.

Hepple Q.C., B. & Choudhury, T. 2001. *Tackling Religious Discrimination: Practical Implications for Policy-makers and Legislators*. London: Home Office. Home Office Research Study No. 221.

Hepple, B. & Szyszczak, E. M. (eds) 1992. *Discrimination: The Limits of the Law*. London: Mansell.

Hindu Forum of Britain 2006. *Connecting British Hindus: An Enquiry into the Identity and Public Engagement of Hindus in Britain*. London: Department for Communities and Local Government.

Hinz, M. O. 2003. Jurisprudence and Anthropology. *Anthropolgy Southern Africa* 26, 3-4, 114-18.

Hodgins, H. 1981. Planning Permission for Mosques: the Birmingham Experience. *Research Papers: Muslims in Europe* 9, 11–27.

Hoekema, A. J. & van Rossum, W. M. 2007. Empirical Conflict Rules in Dutch Legal Cases of Cultural Diversity. In *The Response of State Law to the Expression of Cultural Diversity/Le Droit face à l'Expression de la Pluriculturalité* (ed.) M.-C. Foblets. Brussels: Fondation Francqui (forthcoming).

Home Office 1985. *Tackling Drug Misuse*. London: HMSO.

Home Office 1986. The Ethnic Origin of Prisoners: The Prison Population on 30 June 1985 and Persons Received, July 1984-March 1985. *Home Office Statistical Bulletin 22/84*. London: Home Office.

Home Office 1993. The Prison Population in 1992. *Home Office Statistical Bulletin 7/93*. London: Home Office.

Home Office 1995. *Tackling Drugs Together: A Strategy for England 1995-98*. London: HMSO.

Home Office 1998. *Tackling Drugs to Build a Better London*. London: HMSO.

Home Office 1999. *Statistics on Race and the Criminal Justice System*. London: Home Office.

Home Office 2000. *Statistics on Race and the Criminal Justice System*. London: Home Office.

Home Office 2001. *United Kingdom Anti-Drugs Co-ordinator's Annual Report 2000/1*. London: Home Office.

Home Office 2002a. *Updated Drug Strategy 2002*. London: Home Office.

Home Office 2002b. *Tackling Crack: A National Plan*. London: Home Office.

Home Office 2003a. *The Substance Misuse Needs of Minority Prisoner Groups*. London: Home Office.

Home Office 2003b. *Disrupting Crack Markets*. London: Home Office.

Home Office 2004a. *Tackling Drugs. Changing Lives*. London: Home Office.

Home Office 2004b. *Statistics on Race and the Criminal Justice System*. London: Home Office.

Home Office 2004c. *Working together: Co-operation between Government and Faith Communities*. London: Home Office.

Home Office 2005. *Tackling Drugs. Changing Lives: Turning Strategy into Reality*. London: Home Office.

Honneth, A. 1992. Integrity and Disrespect: Principles of a Conception of Morality Based on the Theory of Recognition. *Political Theory* 20, 2, 187-201.

Honneth, A. 1995. *The Struggle for Recognition: The Moral Grammar of Social Conflicts*. (Tr.) J. Anderson. Cambridge: Polity Press.

Hood, R. et al 2003. *Ethnic Minorities in the Criminal Court: Perceptions of Fairness and Equality of Treatment*, Lord Chancellor's Department Research Series No. 2/03. London: Lord Chancellor's Department.

Hough, M., Clancy, C., McSweeney, T. & Turnbull, P. 2003. The Impact of Drug Testing and Treatment Orders on Offending: Two Year Reconviction Results. *Findings 184*. London: Home Office.

House of Lords 2003. *Religious Offences in England and Wales. Report of Select Committee*. London: HMSO.

Howe, D. 1973. Fighting Back: West Indian Youth and the Police in Nottingham. *Race Today* 5, 1.

Humphrey, D. & John, G. 1971. *Because They're Black*. Harmondsworth: Penguin.

Humphrey, D. 1972. *Police Power and Black People*. London: Panther.

Huntington, S. P. 1993. The Clash of Civilizations. *Foreign Affairs* 72, 3, 22-49.

Hurwitz, M. S. & Lanier, D. N. 2003. Explaining Judicial Diversity: the Differential Ability of Women and Minorities to attain Seats on State Supreme and Appellate Courts. *State Politics & Policy Quarterly* 3, 4, 329-52.

Ignatieff, M. 2003. *Empire Lite. Nation-building in Bosnia, Kosovo and Afghanistan*. London: Vintage.

Jenkins, R. 1967. *Essays and Speeches*. London: Collins.

Johnson, M. & Carroll, M. 1995. *Dealing with Diversity*. Home Office Paper 5. London: Home Office.

Joly, D. 1995. *Britannia's Crescent: Making a Place for Muslims in British Society*. Aldershot: Avebury.

Jones, C. A. 1994. *Science, Medicine, and the Practice of Law*. Oxford: Clarendon Press.

Jones, R. & Gnanapala, W. 2000. *Ethnic Minorities in English Law*. Stoke-on-Trent: Trentham Books.

Juss, S. S. 1997. *Discretion and Deviation in the Administration of Immigration Control*. London: Sweet and Maxwell.

Kalunta-Crumpton, A. 1999. *Race and Drug Trials*. Aldershot: Ashgate.

Kalunta-Crumpton, A. 2003a. Race and Problem Drug Use in an English City. *International Journal of Offender Therapy and Comparative Criminology* 47, 8, 677-97.

Kalunta-Crumpton, A. 2003b. Blacklisted: Race, Drugs and Crime, *DrugLink* 18, 3, 13-14.

Kepel, G. 1997 *Allah in the West: Islamic Movements in America and Europe*. Oxford: Polity Press.

King, M. (ed.) 1995. *God's Law versus State Law. The Construction of an Islamic Identity in Western Europe*. London: Grey Seal.

Kostakopoulou, D. 2006. Thick, Thin and Thinner Patriotisms: Is This All There Is? *Oxford Journal of Legal Studies* 26, 73-106.

Krishnarayan, V. & Thomas, H. 1993. *Planning and Ethnic Minorities: Final Report*. London: Royal Town Planning Institute.

Kymlicka, W. 1989. *Liberalism, Community and Culture*. Oxford: Clarendon Press.

Kymlicka, W. 1995. *Multicultural Citizenship: A Liberal Theory of Minority Rights*. Oxford: Clarendon Press.

Kymlicka, W. 1997. Do we need a Liberal Theory of Minority Rights? Reply to Carens, Young, Parekh and Forst. *Constellations* 4, 1, 72-87.

Kymlicka, W. 2001. *Politics in the Vernacular: Nationalism, Multiculturalism and Citizenship*. Oxford: Oxford University Press.

Kymlicka, W. 2003. Immigration, Citizenship, Multiculturalism: Exploring the Links. In *The Politics of Migration* (ed.) S. Spencer. Oxford: Blackwell, 195-208.

La Font, S. 1996. *The Emergence of an Afro-Caribbean Legal Tradition. Gender Relations and Family Court Use in Kingston, Jamaica*. San Francisco: Austin & Winfield; London: Bethsheda.

Law Society 2003. *Key facts 2003*. London: Law Society. http://www.lawsociety.org.uk/secure/file/147417/d:/teamsite-deployed/documents/templatedata/Publications/Research%20fact%20sheet/Documents/keyfact03_v1.pdf

Lederach, J. P. 1995. *Preparing for Peace: Conflict Transformation across Cultures*. New York: Syracuse University Press.

Lester, A. 2005. Free Speech, Religious Freedom and the Offence of Blasphemy. In *Free Expression is No* Offence (ed.) L. Appignanesi. London: Penguin, 211-39.

Lewis, P. 1994. *Islamic Britain: Religion, Politics and Identity among British Muslims*. London: I.B. Tauris, 13.

Liberty 2005. Terrorism Bill – Liberty's Briefing for Second Reading in the House of Lords. London: Liberty. http://www.liberty-human-rights.org.uk/ (accessed January 14, 2007).

Macdonald, I. A. & Webber, F. (eds) 2005. *Immigration Law and Practice in the United Kingdom*. 6th edition. London: Butterworths.

Malleson, K. & Banda, F. 2000. *Factors Affecting the Decision to apply for Silk and Judicial Office,* Research Report No 2. London: Lord Chancellor's Department Research Unit.

Mamdani, M. 1973. *From Citizen to Refugee: Uganda Asians come to Britain*. London: Frances Pinter.

Margalit, A. & Raz, J. 1990. National Self-Determination. *Journal of Philosophy* 86, 9, 439-61.

Martin, E. & Pyle, B. 2002. Gender and Racial Diversification of State Supreme Courts. *Women and Politics* 24, 2, 35-52.

Mason, D. 1995. *Race and Ethnicity in Modern Britain*. Oxford: Oxford University Press.

Masud, M. K., Messick, B. & Powers, D. (eds) 1996. *Islamic Legal Interpretation*. Cambridge: Harvard University Press.

Melady, T. & Melady, M. 1976. *Uganda: The Asian Exiles*. New York: Orbis Books.

Menski, W. F. 1987. Legal Pluralism in the Hindu Marriage. In *Hinduism in Great Britain* (ed.) R. Burghart. London: Tavistock, 180-200.

Menski, W. F. 1988. English Family Law and Ethnic Laws in Britain. *Kerala Law Times* 1, 56-66.

Menski, W. F. 1991. Change and Continuity in Hindu Marriage Rituals. In *Hindu Ritual and Society* (ed.) S. Y. Killingley. Newcastle: Grevatt & Grevatt, 32-51.

Menski, W. F. 1993. Asians in Britain and the Question of Adaptation to a New Legal Order: Asian Laws in Britain? In *Ethnicity, Identity, Migration: The South Asian Context* (eds) M. Israel & N. K. Wagle. Toronto: University of Toronto, Centre for South Asian Studies, 238-68.

Menski, W. F. 1999. South Asian Women in Britain, Family Integrity and the Primary Purpose Rule. In *Ethnicity, Gender and Social Change* (eds) R. Barot, H. Bradley & S. Fenton. Basingstoke: Macmillan; New York: St. Martin's Press, 81-98.

Menski, W. F. 2001. *Modern Indian Family Law*. Richmond: Curzon.

Menski, W. F. 2003. *Hindu Law: Beyond Tradition and Modernity*. New Delhi: Oxford University Press.

Menski, W. F. 2006a. *Comparative Law in a Global Context: The Legal Systems of Asia and Africa*. 2nd edition. Cambridge: Cambridge University Press.

Menski, W. F. 2006b. Rethinking Legal Theory in Light of North-South Migration. In *Migration, Diasporas and Legal Systems in Europe* (eds) P. A. Shah & W. F. Menski. London: Routledge-Cavendish, 13-28.

Meuleman, J. 2001. Headscarves, Homosexuals, and Imams in the Netherlands. *ISIM Newsletter* 8, 33.

Mirza, H., Pearson, G. & Phillips, S. 1991a. *Drugs, People and Services in Lewisham, Final Report of the Drug Information Project*. London: Goldsmiths College, University of London.

Mirza, H., Phillips, S. & Pearson, G. 1991b. Drug Misuse in a South London Borough. In *Drug Misuse in Local Communities* (ed.) T. Bennet. London: The Police Federation, 115-28.

Mitsilegas, V. 1998. Culture in the Evolution of European Law: Panacea in the Quest for Identity? In *Europe's Other: European Law between Modernity and Postmodernity* (eds) P. Fitzpatrick & J. H. Bergeron. Aldershot: Ashgate, 111-29.

Mnookin, R. & Kornhauser, L. 1979. Bargaining in the Shadow of the Law: the Case of Divorce. *Yale Law Journal* 88, 950-97.

Modood, T. 1990. British Asian Muslims and the Rushdie Affair. *Political Quarterly* 61, 2, 143-60.

Modood, T. 1993. The Number of Ethnic Minority Students in British Higher Education. *Oxford Review of Education* 19, 2, 167-81.

Mole, N. 1987. *Immigration: Family Entry and Settlement*. Bristol: Jordan & Sons.

Munt, I. 1991. Black Organisations, Planning and Access to Premises. *New Community* 17, 4, 583–602.

Murphy, J. 2005. *International Dimensions in Family Law*. Manchester: Manchester University Press.

National Audit Office 2004. *The Drug Treatment and Testing Order: Early Lessons*. London: The Stationery Office.

National Treatment Agency (NTA) 2002a. *Commissioning Cocaine/Crack Treatment*. London: NTA.

National Treatment Agency (NTA) 2002b. *Treating Cocaine/Crack Dependence*. London: NTA.

National Treatment Agency (NTA) 2003. *Update*. London: NTA.

National Treatment Agency (NTA) 2005. *Provisional Statistics for the National Drug Treatment Monitoring System in England 2003/04*. London: NTA.

Nesbitt, E. 2000. *The Religious Lives of Sikh Children*. Leeds: University of Leeds Community Religions Project.

Nielsen, J. 1988. Muslims in Britain and Local Authority Responses. In *The New Islamic Presence in Western Europe* (eds) T. Gerholm & Y. G. Lithman. London: Mansell, 53–77.

Nye, M. 2001. *Multiculturalism and Minority Religions in Britain: Krishna Consciousness, Religious Freedom and the Politics of Location*. Richmond: Curzon Press.

O'Donovan, K. 1993. Marriage: A Sacred or Profane Love Machine? *Feminist Legal Studies* 1, 1, 243-58.

Office for National Statistics 2003. National Statistics Online: Census 2001—Profiles—Birmingham. http://www.statistics.gov.uk/census2001/access_results.asp (accessed January 14, 2007).

Parekh, B. 1990. The Rushdie Affair: Research Agenda for Political Philosophy. *Political Studies* 38, 695-709.

Parekh, B. 1997. Dilemmas of a Multicultural Theory of Citizenship. *Constellations* 4, 1, 54-62.

Parekh, B. 2000. *Rethinking Multiculturalism. Cultural Diversity and Political Theory*. Basingstoke: Palgrave.

Parker, H., Bakx, K. & Newcombe, R. 1986. Heroin and the Young. *New Society,* 24 January.

Peach, C. 1990. The Muslim Population of Great Britain. *Ethnic and Racial Studies* 13, 13.

Peach, L. 1999. *Independent Scrutiny of the Appointment Processes of Judges and Queen's Counsel*. London: Lord Chancellor's Department.

Pearl, D. & Menski, W. F. 1998. *Muslim Family Law*. 3rd edition. London: Sweet & Maxwell.

Pearl, D. 1972. Muslim Marriages in English Law. *Cambridge Law Journal* 30, 1, 120-43.

Pearl, D. 1981. Islam in English Family Law. In *Islam in English Law and Administration* (ed.) J. S. Nielsen. Birmingham: A symposium, 6-10.

Pearl, D. 1986. *Family Law and the Immigrant Communities*. Bristol: Jordan & Sons.

Pearl, D. 1995. The Application of Islamic Law in the English Courts. 1995 Noel Coulson Memorial Lecture at SOAS. http://www.soas.ac.uk/Centres/IslamicLaw/Coulson_Pearl.html (accessed November 18, 2006).

Pearson, G. & Patel, K. 1998. Drugs, Deprivation and Ethnicity: Outreach among Asian Drug Users in a Northern English City. *Journal of Drug Issues* 28, 1, 199-224.

Pearson, G. 1987. *The New Heroin Users*. Oxford: Basil Blackwell.

Pearson, G. 1992. Drug Problems and Criminal Justice Policy. *Contemporary Drug Problems* 19, 279-301.

Pearson, G., Gilman, M. & McLver, S. 1987. *Young People and Heroin*. Aldershot: Gower.

Peers, S. 2004. 'New' Minorities: What Status for Third-Country Nationals in the EU System? In *Minority Protection and the Enlarged European Union: The Way Forward* (ed.) G. N. Toggenburg. Budapest: EURAC & Open Society Institute, 151-62.

Plant, M. 1987. *Drugs in Perspective*. London: Hodder & Stoughton.

Poulter, S. 1986. *English Law and Ethnic Minority Customs*. London: Butterworths.

Poulter, S. 1990. *Asian Traditions and English Law*. Stoke-on-Trent: Runnymede Trust & Trentham Books.

Poulter, S. 1998. *Ethnicity, Law and Human Rights*. Oxford: Oxford University Press.

Probert, R. 2002. When are we married? Void, Non-existent and Presumed marriages. *Legal Studies* 22, 3, 398-419.

Probert, R. 2003. *Cretney's Family Law*. London: Sweet and Maxwell.

Probert, R. 2004. Lord Hardwicke's Marriage Act – Vital Changes 250 Years on? *Family Law* 34, 585-89.

Rawls, J. 1993. *Political Liberalism*. New York: Columbia University Press.

Redmayne, M. 2001. *Expert Evidence and Criminal Justice*. Oxford: Oxford University Press.

Rippin, A. 1990. *Muslims – Their Religious Beliefs and Practices. Vol. 1: The Formative Period*. London: Routledge.

Roberts, S. & Palmer, M. 2005. *Dispute Processes: ADR and the Primary Forms of Decision Making*. Cambridge: Cambridge University Press, 10-11.

Robilliard, St. J. A. 1984. *Religion and the Law*. Manchester: Manchester University Press.

Rolfe, H. & Anderson, T. 2002. *Firm Decision: The Recruitment of Trainee Solicitors*, Research Study 42. London: The Law Society.

Ruggiero, V. & South, N. 1995. *Organised Crime and Drug Markets*, Working Paper 1, BSA.

Runnymede Trust 1997. *Islamophobia, its features and dangers*. London: Runnymede Trust.

Sachdeva, S. 1993. *The Primary Purpose Rule in British Immigration Law*. Stoke on Trent: Trentham.

Samad, Y. 1991. Book Burning and Race Relations: Political Mobilisation of Bradford Muslims. *New Community* 18, 4, 507-19.

Sangster, D., Shniner, M., Patel, K. & Sheikh, N. 2001. *Delivering Drug Services to Black and Minority Ethnic Communities*. London: Home Office.

Sardar, Z. 2004. *Desperately Seeking Paradise*. London: Granta Books, 22.

Sartori, G. 2002. *Pluralismo, Multiculturalismo e Estranei*. Milan: Rizzoli.

Shah, P. A. 2002a. An Unhelpful Approach to the Validity of South Asian Marriage. *Immigration, Asylum and Nationality Law* 16, 1, 32-34.

Shah, P. A. 2002b. Children of Polygamous Marriage: An Inappropriate Response. *Immigration, Asylum and Nationality Law* 16, 2, 110-13.

Shah, P. A. 2003. Attitudes to Polygamy in English Law. *International and Comparative Law Quarterly* 52, 369-400.

Shah, P. A. 2005a. Globalisation and the Challenge of Asian Legal Transplants in Europe. *Singapore Journal of Legal Studies*, 348-61.

Shah, P. A. 2005b. *Legal Pluralism in Conflict: Coping with Cultural Diversity in Law*. London: Glass House.

Shah, P. A. 2007. Thinking beyond Religion: Legal Pluralism in Britain's South Asian Diaspora. *Australian Journal of Asian law* (forthcoming).

Shah, R. 2005. The Phenomenon of the (UK) officially Inspired Forced Marriages. *Immigration, Asylum and Nationality Law* 19, 3, 195-98.

Shah-Kazemi, S. N. 2001. *Untying the Knot. Muslim Women, Divorce and the Shariah*. London: Nuffield Foundation.

Sharma, M. 2005. A View from Inside. In *Free Expression is No Offence* (ed.) L. Appignanesi. London: Penguin, 32-38.

Shaw, A. 1988. *A Pakistani Community in Britain*. Oxford: Oxford University Press, 9.

Shaw, J. 1998. The Interpretation of European Union Citizenship. *Modern Law Review* 61, 293-317.

Shaw, J. 2003. Sovereignty at the Boundaries of the Polity. In *Sovereignty in Transition* (ed.) N. Walker. Oxford & Portland: Hart, 461-500.

Slater, T. R. 1996. Birmingham's Black and South Asian Population. In *Managing a Conurbation* (eds) A. J. Gerrard & T. R. Slater. Studley: Brewin Books, 140–55.

Sondhi, A., O'Shea, J. & Williams, T. 2002. *Arrest Referral*, DPAS Briefing Paper 18. London: Home Office.

Spear, H. 1969. The Growth of Heroin Addiction in the United Kingdom. *British Journal of Addiction* 64, 245-55.

Steffensmeier, D. & Britt, C. L. 2001. Judges' Race and Judicial Decision Making: Do Black Judges Sentence Differently? *Social Science Quarterly* 82, 4, 749-64.

Stephens, J. E. R. 1896. The Growth of Trial by Jury in England. *Harvard Law Review* 10, 3, 150-60.

Stimson, G. & Oppenheimer, E. 1982. *Heroin Addiction*. London: Tavistock.

Sudbury, J. 2002. Celling Black Bodies: Black Women in the Global Prison Industrial Complex. *Feminist Review* 70, 57-73.

Süssmuth, R. & Weidenfeld, W. (eds) 2005. *Managing Integration. The European Union's Responsibilities towards Immigrants*. Washington, D.C.; Gütersloh: Migration Policy Institute & Bertelsmann Stiftung.

Szysczcak, E. 2006. Experimental Governance: the Open Method of Co-ordination. *European Law Journal* 12, 486-502.

Taylor, C. 1994. The Politics of Recognition. In *Multiculturalism: Examining the Politics of Recognition* (ed.) A. Gutman. Princeton, NJ: Princeton University Press, 25-73.

Thomas, H. 2000. *Race and Planning – the UK Experience*. London: UCL Press.

Toggenburg, G. N. 2005. Who is Managing Ethnic and Cultural Diversity in the European Condominium? The Moments of Entry, Integration and Preservation. *Journal of Common Market Studies* 43, 717-38.

Townshend-Smith, R. J. 1998. *Discrimination Law: Text, Cases and Materials*. London; Sydney: Cavendish Publishing.

Tully, J. 1995. *Strange Multiplicity: Constitutionalism in an Age of Diversity*. Cambridge; New York: Cambridge University Press.

Turnbull, P., McSweeney, T., Webster, R., Edmunds, M. & Hough, M. 2000. *Drug Treatment and Testing Orders: Final Evaluation*, Home Office Research Study 212. London: Home Office.

Turning Point 2005. *The Crack Report*. London: Turning Point.

Twining, W. 2000. *Globalisation and Legal Theory*. London: Butterworths.

Vennard, J. et. al 2004. *Ethnic Minority Magistrates' Experience of the Role and of the Court Environment*. London: Department for Constitutional Affairs Research Series 3/04.

Vignaendra, S. 2001. *Social Class and Entry into the Solicitors' Profession*, Research Study 41. London: The Law Society.

Wainwright, M. 2001. Some Bradford Muslims 'act like colonists'. *The Guardian*. http://www.guardian.co.uk/race/story/0,,657655,00.html (accessed March 28, 2006).

Waldron, J. 1992. Minority Cultures and the Cosmopolitan Alternative. *University of Michigan Journal of Law Reform* 25, 3, 751-93.

Walsh, D. 2005. The Rescuers. *The Guardian*. http://www.guardian.co.uk/g2/story/0,,1663179,00.html (accessed March 27, 2006).

Weller, P., Feldman, A. & Purdham, K. 2001. *Religious Discrimination in England and Wales*. London: Home Office, Home Office Research Study No. 220.

Werbner, P. 1986. The Virgin and the Clown. Ritual Elaboration in Pakistani Migrants' Weddings. *Man,* N. S. 21, 2, 227-50.

Werbner, P. 1996. Stamping the Earth with the Name of Allah: Zikr and the Sacralizing of Space among British Muslims. In *Making Muslim Space in North America and Europe* (ed.) B. D. Metcalf. Berkeley: University of California Press, 167–85.

Willis, J. 1973. *Addicts*. Nairobi: Pitman.

Wray, H. 2006. Hidden Purpose: UK Ethnic Minority International Marriages and the Immigration Rules. In *Migration, Diasporas and Legal Systems in Europe* (eds) P. A. Shah & W. F. Menski. London: Routledge-Cavendish, 163-84.

Yilmaz, I. 2004. Marriage Solemnisation among Turks in Britain: The Emergence of a Hybrid Anglo-Muslim Turkish Law. *Journal of Muslim Minority Affairs* 24, 1, 57-68.

Young, I. M. 1990. *Justice and the Politics of Difference*. Princeton: Princeton University Press.

Young, I. M. 1997. A Multicultural Continuum: A Critique of Will Kymlicka's Ethnic-Nation Dichotomy. *Constellations* 4, 1, 48-53.

Young, I. M. 2002. *Inclusion and Democracy*. Oxford: Oxford University Press.

Zaman, M. Q. 2002. *The Role of the Ulama in Contemporary Islam*. Princeton, N.J.: Princeton University Press.

List of Contributors

Dr. Tahir Abbas is a Reader in Sociology and Director of Centre for the Study of Ethnicity at the University of Birmingham. His interests lie in ethno-religious identities of British Muslims and Islam in Britain; education of British South Asians; ethnic minority entrepreneurialism; ethnicity, the judiciary and the criminal justice system; 'race', ethnicity and multiculturalism theory, policy and practice.

Dr. Roger Ballard is founder and Director of the Centre of Applied South Asian Studies (see http://www.art.man.ac.uk/CASAS/). Having acted as expert adviser to the Ethnic Minorities Advisory Committee of the Judicial Studies Board, he now devotes much of his time as a consultant anthropologist.

Meena Bhamra, formerly a practising solicitor, is now writing a PhD thesis at University College London.

Dr. Richard Gale is a Research Fellow at the Department of Sociology, University of Birmingham. His research interests lie in social geography and urban sociology, divided cities, place and the politics of identity, religion and ethnicity, the interaction between religious identity and planning law, and the relationships between youth and ethnicity in patterns of political participation.

Prof. Ralph Grillo is Emeritus Professor of Social Anthropology at the University of Sussex and has researched on migration, ethnicity and multiculturalism in France, Italy and the UK.

Dr. Anita Kalunta-Crumpton is a Lecturer at the School of Business and Social Sciences, Roehampton University. Her research interests lie in race and criminal justice, drugs use and drug trafficking, and comparative criminal justice.

Mohamed M. Keshavjee, a barrister, has practised law in Kenya, Canada and England. He has taught at the Institute of Ismaili Studies, London, and is a doctoral student at SOAS, University of London researching ADR in a diasporic Muslim community in the UK. He also serves on the Steering Committee of the World Mediation Forum, and is a member of the Advisory Board of the Festival of Muslim Cultures in Britain.

Dr. Valsamis Mitsilegas, Legal Adviser to the House of Lords European Union Committee between 2001 and 2005, is now Senior Lecturer at the Department of Law, Queen Mary, University of London. His expertise lies in EU Justice and Home Affairs and national and international legal responses to transnational organised crime, money laundering and terrorism.

Dr. Prakash Shah is a Senior Lecturer at the Department of Law, Queen Mary, University of London. His research interests lie mainly in the field of ethnic minority laws and immigration, asylum and nationality law.

Index

C

D

Immigration and Asylum Law and Policy in Europe

1. E. Guild and P. Minderhoud (eds.): *Security of Residence and Expulsion.* 2000
ISBN 90-411-1458-0
2. E. Guild: *Immigration Law in the European Community.* 2001
ISBN 90-411-1593-5
3. B. Melis: *Negotiating Europe's Immigration Frontiers.* 2001
ISBN 90-411-1614-1
4. R. Byrne, G. Noll and J. Vedsted-Hansen (eds.): *New Asylum Countries?* Migration Control and Refugee Protection in an Enlarged European Union. 2002
ISBN 90-411-1753-9
5. K. Groenendijk, E. Guild and P. Minderhoud (eds.): *In Search of Europe's Borders.* 2003
ISBN 90-411-1977-9
6. J. Niessen and I. Chopin (eds.): *The Development of Legal Instruments to Combat Racism in a Diverse Europe.* 2004
ISBN 90-04-13686-X
7. B. Bogusz, R. Cholewinski, A. Cygan and E. Szyszczak (eds.): *Irregular Migration and Human Rights: Theoretical, European and International Perspectives.* 2004
ISBN 90-04-14011-5
8. H. Battjes: *European Asylum Law and International Law.* 2006
ISBN 90-04-15087-7
9. Elspeth Guild and Paul Minderhoud (eds.): *Immigration and Criminal Law in the European Union: The Legal Measures and Social Consequences of Criminal Law in Member States on Trafficking and Smuggling in Human Beings.* 2006
ISBN 90-14-15064-1
10. Georgia Papagianni: *Institutional and Policy Dynamics of EU Migration Law.* 2006
ISBN 90-04-15279-2
11. Elspeth Guild and Anneliese Baldaccini (eds.): *Terrorism and the Foreigner: A Decade of Tension around the Rule of Law in Europe.* 2006
ISBN 90-04-015187-7
12. Steve Peers and Nicola Rogers (eds.): *EU Immigration and Asylum Law: Text and Commentary.* 2006
ISBN 90-04-15374-8
13. Prakash Shah (ed.): *Law and Ethnic Plurality: Socio-Legal Perspectives.* 2007
ISBN 978-90-04-16245-7

Martinus Nijhoff Publishers – Leiden • Boston